# Windows® Server

## UNDOCUMENTED SOLUTIONS

# Beyond the Knowledge Base

# Windows® Server

## UNDOCUMENTED SOLUTIONS

# Beyond the Knowledge Base

Serdar Yegulalp

**McGraw-Hill**/Osborne

New York   Chicago   San Francisco
Lisbon   London   Madrid   Mexico City   Milan
New Delhi   San Juan   Seoul   Singapore   Sydney   Toronto

The *McGraw-Hill* Companies

**McGraw-Hill**/Osborne
2100 Powell Street, 10th Floor
Emeryville, California 94608
U.S.A.

To arrange bulk purchase discounts for sales promotions, premiums, or fund-raisers, please contact **McGraw-Hill**/Osborne at the above address. For information on translations or book distributors outside the U.S.A., please see the International Contact Information page immediately following the index of this book.

### Windows® Server Undocumented Solutions: Beyond the Knowledge Base

1234567890 FGR FGR 019876543

ISBN 0-07-222941-1


**Publisher**
   Brandon A. Nordin
**Vice President & Associate Publisher**
   Scott Rogers
**Editorial Director**
   Tracy Dunkelberger
**Project Editor**
   Mark Karmendy
**Acquisitions Coordinator**
   Athena Honore
**Technical Editor**
   Steve Thomas
**Copy Editor**
   Mike McGee

**Proofreader**
   John Gildersleeve
**Indexer**
   Claire Splan
**Composition**
   Tara A. Davis, John Patrus
**Illustrators**
   Kathleen Fay Edwards,
   Melinda Moore Lytle, Lyssa Wald
**Cover Design**
   Tree Havener
**Series Design**
   Tracy Dunkelberger, Peter F. Hancik,
   Mark Karmendy


This book was composed with Corel VENTURA™ Publisher.

For Lori, without whom I would never have gotten into all of this.

# About the Author

Serdar Yegulalp has been writing about Windows, PCs, and related subjects for over ten years. From 1994 to 2001 he served on the staff of *Windows Magazine*—reviewing products, writing feature articles, and eventually editing his own column on Windows 2000. After *Windows* folded, he continued the column in his *Windows 2000 Power Users Newsletter*, available online at http://www.win2kpowerusers.com. He also contributes regularly to *Australian PC Magazine* (where he writes the "Windows Workshop" monthly column) and Techtarget.com (where he offers his expertise with Windows 2000, Windows XP, and Exchange Server). His side projects include running a free and user-supported web-based role-playing game system, Illusionary Minds Chat (http://im-chat.com)—a project built entirely from scratch using Windows 2000, SQL Server, and IIS 5.0. Finally, when he has spare time, he records music under the moniker The Gline (http://www.thegline.com), and has three albums to his credit. He has a wife, Lori, of eight years, and lives in New York.

# About the Technical Editor

Steven B. Thomas is President and Chief Technical Officer of Meridian Networks—a network system integration and consulting firm in West End, N.C. Recently, he spent five years as a full-time faculty member at Sandhills Community College in Pinehurst, N.C., where he taught Microsoft, Cisco, and general networking and system administration topics. Steve holds most major networking certifications including the MCSE, MCP, MCSA, MCT, Network+, CCNP, CCNA, and CCDA. Steve is also the author of several books on various Microsoft and networking topics, including *Windows NT 4.0 Registry: A Professional Reference* (Osborne/McGraw-Hill, 1997, ISBN: 0079136559; despite being three versions back on Windows by now, this remains a useful reference to this day). In his spare time, Steve glories in Windows tips, tricks, and administrivia, and his love for the subject shows in everything he writes. For more information, please contact Steve at sthomas@meridiannetworks.com.

# AT A GLANCE

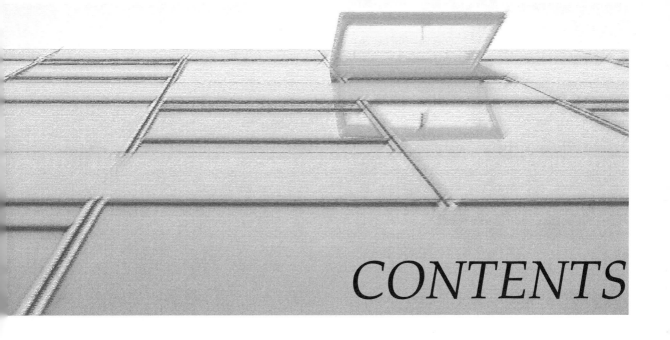

# CONTENTS

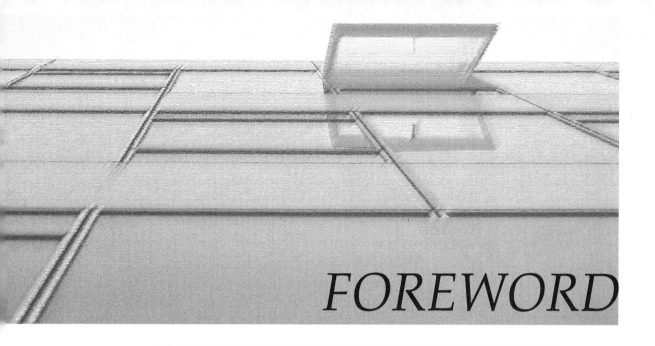

# FOREWORD

Undocumented Solutions. Could a tome be any more timely?

While Microsoft has remained steadfast in its position that ever since Windows 95, Windows has been an open book, others have begged to differ.

In recent months, Microsoft has been criticized, both by the European Commission and the U.S. Department of Justice—not to mention by its myriad competitors—for failing to document fully all of the programming interfaces and features of its flagship Windows operating systems. Just this past summer, Microsoft agreed to publish more of the Windows communications protocols in order to alleviate government concerns.

It's not just legal trials that are making for Windows tribulations. In April, Microsoft began shipping its latest, major server release, Windows Server 2003. Currently, the company is working feverishly on its next-generation Windows client, code-named Longhorn. Meanwhile, Linux is nipping at Windows' heels. Customers are demanding access to Windows source code and interfaces like never before.

Interesting. At the very time that Microsoft is seeking to make Windows more intuitive and to isolate customers from the inner workings of Windows, software developers, systems administrators, and customers all are becoming increasingly interested in what makes Windows tick.

Microsoft offers its users some information on the inner workings of Windows in its Knowledge Base articles that it publishes to its web site. But many customers want and need information that goes beyond these pieces.

That's where this book comes in.

Technology veteran Serdar Yegulalp has been in the Windows trenches since Microsoft released NT 3.51 in 1995. For the past eight years, he has been writing about and working with Windows. As a result, Yegulalp is full of tips and tricks for individuals who want to customize Windows in order to make their home and business systems work and play better.

This work is part of an esteemed and growing tradition of documenting the undocumented features in Windows. Microsoft history buffs may recall the uproar around Andrew Schulman's *Undocumented DOS* and *Undocumented Windows* books when they hit the market several years back. I expect *Undocumented Solutions* to take its rightful place right alongside those classics.

—Mary Jo Foley, Editor, Ziff Davis *Microsoft Watch* newsletter

# ACKNOWLEDGMENTS

First, I need to thank Tracy Dunkelberger, the editor of this title, who brought the rough idea to me and helped me whip it into shape. She walked me though the sometimes bumpy creation process and did a fantastic job coordinating everything.

I also need to thank Athena Honore, my acquisitions editor, and both Steve Thomas and Mike McGee, my tech and copyeditors, who all helped tame the beast and give it the proper form. They were especially helpful in pointing me towards some resources and ideas that I hadn't originally considered (especially in the networking chapter), and were instrumental in thoroughly fleshing out several sections of the book.

Some major family thanks are also in order: my parents, Sevinç and Tunçel; Linda and Alfred, my in-laws; and finally my wife, Lori, all of whom were incredibly supportive during the long months during which I holed myself up in the "lab" and tested, researched, checked, wrote, and rewrote. You guys are the greatest.

I should also thank the thousands of readers of the *Windows 2000 Power Users Newsletter*, who provided me with feedback on many topics; the friendly folks at the PCNineOneOne.com forum—especially my former co-worker Jason Levine—who were also full of interesting ideas and hints; the 2CPU.com forum readers and participants, with many suggestions and notes about dual-CPU systems; and the many endless folks on USENET who had questions *and* answers alike on just about every subject out there.

Lastly, I want to thank two people who might never read this book: Eva Kafka Barron, my first *real* writing instructor; and Harlan Ellison, who showed me that you can write about *anything* and make it interesting—provided *you* have something to bring to it.

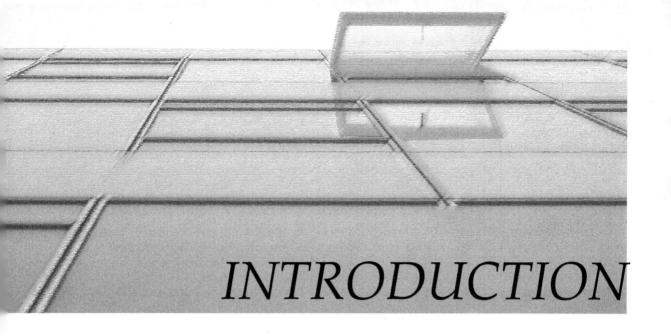

# INTRODUCTION

You now hold in your hands a powerful and eclectic collection of largely undocumented features, fixes, tips, tricks, and tools for Windows 2000 Server and Windows 2003 Server. "Undocumented" means that for whatever reason, most of the information in this book has never stood together under one roof, and has rarely, if ever, been explained in a detailed fashion.

Many conventional users never come across this stuff, and there are also many experts who don't, either. By writing this book, I'm hoping to put these things into as many people's hands as possible and empower them to make use of all of it. You are not obliged to use every tip in this book, but you're welcome to use any or all of them as you see fit. Also, don't feel that you have to read the book straight through (barring this introductory section, where some important high-level information is laid out); you can skip around, take what you need, and leave the rest for later.

## What this Book Covers

This book describes a great many techniques and methods for Windows 2000 and Windows 2003 Sever that for one reason or another are relatively obscure but still immensely useful. They are also, by and large, not supported by Microsoft—in other words, if you use the techniques described herein, you need to do so carefully and at your own risk.

Many of these tricks *do* exist in some documented form, but that documentation is usually so scattershot or so hard to track down (or hard to read!) that it might as well not even exist. Some of them are genuinely undocumented and have only come to light more or less by accident. All of them are useful in some way, and you may find yourself surprised at how a tip you never imagined would be useful at first has suddenly become indispensable.

Most of the tips used in this book come directly out of my own personal experience with Windows 2000 / 2003 Server. I spent endless hours foraging through the bowels of Microsoft's on-line libraries, including the venerable Knowledge Base, for every scrap of fact and technique I could unearth. I also owe a debt for life to Google's® USENET search engine, from which I was able to exhume endless additional information, and where I was able to confirm and double-check a good deal of what I had unearthed. I also received a fair number of these tips from people who wrote to me as readers of my *Power Windows 2000 Newsletter*, and who had many secret techniques of their own to share.

## How to Use this Book

Each chapter and appendix in this book comes with a prevailing theme:

- "Automatic Setup" concentrates on techniques and information used when setting up or installing Windows 2000 / 2003 Server.

- "Hardware Tweaking" discusses methods relating to hardware, such as device drivers and tweaks for hardware performance.

- "Desktop and UI" concerns itself with modifying the look-and-feel of the operating system—desktop layout, visual themes, the behavior of objects, and so on.

- "Memory" deals with the core of the OS, including things like CPU tweaks.

- "Networking" is self-evident, but covers hardware, protocols, and some third-party solutions to networking problems.

- "Management" deals with the tools and components used to manage or maintain Windows servers.

- "IIS and Active Directory" covers the server components native to Windows 2000 and 2003 Server.

- "Upgrades and Updates" deals with how to find the latest versions of many Windows components—not just from Microsoft Update, but from many of the more obscure areas of the Microsoft site—as well as some tools for learning if you have the most recent revisions of many less-documented system components.

- "Links" (Appendix A) compiles a list of useful websites and links for Windows admins, and "Freeware, Shareware, and Trialware" (Appendix B) contains references to first- and third-party downloads and add-ons for administering and performing under-the-hood adjustments to Windows 2000 / 2003 Server.

 # Building a Bootable CD with a Slipstreamed Service Pack Installation

| High |
|------|
| Moderate |
| Low |

Each tip has a margin icon to signify that it pertains to Windows 2000 Server, Windows 2003 Server, or to both (like the one shown here). The tips described in each chapter also come with a risk rating—HIGH in this case—which describes how dangerous or potentially disruptive the tip in question can be:

- **Risk Level LOW:** You can use this tip safely on a production server without worrying about data loss or crippling functionality. No reboot is needed, and you do not need to back up any data.

- **Risk Level MODERATE:** You can use this tip on a production server, but there will almost certainly be an interruption of workflow since a reboot may be needed. There is still no danger of data loss, but having a recent backup is a good idea.

- **Risk Level HIGH:** Tips and techniques with this rating can result in data loss if the instructions are not followed to the letter. A reboot will usually be needed. These tips should be considered experimental and should *not* be performed on a production server the first time you try to use them.

Note that most of the tips in this book are written for single-processor machines that are not part of a cluster, since those make up the majority of Windows 2000 servers out there. There are, however, some tips that specifically talk about multiple processors. Such tips will be broken out and discussed separately from the rest of the tips, since many of them cannot be used interchangeably with regular (non-clustered, single-CPU) machines.

Every tip in this book has been tested on one or more real-world systems to ensure that it behaves as described. There may be the occasional tip that doesn't behave as expected, but the odds of this happening are usually fairly low unless something is already wrong with the system. Whenever there is the possibility of a tip or technique going awry when something else is already wrong, I've tried to do my homework to make sure I know when the odds of this happening are more likely.

## What this Book Doesn't Cover

First and foremost: this book is *not* a guide to installing, maintaining, or using Windows 2000 / 2003 Server.

In other words, it's assumed that anyone reading this already knows their way around Windows 2000 / 2003 Server—how to install it, how to keep it running, how to make changes, and how to do some basic disaster recovery. That information should be par for the course for any administrator who wants to use the information in this book, and will *not* be covered here in any form.

In addition, a great many assumptions are made about what the reader will know. If you don't know how to perform Registry editing or make changes in the Metabase, you won't find it spelled out for you here; all of this is assumed knowledge in this book. If you want to get some basic understanding of Windows 2000 / 2003 Server, I'd recommend taking a look at *Windows® Server 2003: The Complete Reference* (McGraw-Hill/Osborne, 2003, ISBN 0-07-219484-7), where you'll find basics explained in all the detail you need.

This book is also written from the presumption that you not only have the *ability* to make the changes described within this book, but the *privilege* to do so. If you're not the sysadmin of the server you want to make any of the described changes to, *don't do it*, as you can get into enormous amounts of hot water for tinkering with things that are not yours to tinker with. If you're not the sysadmin but you see something you think your server might benefit from, bring this book to your sysadmin and talk it over with him or her, but *don't* try to make the changes yourself. (This warning should be assumed knowledge, but by putting it here in black and white, I can also put my *own* mind at ease.)

If you *are* the sysadmin who can make changes like the ones described in this book, avoid using any of these tips on a production system—i.e., a system with live data or that's "in use" in some form—until you're certain that they can be implemented safely. I have done my best to make sure that I have documented any possible pitfalls that may come up when implementing these tips, but you should do the smart thing on your own and take steps to be safe. If you can, set up a "guinea pig" computer—a test machine—which you can try out these tips on first.

The reason I am emphasizing absolute caution is that many of these tips and techniques have the power to *totally* mess up your system. Go back and read that last sentence again, because there's no reason for you to have to be staring down at a tear-stained keyboard while ripping out your hair. Keep backups of all your critical data, and remember that there can always be unforeseen side effects to any changes you make. Again, how you do this and to what extent is up to you, but have it in some form.

Finally, don't use any of the information in this book in a malicious or disruptive fashion, or use it to circumvent licensing restrictions or copyright laws. (I shouldn't have to say that either, but it allows everyone's lawyers to sleep easier at night.)

Now that we have the dire warnings out of the way, let's start digging!

# CHAPTER 1
## *Automating Setup*

**In This Chapter:**

- ☐ Slipstreaming a Service Pack into a Network-Shared Repository
- ☐ Building a Bootable CD-ROM with a Slipstreamed Service Pack Installation
- ☐ Switching an Existing Windows Installation from Standard to ACPI HAL or Vice Versa
- ☐ Cloning to a System with a Different Disk Controller
- ☐ Moving Windows to Another Partition or Hard Drive on the Same System
- ☐ Dual-Booting with Multiple or Earlier Versions of Windows

A good deal of any Windows administrator's time is taken up with the tedium of installing (or reinstalling) copies of Windows onto various machines, or updating Windows. That's why administrators welcome any way of expediting the process with open arms.

In this chapter, I'll be exploring some common and not-so-common methods meant to keep that tedium at a minimum, such as: slipstreaming a bootable installation CD-ROM or a network repository of installation files; cloning workstations; conducting unattended installs; as well as other time- and sanity-saving techniques.

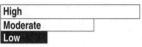

# Slipstreaming a Service Pack into a Network-Shared Repository

| High |
| Moderate |
| **Low** |

Slipstreaming is the art—and science—of taking the most recent service pack for Windows and merging it with the distribution media. It's most commonly done in networked environments, where the slipstreamed product can then be offered across the network to all users.

## Overview

Rather than install the operating system and then apply the necessary hotfixes after the fact (the by-the-book way of doing things), slipstreaming lets you roll the hotfixes up into the distribution media itself. It's trickier than doing things "the hard way"—at least the first time—but if you're rolling out Windows installations on a whole slew of systems, or just want to save yourself time by not having to patch in the future, this is a good way to do it.

---

## The Party Line                                   Company X

```
Microsoft does indeed talk about slipstreaming a service
pack in this fashion, although they downplay it in favor
of pushing out service packs to individual workstations or
cloning a pre-patched system.
```

## *The Undocumented Solution*

*There are also a few potential disadvantages to using a slipstream-patched install. For one thing, in some machines, a slipstream installation does not work correctly—sometimes incompatibilities between hardware and patched versions of drivers make it difficult to install Windows, which is another reason Microsoft may not be crazy about doing this. But if you're diligent and careful, you can get a lot of benefit out of this trick.*

## What You'll Need

- The original distribution media (CD-ROM) for Windows 2000/2003
- Complete downloads of the particular service packs and post-SP hotfixes to add
- At least 1GB of free hard drive space
- Network connectivity for your clients

CHAPTER
1

Automating Setup

Follow these steps to create a slipstreamed network repository for Windows:

1. If you haven't done so already, download a complete copy of the service pack you want to slipstream. Note that service packs come in two versions—one that downloads the needed components on-the-fly from Microsoft, and another which contains the entire service pack in one archive. The latter is the one you want, although by some weird quirk of Microsoft naming conventions, that one is called the "Network Install" version. (My guess is the reason they called the full install "Network Install" is because it can be installed by administrators across a local network. Nevertheless, it can still be needlessly confusing.)

   As of this writing, the last full service pack for Windows 2000 is Service Pack 3 (published 7/29/2002), a 127MB download. The URL for this download sometimes changes, but it can be found by going to the Microsoft site (www.microsoft.com), clicking Downloads, and then Windows (Security and Updates) from the left-hand menu.

   If you're slipstreaming a copy of Windows that's *not* in English, be sure to get the correct service pack version for your edition of Windows. English is the default language for all service packs unless you specify otherwise.

2. Copy the entire contents of the Windows 2000 installation CD-ROM to a folder on your hard drive. "Entire contents" means exactly that, including hidden and

system files. If you want to do this from a command line, which is probably the best way to go, use:

**xcopy** *<cd-drive-with-Win2K-disk>*:**\\\*.\*** *<target-folder>* **/E /H /K /O**

This will copy over all the files, including hidden and system files, and re-create the directory structure of the CD-ROM, as shown in Figure 1-1. The name of the target folder is not important, but use something like "slipstream CD" to make it stand out. There are 7817 files on the CD-ROM totaling 404MB, so the copy process should take some time. A complete copy of the Windows 2000 CD-ROM has been made to this system's hard drive, in the folder H:\WIN2KSP3CD.

Create a new folder for the service pack itself and copy the service pack into it. Unpack the service pack in that folder by using the **w2ksp3 -x** command. The name of the actual service pack executable may change if you're using something other than Service Pack 3, of course, but the -x switch (which

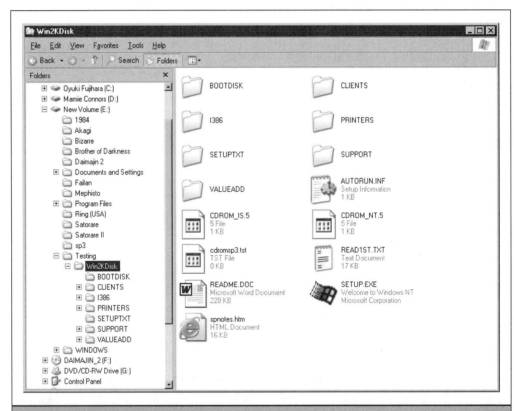

**Figure 1-1.**    A local copy of the contents of the Win2K CD-ROM. The files can be copied to any drive or folder as long as there's space available.

unpacks the files for redistribution) is mandatory. You will be prompted as to which folder to unpack the service pack into; if you specify a folder that doesn't exist, it'll be created for you.

3. Go to the directory \i386\update\, in the folder you saved the service pack files in, and type **update -s:<drive-and-path-to-copied-CD-files>**

---

**NOTE**    You can save yourself a step by copying over the CD-ROM files and then unpacking the service pack *directly into the CD directory* by typing **win2ksp3.exe -s:<*drive-and-path-to-copied-CD-files*>**. For this to work, the \i386 directory from the CD must be exactly one level below the folder you created. So, if you created the folder D:\CD-FILES and placed the contents of the CD-ROM in there, the \i386 folder must be located at D:\CD-FILES\i386 for this to work. You should then see the screen shown in Figure 1-2.

---

4. The slipstreaming process will take a few minutes. When it's done, you'll see a dialog box that says "Integrated install has completed successfully."

You can also add any post-service pack hotfixes at this point in the same manner. Hotfixes, when unpacked with an -x switch, can be directed to a system folder. You do need to be mindful of what order to install hotfixes in, as some of them may need to be installed before others to work correctly. One thing that is *not* possible to do at this stage is slipstream in Internet Explorer 6 Service Pack 1,

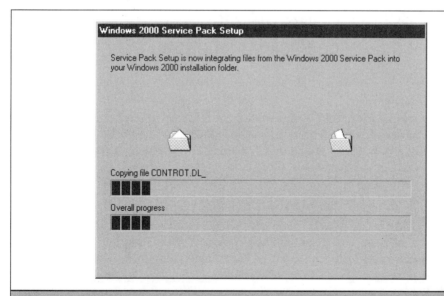

**Figure 1-2.**    Slipstreaming a service pack into the locally-copied files. This may take several minutes and should not be interrupted.

**CHAPTER 1**

Automating Setup

because of the way IE deals with system components. The only way to do this is to wait until it becomes part of a service pack itself.

5. Share out the folder for use by your remote clients.

If you have a server with Remote Installation Services (RIS), you can use the slipstreamed network repository as a way to remotely install Windows on a machine with nothing more than the RIS startup disk and a compatible network card. A step-by-step walkthrough of how to accomplish this is detailed in Microsoft KnowledgeBase article 300483. There are several downsides to using RIS, however:

- RIS must be controlled from the back end using a server.

- RIS requires at least 2GB of dedicated space on the server—Microsoft recommends setting aside an entire disk or partition for this.

- The server in the network must also be running DNS, DHCP, and Active Directory.

- The client has to be accessible through a network that has a great deal of spare bandwidth and low latency (to keep the installation from taking a long time).

If you don't have, or can't dedicate, a server to do this, or if you are dealing with a lot of workstations that are very far apart and not always network-accessible, then the best way to distribute the latest-and-greatest version of Windows may be to build a slipstreamed boot CD-ROM.

## 2000/2003 Building a Bootable CD-ROM with a Slipstreamed Service Pack Installation

| High |
|------|
| **Moderate** |
| Low |

If slipstreaming service packs and post-service pack hotfixes into a shared repository won't satisfy your needs, consider building a slipstreamed Windows boot CD-ROM. This is a copy of the Windows installation CD with all of the most recent service pack files and post-service pack hotfixes installed on it.

### Overview

Why create a slipstreamed CD-ROM? For one thing, the convenience of having a slipstreamed CD handy is hard to beat. Install Windows with it and there's no need to patch anything; everything comes off the CD pre-patched with the latest updates.

---

**NOTE**   I owe thanks to Steven Bink for this particular technique. Visit his web site for many other Windows techniques at www.bink.nu.

---

## The Party Line

Microsoft doesn't endorse or condemn slipstreaming onto a CD-ROM, although they do offer instructions on how to slipstream a network install from a file repository (see the preceding). It's possible they don't provide details on rolling your own CD-ROM because it's not as straightforward as doing a network-slipstream install—and they probably don't want to give people the impression that they can freely make their own installation CDs without respecting license restrictions.

## *The Undocumented Solution*

*The solution, of course, is to assemble your own installation CD. This requires software that isn't included with Windows, but it isn't difficult to acquire. Nor are the techniques needed to create the CD hard to learn. (As mentioned earlier, you also need to be mindful of Windows licensing restrictions and not install more copies of Windows with your newly-minted CDs than you have licenses for!)*

## What You'll Need

- Nero Burning Rom, or equivalent CD-burning program

  Most of what's required should not be hard to come by. The program I've used as the example for this solution is Nero Burning Rom, but any program that can burn bootable CD-ROMs will work; you just need to modify the instructions to match the same steps listed here.

- The original distribution media (CD-ROM) for Windows 2000/2003

- Complete downloads of the service pack and post-SP hotfixes to add

- At least 1GB of free hard drive space

- A CD-ROM burner (optional, but necessary if you plan on making CD-ROMs from the slipstreamed installation)

- A CD burning program that can create bootable CD-ROMs, such as Nero Burning Rom

- Blank CDs

> **NOTE**   You may want to practice doing this on a CD-RW, since if you make a mistake it can be erased and re-used. If you re-use the same CD-RW more than once, choose "full erase" rather than "quick erase" to prevent problems, especially on a bootable CD-ROM. It is possible to use CD-RWs for the actual distribution, but it isn't the best idea. It may require BIOS-level UDF support on the machine in question (something not supported on all machines yet). CD-RWs are also more expensive.

Perform steps 1–5 from the previous "Slipstreaming a Service Pack into a Network-Shared Repository" section, then following these steps:

6. The next step is to extract the boot sector information from the CD-ROM so you can create a bootable CD. This step is optional, but useful. With it, you can provide people with only the CD (not a cumbersome set of four boot floppies) and they can easily install this patched copy of Windows on a system that has no operating system.

   Most CD-burning programs do not have built-in support for extracting boot sectors from a CD-ROM. There is a simple program, which is freeware, called BBIE—Bart's Boot Image Extractor—which you can use to create an image file of the boot sector from a CD. It's available at www.nu2.nu/bbie/, and it's easy enough to use: run the program, and specify the CD drive to extract the image from as a command-line option. (See Figure 1-3.) The boot sectors will be written to a file named image1.bin.

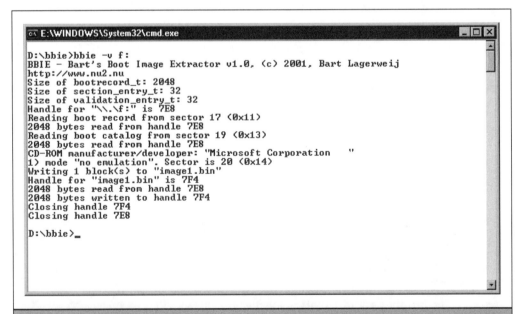

**Figure 1-3.**   Sample output from BBIE, a boot-image extraction utility that runs from the command line

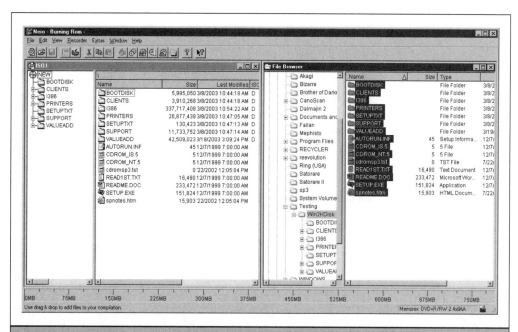

**Figure 1-4.**    Creating a new CD-ROM image in Nero. This is just one of many programs that can be used for creating a slipstreamed boot CD, however.

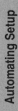

7. Start Nero (or an equivalent CD-ROM burning program) and create a new CD-ROM with it. Copy everything in the CD image folder you patched with the service pack to the new disk you're creating, as shown in Figure 1-4. For all other programs, just add the contents of the CD image folder through whatever procedure is used.

8. If you're creating a bootable CD-ROM, follow this step; otherwise, skip to step 9.

   In Nero, when you select New Compilation, choose CD-ROM (Boot) from the left-hand menu, as shown in Figure 1-5. Under the Boot tab, set Image File to the image file you extracted in step 6. Check Enable Expert Settings and set Kind Of Emulation to None, the listing for Load Segment Of Sectors to 07C0 (which should be the default), and Number Of Loaded Sectors should be set to 4. The Boot Message section is unimportant and can be left as is.

9. Under the ISO tab shown in Figure 1-6, set File/Directory Name Length to ISO Level 2, adjust Format to read Mode 1, and change the Character Set listing to ISO 9660. Check off the box listed next to Joliet, and also check off all three boxes under Relax ISO Restrictions: Allow Path Depth Of More Than 8 Directories; Allow More Than 255 Characters In Path; and Do Not Add The ';1'

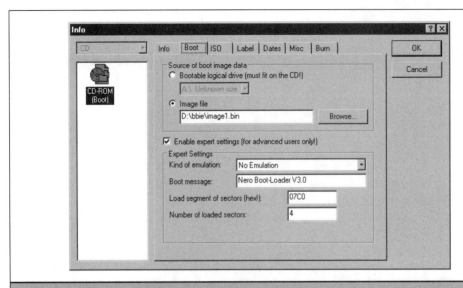

**Figure 1-5.**   The Boot tab for creating a CD-ROM in Nero. Note that "Enable expert settings" must be checked and the options below filled in.

ISO File Version Extension. If you're using another CD-ROM creation program, set all of these options appropriately in your own application. The last option, for the ISO File Version Extension, is extremely important if you're creating a bootable CD-ROM, since the CD will not boot if you add ";1" to the ISO version.

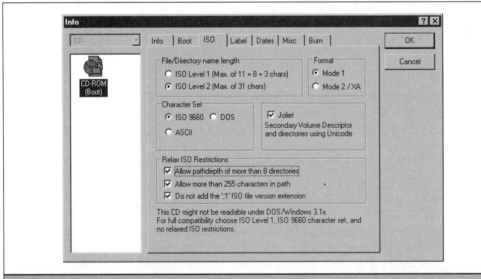

**Figure 1-6.**   The ISO tab for creating a CD-ROM in Nero. Make sure the options are set as shown.

10. Under the Label tab, set the volume label to whatever you want. You can always change it to conform to the existing volume labels for the Windows 2000 CDs:

- Professional: W2PFPP_EN

- Server: W2SFPP_EN

- Advanced Server: W2AFPP_EN

- DataCenter: W2DFPP_EN

In fact, this is probably a good idea, since there are some third-party programs which look for the Windows 2000 CD-ROMs by volume label and not disk manifest.

11. Burn the CD. Once it's finished, try test-booting it to see if it works correctly. If it boots and brings you to the first setup screen, it's almost certainly working correctly, although making a full installation on a test system is always worth doing to make sure everything is in order.

If everything seems to be in order but the disc still refuses to boot, try re-burning it at a lower speed. Some discs that play acceptably may not boot when burned at 8× or higher speeds, and some drives are not as tolerant of discs burned at higher speeds than others.

Under *no* circumstances should you try overburning, a technique where more information is written to the CD than is normally allowed by the disc's specifications. This may work in some drives but not others, and there is no guarantee you will have a useable disc at *all* afterwards.

---

**NOTE**   If you have an installation of Windows 2000 Datacenter Server, you won't be able to slipstream a conventional service pack onto the disk. If you try to install a non-Datacenter service pack into Datacenter, you'll get an error message that reads "This Service Pack has not been qualified by your hardware vendor for installation on this copy of Windows 2000 Datacenter Server." Microsoft maintains strict vendor-level control over what components are to be included in service packs and installation disks for Datacenter as a way of guaranteeing uptime and compatibility. However, if for some reason you do want to get around this, a site called WinXP.bink.nu has published slightly modified versions of the service pack installers that will allow you to use conventional service packs in Datacenter Server. This isn't something you should attempt casually, of course, since Datacenter is kept closed-ended for a reason.

---

Another good reason to have a slipstreamed copy of a Windows 2000 installation disc is if you need to update a Recovery Console installation. When you install a service pack on a running copy of Windows that has the Recovery Console also installed, the Recovery Console does *not* automatically get updated. To do this, insert your slipstreamed Windows 2000 CD-ROM, type **winnt32 /cmdcons**, and then follow

**CHAPTER 1**

**Automating Setup**

the prompts. You can also upgrade the Recovery Console manually by following steps 1–5, shown earlier, and running **winnt32 /cmdcons** from the \i386 folder of your patched Windows 2000 installation. This has to be done on the machine you're updating; it can't be done remotely.

 # Switching an Existing Windows Installation from Standard to ACPI HAL or Vice Versa

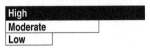

Most Windows NT/2000 experts know about the Hardware Abstraction Layer, or HAL—it's a system component that stands between the operating system and the hardware itself. All system calls made to hardware are *abstracted* through the HAL—this way, no program can do something naughty like try to write directly to the hard drive. This is also the reason why a great many MS-DOS mode programs, especially disk utilities, won't run in NT or 2K—the HAL stops these programs cold. There's more than one variety of HAL, and again, longtime NT/2K mavens will be familiar with this. Sometimes there's a need to change from one HAL to another.

When you install Windows, you can either let the installation program autodetect the HAL to use (usually "Standard" or "ACPI PC"), or press F6 during the first phase of setup to supply one yourself if you have a system that requires a vendor-supplied HAL to work correctly. Many of the earlier multiprocessor machines came with a custom HAL and wouldn't work correctly with anything else. To be scrupulously fair, they *might* work with the "generic" HAL, too, but a) multiprocessor support wouldn't be available, and b) a great many other functions would also probably be disabled.

## Overview

Once you install a given system's HAL, the popular perception is that you are stuck with it and that you will need to tear the whole system down to change to another HAL. The truth is that you *can* change HALs on-the-fly, with a little work.

Why do this? If you move from one machine to another, for instance (a process elaborated on elsewhere in this chapter), or if you change motherboards, or are switching HALs to defeat a problem. Some people who run servers or workstations with esoteric hardware use the Standard PC HAL rather than the ACPI PC HAL due to problems with that machine's implementation of ACPI. (If you don't really need sleep mode or standby mode in a machine that doesn't support it that well to begin with, why not do away with it entirely and save yourself some trouble, as well as a possible incompatibility or three?)

## The Party Line    `Company X`

What does Microsoft say about changing HALs? *No, no, a thousand times no.* According to Microsoft's own literature on the subject, changing HALs can cause a drastic malfunction because of the way the Plug-and-Play device tree is enumerated. The device tree is set up differently for each HAL, and can only be reconstructed by reinstalling Windows. They *do* say that you can change from a single- to a multi-processor HAL without going through the rigmarole of a reinstall, but they *don't* advise switching from a standard HAL to ACPI HAL at all.

## *The Undocumented Solution*

*Despite the preceding warnings, it can be done—you can change from one HAL to another. You just need to be incredibly careful about it.*

## What You'll Need

- Windows 2000/2003 installation CD-ROM
- A set of Win2K boot floppies in case CD booting doesn't work
- A backup of all your existing data. I'm not joking—don't even think about attempting this on a system without a full and total backup, and never do this on a production system before taking it officially offline.
- Copies of your updated device drivers

Keep in mind that if you set up Windows 2000/2003 with an ACPI HAL, you can convert to a Standard HAL by simply following steps 1–3 and rebooting. You can switch back to an ACPI HAL at any time the same way. The ACPI device tree enumeration seems to be downwardly compatible with the standard device tree, but the reverse is not true.

Follow these steps to switch HALs:

1. To be safe, run a system cleanup—get rid of any unneeded Registry entries, deinstall any applications that don't need to be there, and just swab the decks in general. It can't hurt.

CHAPTER
1

Automating Setup

**NOTE**   You may want to boot in Safe Mode to change HALs, as this will keep other problems at a minimum.

2.  Open the Windows 2000 Device Manager and get the Properties for the icon under Computer. This will either be listed as Standard PC or Advanced Configuration And Power Interface (ACPI) PC. You may also see HALs for multiprocessor machines.

**NOTE**   In Windows 2003, you will only see Standard and Advanced Configuration and Power Interface (ACPI) PC HALs, unless you are using Windows 2003 Advanced Server. The HALs in Windows 2003 Server support 1–2 processors by default.

3.  Under the Driver tab, click Update. Tell the wizard you want to specify or search for the driver to install, and then choose the appropriate HAL from the list shown in Figure 1-7. If you're switching to a HAL from a vendor, click Have Disk and provide the disk with the HAL on it.

**NOTE**   If you're changing HALs on a multiprocessor motherboard that only has one processor installed, use a uniprocessor HAL.

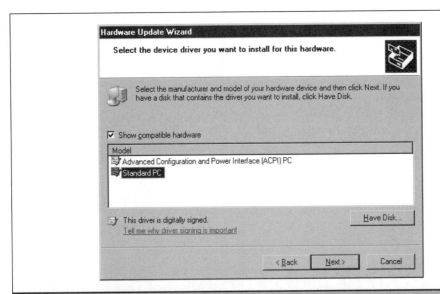

**Figure 1-7.**    Changing HALs. More than one HAL may be available depending on which version of Windows Server you're running.

4. Complete the wizard and reboot. The system at this point will crash and deliver a STOP error, occasionally with some complaint about not being able to find the correct HAL, and may also reboot automatically.

5. Insert the Windows 2000 CD-ROM, reboot, and start the install process. Don't select Repair. (If you need to supply drivers only during setup, for things like mass-storage controllers, press F6 during the boot process and have the drivers ready.)

6. Specify the existing Windows 2000 directory as the target directory for the installation. Then you'll be prompted to repair the installation; do this by pressing R.

7. During the file copying process, you may be prompted to overwrite NTOSKRNL.EXE. Say No to this option. This is very important—if you copy over the existing kernel, you'll wreck things for good. (You will usually only get prompted for this if you are working with an installation of Windows that has had a service pack applied to it that is a later version than the revision on the installation media.)

8. You'll also be prompted to copy over HAL.DLL. For this option, say Yes.

9. Let the process complete. Upon reboot you should have the correct HAL and a properly re-enumerated device tree. You may also be prompted to reboot because of "newly detected / installed hardware."

---

**NOTE**    If you are *only* switching from a single to a multiprocessor HAL, you can do this in the Device Manager without having to go through the repair/reinstallation process (steps 4–9).

---

# Cloning to a System with a Different Disk Controller

| High |
|------|
| **Moderate** |
| Low |

If you think of the late Dolly the Sheep when you read the word *cloning* in a book like this, you're actually not far off the mark. In biology, a clone is an exact genetic replica of a living organism created outside of conventional reproductive methods. In computers, a clone is a bit-for-bit replica of another computer's software and operating system installation, usually made from a single master copy. Cloning is one of the fastest ways to set up a whole batch of computers with the same OS and software without having to tediously reinstall everything from scratch.

## Overview

One of the things often not spelled out very clearly is that in Windows, you cannot clone a system image to a machine that has a different controller driver setup.

CHAPTER
1

Automating Setup

What if, for instance, you have a slew of machines—some with one variety of disk controller and some with another? Cloning a disk image to all of them indiscriminately, *even if it contains driver support for both controllers,* may not work—if only because the cloned image's BOOT.INI references may no longer be accurate on the new disk setup. If you clone from a system with an IDE controller and you try to deploy it on a system with a SCSI controller, even if you have the same number of disks and the same partition layout, as well as the right drivers present, it still won't work.

---

## The Party Line                                          Company X

Microsoft makes a point of only deploying a system image on
a machine that has the same mass storage controller, and
doesn't offer any advice for how to do this. Is it possible?
Yes, but it'll take some work.

---

## *The Undocumented Solution*

*The only way to make it work is to post-configure BOOT.INI after the cloning process to point to the right place. In the abstract, this isn't difficult, but it's one extra step that needs to be considered. Usually this does not involve much more than replacing a multi(0) reference in BOOT.INI with a scsi(0) reference. Sometimes no changes are required at all (depending on the configuration of the controller), but the only way to be sure is to experiment.*

*Another way to get around this—and probably the most reliable method—is to provide a boot floppy that contains the appropriate startup files and BOOT.INI reference for that specific machine's hardware configuration, and then run a batch file on first boot that copies the BOOT.INI file from the floppy onto the system. (Note that BOOT.INI is a hidden system file and so would need to be marked as normal first.) Simply build two versions of the floppy—one for each type of setup—and provide them, as needed, with each system. After the first boot, the floppy can be discarded since it is no longer required.*

## What You'll Need

- The SYSPREP tool. On the Windows 2000 Server and Advanced Server CD-ROMs, it's in the DEPLOY.CAB archive in the folder \SUPPORT\TOOLS.
- Controller drivers for all the controllers to be configured
- A blank floppy disk

Follow these steps to clone a system with a different disk controller:

1. Set up a system to be cloned that includes *both* controller drivers. One way to do this is to install first one controller, then the other, then remove whichever controller is used less often (most likely the SCSI controller), and edit the startup parameters for the drivers so they both start.

   In Windows 2000 and 2003, boot-time device drivers aren't enumerated in Services the way they were in NT 4.0; they're simply listed as devices in the Device Manager. However, they are still stored in the Registry in the same fashion as in Windows 2000, and can be edited in the same way.

   All system device drivers are kept in the subkey HKEY_LOCAL_MACHINE\ SYSTEM\CurrentControlSet\ Services. For instance, if you look in that key for the subkey atapi, you'll see a set of entries that describe how the ATAPI service is handled. To set the ATAPI service's startup parameters, edit the Start value to one of the following decimal values, depending on what you want it to do:

   | | |
   |---|---|
   | 0 | Load the device driver at boot time. |
   | 1 | Load the device driver with the system files. |
   | 2 | Load the device driver automatically after the system files have loaded. |
   | 3 | Load the device driver on demand after the system files have loaded. |
   | 4 | Disable loading of this device driver. |

   The choice will generally be between 0 or 4, since most boot-time device drivers are either loaded at boot time or not at all.

2. Create a batch file that follows this example:

   ```
   echo If you have removed the floppy disk from the A: drive,
   echo please reinsert it now.
   Pause
   Copy A:\BOOT.INI C:\
   echo Please remove the floppy disk from the A: drive.
   echo You will no longer need it.
   Pause
   ```

CHAPTER

1

Automating Setup

3.  Save the batch file to the system to be imaged, and then add the following REG_SZ Registry key:

    *   HKEY_LOCAL_MACHINE\SOFTWARE\Microsoft\Windows\ CurrentVersion\RunOnce

    *   String Name: (Arbitrary—this can be anything; make it something descriptive like "ResetBOOTIni")

    *   Value: (Full drive and path to the batch file)

**NOTE**   This assumes the A: drive is the floppy drive.

4.  Create a floppy disk that has the Windows 2000 boot files, one for each machine to be cloned. This can be done by simply formatting a floppy disk in Windows 2000 and copying the files BOOT.INI, NTLDR (hidden) and NTDETECT.COM (also hidden) to the disk. The BOOT.INI file should have the appropriate references for each machine's controller type.

    A common BOOT.INI file looks like this:

```
[boot loader]
timeout=0
default=multi(0)disk(0)rdisk(0)partition(2)\WIN2K
[operating systems]
multi(0)disk(0)rdisk(0)partition(2)\WIN2K="Microsoft Windows 2000
Server" /fastdetect
```

    To determine the differences between the BOOT.INI files for systems with each type of controller, you may want to try installing Windows separately on each kind of machine and compare the two files.

    In some cases, the two may be exactly the same and you may not need to create discrete BOOT.INI files. The one main difference you may see is the presence of scsi(0) rather than multi(0), which only appears when the on-board SCSI controller has no boot BIOS support. In such a case, the driver for the SCSI adapter also needs to be present on the boot floppy, but there are very few SCSI controllers that do not have boot-BIOS support enabled by default.

5.  Sysprep the system and copy off the disk image.

6.  Deploy the image on both types of systems and package the systems with the appropriate floppy disk.

7.  Disable the unneeded disk controller after the system has been set up. This is optional, but one way to do this is to have the floppy disk batch file make the

appropriate driver changes to the Registry by running a .REG file, either on the floppy disk itself or on the cloned system, which sets the controller in question to Disabled.

# Moving Windows to Another Partition or Hard Drive on the Same System

| High |
|---|
| Moderate |
| Low |

Odds are, this has happened to you more than once: You've got a Windows 2000 system, tweaked and tuned just the way you want it, with all the applications you need and everything as it should be. Except for one thing: the hard drive. You've only got a 20GB partition available for the operating system, and you want to move the OS to the big, jumbo drive you just bought—without having to tediously reinstall everything.

> **NOTE**   I owe thanks to Viktor Heimonen for the details of this trick. You can visit his web site at http://netti.nic.fi/~point.

## Overview

In some cases you can solve the problem by using a partition-copying utility such as PowerQuest's PartitionMagic, but what if you want to preserve your existing drive lettering or partition layout? This can often turn a simple operation into a huge headache, and you may find yourself with a lot of unintentionally broken applications because of bad drive mappings—or, worse, a completely unbootable system, since many drive letter references are hard-wired into the Registry and cannot be easily swapped out. Sometimes the only way to do this properly is to relocate the OS "by hand"—in other words, by manually copying Windows to another partition and hacking its drive letter references directly.

---

## The Party Line                    Company X

```
Microsoft's official stance on this can be summed up in
one word: No. Like a lot of other operations that involve
major-league fiddling with the location of the Windows
binaries, they frown on this heavily. It's not hard to see
why: any operation that involves moving Windows around is
inherently dangerous, because you can screw up your system
```

CHAPTER
1

Automating Setup

for keeps. Microsoft *does* talk about using a parallel installation of Windows for rescue operations, but the sort of work we'll be talking about here is of a different ilk.

## *The Undocumented Solution*

*With a little planning and forethought, however, it's possible to safely relocate your OS to any partition you like without breaking everything (and without rendering your system unstartable).*

## What You'll Need

- Your new hard drive(s), of course
- A partition-copying program, or the installation CD for your OS

If you don't have a commercial partition copying program available, look into BootIt Next Generation from Terabyte Unlimited (www.terabyteunlimited.com/), an inexpensive partition-copying program that's just as good as any pricey commercial product. Note also that some hard drives come with partition copying applications (Western Digital's drives, for instance), but some of those will only work to or from that particular manufacturer's brand of drives.

Follow these steps for moving Windows to another partition or hard drive on the same system:

1. Install and prepare the new hard disk's partitions. You can do this either with your existing Windows installation, or with the utilities provided with many hard drives; either one works. Whichever course you take, make sure the new partition has a drive letter assigned to it before you continue.

2. This step—copying the OS directory over to the new hard drive—can be accomplished in several ways.

    One possible method is to make a parallel installation of Windows 2000 that is nothing but the OS—no additional programs, nothing else—boot into it, and copy the original OS directory using the XCOPY command. The problem with doing this is that finding the right target location for the temporary OS can be a little troublesome—if you put it into the same partition as either your source or target partition, problems can develop. For one, if you install it on the same partition as your existing copy of Windows, your Documents and Settings folder will be trashed. Put it on the target partition, and the existing Documents and Settings folder may not copy over correctly, since it's "in use" when you're doing the copy operation. The ideal way to do this may simply be to image the partition and then boot back into your regular Windows installation to perform the rest of this trick.

If you *do* wind up using a "rescue OS" installation to do the copying, be sure to use the command-line xcopy function to do the copying. *Don't use Explorer.* You can use xcopy like this:

```
xcopy c:\*.* d: /e /k /x /h /o /g
```

This is assuming that C: is your source drive and D: is your target drive, of course. The switches with xcopy insure that everything, including hidden and system files, are copied over, with their NTFS metadata intact. *This is extremely important*—if you copy over the files without preserving their NTFS permissions and ownership information, the resulting copy of the OS will not work correctly. What's worse is that it may not be immediately apparent. I've seen some situations where people have copied over the OS, booted it, and then got as far as the login screen before experiencing an error of some kind. This is yet another reason why making a disk image of the original partition may not be a bad idea, since it eliminates many of these variables in one fell swoop.

If you decide to use a partition-copying tool to make the copy, check to see if the program supports what some partition programs refer to as "forensic mode." This insures that the copy is an exact bit-for-bit replica of the original and has not been time-stamped or otherwise messed with. Norton Ghost, for instance, explicitly supports forensic copying.

Edit your system's BOOT.INI file to contain an entry that points to the new copy of Windows. Usually the easiest way to do this is to copy an existing line from BOOT.INI and edit it, although if you are dealing with an exotic combination of controllers or disks, you may need to play with the entries a bit to get the right one. Creating a BOOT.INI entry for another partition or hard drive is somewhat outside the scope of this discussion, though; if you want the full lowdown on how to do this, see Microsoft KnowledgeBase Article 102873, "BOOT.INI and ARC Path Naming Conventions and Usage."

Make sure this new BOOT.INI line also has a distinctive name—"New Windows Installation" should do the trick.

3. Start regedt32 (*not* regedit, there's a big difference!) and select Load Hive from the Registry menu. Go to the \%SystemRoot%\System32\Config folder in your copied Windows installation (where %SystemRoot% is, of course, the name of the system folder—usually WINDOWS) and open the file named SYSTEM, as shown in Figure 1-8. Give this hive file a name, any name— "Temp" will do just fine. The hive file will then appear as a new branch of the Registry.

CHAPTER 1

Automating Setup

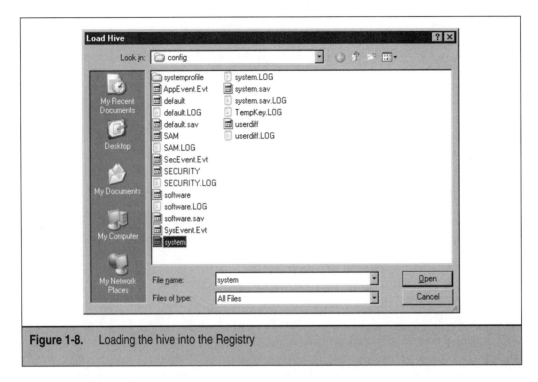

**Figure 1-8.** Loading the hive into the Registry

4. Open the new Registry branch you just created and then open the subkey MountedDevices. Look for two subkeys in the right-hand pane with the drive letters of the source and destination partitions:

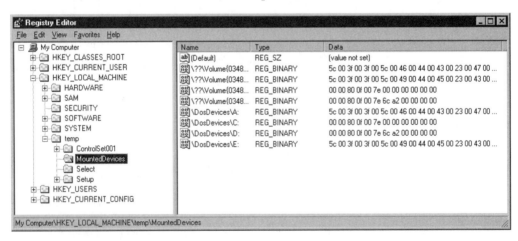

5. Open Notepad or some other text editor, double-click the subkeys in question, and copy out their binary values to Notepad. Make certain you label them so you know which is which, and be sure to copy and paste in Hex mode, as shown next.

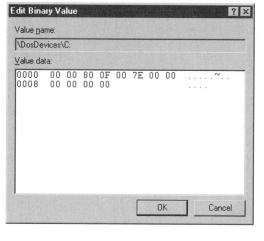

6. Swap the binary values for these two subkeys, so that the source drive has the target drive's binary data and vice versa.

7. Unload the hive from the Registry menu and close regedt32.

8. Reboot to the new installation of the operating system.

---

**NOTE**   When you move applications to another partition, the drive lettering of the destination partition should be the same as the drive lettering you had in the original partition. In other words, if you had your applications on a drive named C:, they should *still* be on a drive named C: when you're done. The last few steps of this operation are designed to insure that. If you want to move your applications separately to another partition, that's way outside the scope of this book—you're best just deinstalling and reinstalling the application in the new target partition. (There are programs that claim to do this for you seamlessly, but I have not tested any of them.)

---

2000/2003 # Dual-Booting with Multiple or Earlier Versions of Windows

A dual-boot system, or multiboot system, is a computer with more than one operating system installed and some way for a user to select which one to boot into. Dual-boot systems used to be highly uncommon, but are becoming more and more prevalent—people are installing Windows and Linux on the same system, or multiple versions of Windows for migrating or testing.

## Overview

Setting up a Windows system to dual-boot into other operating systems—or other versions of Windows—is a subject you could easily write a whole book on. While we don't have a whole book's worth of room to devote to the subject, we can certainly talk about the basics of it in this space, as long as we confine the discussion to dual-booting between different versions or installations of Windows.

---

# The Party Line

Microsoft doesn't warn against multibooting—in fact, their own boot loader is designed to support it. Where they fall short, however, is in providing detailed instructions on how to do this with a mixture of different operating systems, especially when you want to add Windows 9x (95, 98, or Me) after the fact to a system with Windows NT/2K on it, or when you are adding any earlier version of Windows to a machine with a later version on it. This will be the focus of this section.

---

## *The Undocumented Solution*

*The way to handle multibooting when you're installing operating systems "out of order" (NT on a 2K box, for instance) is to repair the system after the install process using the most recent version of Windows.*

## What You'll Need

- Copies of all the appropriate operating system CD-ROMs
- A DOS boot floppy—you can create one from an existing Windows 9x installation. This disc should also contain the SYS.EXE utility.

There are two big issues with dual-booting that need to be considered. The first is the boot sector and the Master Boot Record (MBR), both of which must be kept current with the most recent version of Windows on that machine. For instance, if you have Windows 2000 Server and Windows 2003 Server both installed on the same computer, the boot sector and MBR must both be placed there by Windows 2003. Otherwise, Windows 2003 itself may not boot correctly. The key to this is remembering that the boot sector and MBR must be *downwardly* compatible.

The second is the location of the other installations. For the reasons mentioned earlier (the Documents and Settings folder, for one) don't try to install two copies of Windows on the same partition. Place each copy on its own partition. If you're installing Windows 9x on a system with Windows 2000 on it, bear in mind that Windows 9x may not be able to recognize an individual partition larger than 2GB. For that reason, it may be best to install Windows 9x on any system first, but in some cases that may not be possible.

If you're installing Windows 9x on a system that has Windows 2000 or 2003 on it already, follow these steps.

1. Boot Windows 2000/2003 and create a FAT16 partition no bigger than 2GB to hold the Windows 9x installation.

2. Copy the entire contents of the Win9x directory to a matching folder in the new partition.

3. Boot the system with the DOS boot floppy. Make sure the newly created FAT16 partition is accessible. If it isn't, you may need to re-create it in a different part of the disk—a partition too far out from the beginning of the disk may not be DOS-accessible. Use the SYS utility (found in the Windows 98\WINDOWS\COMMAND directory) to make the new partition DOS-bootable.

4. CHDIR to the new partition with the Windows installation files on it and run the setup.exe file to begin the setup process.

5. At some point during setup you may be warned that the system you are installing on contains Windows NT files. This is normal, and once you click through this, the setup process should continue as before.

6. Let the setup process finish, and then insure that your new copy of Windows runs correctly.

7. Boot the Windows 2000/2003 CD-ROM and run the Manual Repair option. Select the option to repair the boot sector only.

8. In Windows 2003 Server, you will need to run both the Recovery Console and BOOTCFG /REBUILD. This command scans through the whole system and repairs the boot loader so that all available operating systems have an entry and can be booted separately.

9. Reboot. You should see the Windows boot loader with a separate entry for your new Windows installation.

**CHAPTER 1**

**Automating Setup**

# CHAPTER 2

## Hardware Tweaking

**In This Chapter:**

- [ ] Setting IRQ Priorities
- [ ] Enabling/Disabling Hardware Write Caching for Hard Drives
- [ ] Hard-Enabling DMA for Hard Drives
- [ ] Optimizing Windows 2000 Processor Time
- [ ] Permanently Setting Processor Affinity for an Application
- [ ] Setting Device Driver Affinity in a Multiprocessor System
- [ ] Disabling Last Access Time Stamp in NTFS
- [ ] Disabling 8.3 Filename Generation in NTFS
- [ ] Changing Cluster Sizes in NTFS Volumes
- [ ] Changing Master File Table Allocations for NTFS to Offset Fragmentation
- [ ] Using a Third-Party Defragmentation Program

Generally, the only time a Windows 2000/2003 Server administrator deals directly with a system's hardware is when he has to service it—for example, replacing or upgrading hard drives, adding memory, and so on. This is because Windows usually insulates the administrator from the burden of having to configure hardware "by hand," something which, thanks to standards like Plug and Play, have become a thing of the past.

Well, *almost*. One of Windows' secrets is that you can still make a good many changes to how the system interacts with its hardware, but most of the mechanisms for doing so are concealed from the end user. There are a few obvious explanations for why this is the case: for one, by not burdening the user upfront with unneeded options, they aren't needlessly preoccupied by them ("Do I need to change this setting or not?"). Also, it keeps an overly curious user from pushing the wrong button, so to speak, and making a mess of things.

But what if you're an expert, and you *do* want to tinker with the way Windows handles certain hardware functions? What if you're running a system which is going to be performing some extreme function, such as serving thousands or millions of files? If that's the case, the out-of-the-box defaults may not be the best choice, and you may need to make some low-level changes. One of the ways you can do this, of course, is by editing the Registry. Many low-level hardware handling functions can be modified with Registry edits—provided you know what they are and how to apply them.

Microsoft doesn't always discuss these modifications openly, and when they do, they pepper talk of them with broadly worded disclaimers. They also usually don't provide a lot of hard information about the real value or utility of many of these modifications, or what kinds of performance advantages result from such changes.

To that end, this chapter will discuss these types of modifications—not just *what* you can hack, but what you can *expect* from implementing those hacks. Some hacks are useful but oversold, providing marginal benefits, while others may only be useful to a few users—nevertheless, those few users might find them immensely useful. I'll also describe changes you may have read about elsewhere (sometimes described as "undocumented" or "secret") and why they may be a waste of time, effort, and hope.

## 2000/2003 Setting IRQ Priorities

| High |
|------|
| Moderate |
| **Low** |

Despite all the changes made to the PC's basic architecture, Intel- and AMD-based systems are still interrupt-driven. A good deal of work has been done to isolate the user from the agony of assigning interrupts (IRQs) to devices. Part of this is handled through the virtualization of IRQs on ACPI-compliant computers—many devices will appear to share the same IRQ, when in fact all that is happening is that the IRQ contentions are being managed without the intervention of the user. On top of this, there are also "virtual" interrupts interpolated into the operating system through the HAL (Hardware Abstraction Layer).

## Overview

It is possible to force some IRQs to be handled at a higher priority than others. By default, IRQs are left unprioritized by the operating system. The assumption is that the machine, and the devices themselves, will contend as

needed for system resources. Up to a point, this is valid, but what if there are some devices that don't contend as aggressively and need to be given a "boost?"

# The Party Line                    Company X

For many of the preceding reasons, Microsoft prefers to keep discussion of IRQ priority changes away from most users. When editing the properties of a Plug-and-Play device, for instance, it's not possible for the user to make any changes to the memory or IRQ assignments.

**CHAPTER 2**

Hardware Tweaking

## *The Undocumented Solution*

*As it turns out, there is a way to modify IRQ priorities in the system by editing a Registry setting that indicates which IRQs receive higher priority.*

## What You'll Need

A Registry editor, such as REGEDIT or REGEDT32

Be sure to reboot after following these steps:

1.  Open the Registry editor and navigate to the following key:
    HKEY_LOCAL_MACHINE\SYSTEM\CurrentControlSet\Control\
    PriorityControl.

2.  Create a new DWORD value named IRQ#Priority, where "#" is the IRQ number to affect. For instance, if you want to make IRQ 11 highest priority, the name of the DWORD value would be IRQ11Priority.

3.  Set the value of the key to **1**.

Most of the way this tip has been publicized has been by using it to raise the priority for IRQ 8, which is hard-assigned to the real-time system clock. Since IRQ 8 is already the third-highest priority IRQ in the system, with only the keyboard and the system timer (IRQ 0) being higher, raising it that much more wouldn't generate any appreciable change in performance.

On the original PC (the XT/AT line of systems), the priority of the interrupts was in linear order: 0 being the highest and 7 being the lowest. On more recent PCs, the order is a little more complicated—0, 1, then 8–15 (initially all the same), followed by 3–7. The best way, then, to get any real performance improvement when using this tip is to change an IRQ in the 3–7 range. Changing one of the IRQs in the 8–15 range *may* improve things a bit.

Some people have reported getting higher speeds by kicking up IRQ 8, but from what I've been able to tell, those changes appear to be subjective and hard to quantify. This is partly why I've listed this with such a major chunk of salt: you can't do any damage with it, but you *can* badly overestimate what sort of benefit it'll have.

An example from my own system is worth mentioning. I have a computer with IRQ 11 assigned to the USB controller. By boosting IRQ 11's priority, I was able to reduce the latency from one of my USB-based audio devices. However, I got better, and far more substantial, results by replacing my USB filter driver with a more recent version from the manufacturer. I've since set the tweak back to IRQ 8 just to see if anything changes, but the difference is hardly perceptible to me—so the jury is still out.

Also, given how priorities are handled by the system in general, adding more than one IRQ to the priority list is probably useless, and may not improve the system's efficiency at all. So if you do choose to use this, apply it to an IRQ that is key to your system's performance—for instance, a network adapter, if you're running a server.

The best thing to do before making any changes is to perform some research and determine what IRQs are being shared by what devices, and work from there. To do this, bring up the Device Manager in Windows, either through the Properties panel of My Computer or through the Computer Management Console, then select View | Resources by Type. Expand the "IRQ" branch of the device tree and you will see each device in your system categorized by IRQ. From this, you can see devices that share common IRQs.

The exact IRQs in question may vary heavily, and some of them may be completely virtualized. For instance, on a single-processor machine running Windows 2003, many devices share IRQ 9, as in Figure 2-1. On a dual-processor computer, three devices share virtual IRQ 17—which doesn't actually exist in hardware, but is manifested in the HAL for the sake of the rest of the OS. Most of the time, the machine will do a good job managing such virtualization for you, so tweaking to boost performance for them is unnecessary. On dual-processor systems, rather than boosting IRQ priorities, you may be better off assigning affinity for device drivers. This will be discussed later in the section "Permanently Setting Processor Affinity for an Application."

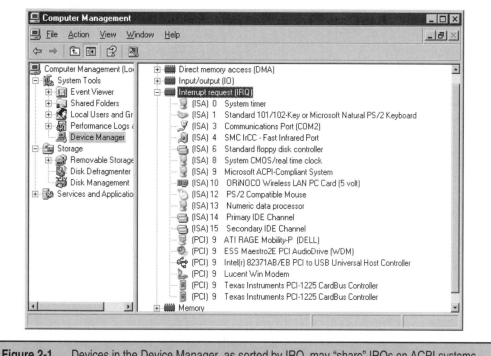

**Figure 2-1.**    Devices in the Device Manager, as sorted by IRQ, may "share" IRQs on ACPI systems.

 # Enabling/Disabling Hardware Write Caching for Hard Drives

| High |
| --- |
| Moderate |
| Low |

Improvements in hard drive speed are not only due to throughput advances but are also the result of more intelligent management of data flow. One of the ways hard drives routinely manage the flow of data is through on-drive or on-controller caching (as opposed to software caching, which I'll talk about separately).

## Overview

Hardware caching involves keeping a memory buffer, either on the drive itself or on the controller used to manage the drive, so that data can be read and written in large chunks. This makes data gathering/writing operations much faster, since the drive doesn't have to seek out data as precisely; it can grab a whole "slice" of data from the drive in one quick pass and deal with the results in memory, which is many times faster than trying to pick up the pieces individually from the drive. Most IDE hard drives made today have an on-disk cache of anywhere from 512KB to 1MB. As of this writing, Western Digital makes a special "Limited Edition" version of their high-end 7200-RPM IDE hard drives that sport a whopping 8MB of on-disk cache (and are phenomenally fast because of it).

To support this, Microsoft lets you set a flag that enables or disables the on-disk cache for an individual drive. This flag can be found in the Policies tab of the Properties pane for the drive's entry in the Device Manager, shown in Figure 2-2.

In Windows 2003, another option is available, labeled "Enable enhanced performance." When selected, Windows 2003 performs aggressive read/write caching on the disk in question, which improves performance even further, but again at the risk of possible data loss if there is a power outage.

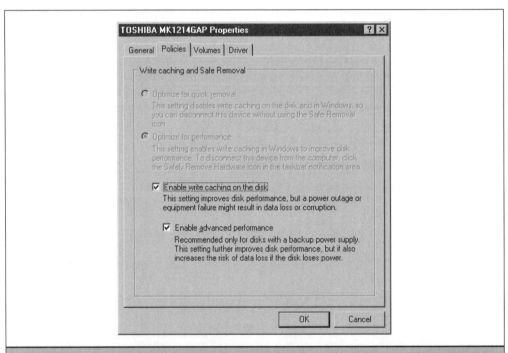

**Figure 2-2.** The "enable advanced performance" and "enable write caching" check boxes can significantly boost performance in Windows 2003, but should only be used on a stable, power-protected system.

## The Party Line                    Company X

Microsoft leaves both of these options unchecked by default. The reason for this is simple: if there's a power failure or other calamity, any data in that buffer that has not been flushed to disk will be lost. The results of such a loss could range from mildly annoying (a lost file) to wholly disastrous (a slew of lost files, or an unbootable system, or a trashed directory table, or... you name it).

## *The Undocumented Solution*

*When dealing with the write-caching option, what Microsoft does not explicitly say about this solution is that it is operating-system independent. In other words, if you enable it, its behavior is going to be entirely governed by the way your hardware behaves and not the way Windows itself behaves or how your disk controller drivers act.*

*Checking the box will enable hardware-level write caching for that drive, of course, but you should generally only do this on systems that have some form of redundant power protection, such as a UPS, and have a good history of stability. If you are debugging a system that has stability problems (BSODs due to possibly flaky hardware or drivers, and so on), turn this option (or both options, if you're using 2003) off while doing your debugging to minimize data loss and possible damage. Also, shutting it off may help you determine if problems with a disk are due to defective cache memory on the drive itself rather than some other factor.*

## 2000 Hard-Enabling DMA for Hard Drives

DMA, or Direct Memory Access, is a transfer mode used by EIDE-compatible hard drives that allows the hard drive controller to transfer data from the disk directly into memory. This allows the controller to work independently of the CPU, in a fashion similar to SCSI controllers. The older IDE transfer mode, Programmed I/O (PIO), is still maintained by newer controllers for backwards compatibility, but it is markedly slower than DMA since it requires the CPU to manage throughput.

## Overview

Windows support for DMA is quite robust, and encompasses both hard drives and removable drives such as CD-ROMs (which are classified as removable drives in Windows). Since IDE and SCSI hard drives are nearly identical at this point in terms of performance, many people who want to build a simple departmental server are opting for EIDE rather than SCSI, since EIDE is less expensive. The reason for SCSI drives costing more than IDE has more to do with the quality testing done on the drive platters than with the cost of the SCSI controller itself. Since SCSI drives are designed for long-term usage, they must be rated to have a higher MTBF (mean time between failures) than IDE drives. That said, IDE drives have been observed to perform for years without problems, so they are growing in popularity as a choice for those who want to build a simple server. (For the sake of dependability, however, SCSI is still generally considered the one to opt for, especially when building mission-critical systems that require 99.999 percent uptime or better.)

There are several breeds of DMA for hard drives: UDMA33, UDMA66, UDMA100, and UDMA133, each progressively faster than the last. The number describes the theoretical top speed of the device: 33 meaning 33 MBps, 66 meaning 66 MBps, and so on. By default, Windows 2000 only supports UDMA33 natively, since support for anything faster than that is disabled as a preventative measure against data loss.

To that end, many users enable DMA support for disk controllers that provide it, but are not aware that on certain machines DMA support must be forced in order to work properly—and that even if enabled through the standard driver interface, it also has to be enabled through a Registry hack when using a system that has an Intel-brand chipset.

---

## The Party Line                              `Company X`

Microsoft understands that not all systems that use UDMA will have it natively supported under Windows, and have documented this particular problem. The incompatibility, however, should also be seen outside the Microsoft articles' narrow context. Available documents include

**Article 269555, "Device Manager Lists ATA-100 Device Incorrectly as Using PIO Instead of UDMA"** This merely describes how devices that use UDMA100 are listed as being

PIO instead, but says nothing about whether or not UDMA100 is, in fact, patched or working as advertised.
**Article 260233, "Support for ATA 100 (Mode 5) in Windows 2000"** This contains a hotfix (later rolled into Service Pack 2) which addresses the use of UDMA100 in Windows 2000. As far as I can tell this does *not* mean that the hack is not needed if you use Windows 2000 with Service Pack 2 or greater, but only that problems with UDMA100 support *specifically* are addressed in SP2. The hack may still be needed on systems that require it.
**Article 247951, "HOW TO: Enable UDMA66 Mode on Intel Chipsets"** This is the actual hack (which is reprised with some modification). The title of the article might imply to readers that it's for Intel chipsets only, but that apparently hasn't stopped people from misusing it.

## *The Undocumented Solution*

    *First off, quite simply, this procedure is dangerous unless you are certain it is supported by your motherboard. This is why Microsoft hints that it should only be used for Intel chipset motherboards only.*

    *The best way to determine if this technique is supported is to check with your motherboard's manufacturer. If the motherboard manufacturer supplies their own drivers for the IDE controller (as a download, or bundled on a disk or CD-ROM) rather than use the default ATAPI.SYS driver bundled with Windows, then the chances are they support UDMA66 and higher natively. In that case, this hack may be not only redundant but may have the potential to trash your system.*

Promise-brand disk controllers register themselves as SCSI controllers rather than IDE to avoid problems with IDE DMA issues like this; if you're using a Promise controller that does this, the hack is not required unless you're trying to enable advanced UDMA support on *another* controller in the same system. Many VIA chipset computers, which use the VIA "4-in-1" drivers, have UDMA66 and higher enabled natively. Lastly, systems with IDE RAID controllers should *never* use this hack, as IDE RAID controllers are usually registered as SCSI controllers to get around the disable-IDE-UDMA-by-default limitation. In their hardware driver development documentation, Microsoft actually recommends against doing this, but that hasn't stopped Promise Technologies and a number of other manufacturers from doing exactly that.

## What You'll Need

A Registry editor, such as REGEDIT or REGEDT32

---

**NOTE**    Make sure your drives are set up correctly. Most administrators are aware UDMA drives require a special 80-pin cable, which must be installed according to the labeling on the cable itself; one end is designed to be attached to the motherboard *only*. Also note that all drives on a chain will default to the speed of the *slowest* device on that chain: if you have a UDMA33 and a UDMA100 drive on the same chain, the whole chain will run at 33, *not* 100.

---

Once you're sure this is the right hack for your system, here's what to do:

1. Open the Device Manager, navigate to the disk controller, and set it to use UDMA66 and higher. You are not looking for the controller itself, but rather the controller *chains*, which are usually listed as "Primary/Secondary IDE Channel."

2. Open the Properties for each controller chain, select the Advanced Settings tab, and set the Transfer Mode option for each device in the chain to "DMA if available." Some devices may be disabled, as they may not support DMA natively, or there may simply be no device on that chain.

**Primary IDE Channel Properties**    ? X

General   Advanced Settings | Driver | Resources |

Device 0

Device Type:    Auto Detection

Transfer Mode:    DMA if available

Current Transfer Mode:    Ultra DMA Mode 2

Device 1

Device Type:    Auto Detection

Transfer Mode:    DMA if available

Current Transfer Mode:    Not Applicable

3. If you do not see an Advanced Settings tab for your particular controller, *stop here*. Odds are, UDMA66 and later are supported natively by your drivers, and you need not do anything.

4. Open your favorite Registry Editor and navigate to the following key: HKEY_LOCAL_MACHINE\System\CurrentControlSet\Control\Class\ {4D36E96A-E325-11CE-BFC1-08002BE10318}\0000

5. Add a new DWORD value under this key named **EnableUDMA66** and set it to **1.**

6. Shut down the system and reboot.

**NOTE**    If at this point you experience an error, reboot with the Last Known Good configuration to restore the version of the Registry you had before you made these changes.

# Optimizing Windows 2000 Processor Time

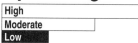

Windows 2000 maintains a set of defaults that control how much processor time is allocated to a thread, and also the relative time allocated to threads in the foreground versus threads in the background.

## Overview

The out-of-the-box turnings for these settings are good for most machines, but a discriminating administrator may want to fine-tune them. For instance, a system that gets virtually no desktop or user-interface activity may perform a little better if tuned to give more priority to background processes. That way, even if someone does log

**CHAPTER 2**

Hardware Tweaking

on to the system locally, the machine's main priorities will focus on its back-end functions, not on what is being run in the foreground (which, for a server, is as it should be).

---

# The Party Line

```
Microsoft has actually exposed part of the functionality for
this setting without requiring a Registry edit. If you open
the Control Panel, launch System, and then select Advanced |
Performance | Settings, followed by the Advanced tab, you
can adjust whether or not Windows prioritizes processes that
run in the foreground or background, as shown in Figure 2-3.
But there's no way to change any of the other settings that
govern this behavior; to do so requires a little Registry
hacking.
```

---

## *The Undocumented Solution*

*A Registry setting named Win32PrioritySeparation controls how threads are handled by the processor. The Registry setting is a bitmask, so it requires some deciphering to know how to use it correctly, as well as a little planning so you use values which best complement the server type you're using.*

## What You'll Need
A Registry editor, such as REGEDIT or REGEDT32

Follow these steps to optimize Windows 2000 processor time:

1. Fire up the Registry editor and navigate to HKEY_LOCAL_MACHINE\ System\CurrentControlSet\Control\PriorityControl. Win32PrioritySeparation should appear in that subkey as a DWORD value.

2. Win32PrioritySeparation is a six-bit value. The default value is 0×02 (hex). The best way to determine the value for this entry is to fire up the Calculator applet, set it to binary mode (select Scientific under the View menu if you don't see the option to enter binary), compile the value you're going to use from the choices below, switch the calculator to Hex or Dec(imal), and then enter the value listed.

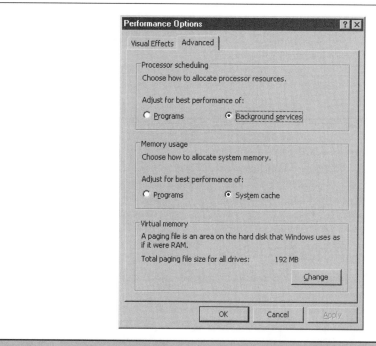

**Figure 2-3.**   The Advanced tab in Performance Options only allows you to choose giving priority
scheduling to either background or foreground services.

3.  The two leftmost bits, or the two highest bits, represent how long threads are
    permitted to run when they are scheduled. Setting them to **10** makes them run
    at shorter intervals. Setting them to **01** makes them run at longer intervals.

4.  The two middle bits determine whether the length of each thread cycle, or
    *quantum,* is fixed or variable. This has several consequences: if you set this to
    fixed, the same quantum value applies for both background and foreground
    threads. If you set it to variable, the length of each thread's execution time will
    vary, but the *ratio* of foreground to background time remains fixed. (However,
    we can change that to some degree as well, which will be revealed later.) Set
    these two bits to **01** to use variable-length quanta, and **10** to use fixed-length
    quanta.

5.  The lowest, or rightmost, two bits determine the ratio of foreground to
    background threads. A value of **00** means that foreground and background
    threads get the same ratio of time, and overrides any variable-length specification
    (as seen in #4). A value of **01** means that foreground processes get allocated
    twice the amount of time as background processes. A value of **10** or **11** means
    foreground processes get *three* times the amount of processor time as background
    processes.

> **NOTE** These values apply for Windows 2000 Server and Windows 2003 Server *only*. They are not valid for Windows 2000 Workstation or Windows XP Home or Professional. They can be added, but the system won't recognize them.

6. Set the value and reboot.

By default, the settings in Windows 2000/2003 Server provide foreground and background threads with equal processing priority. The importance of quanta only really becomes significant on a system where there is 100 percent CPU utilization. With that in mind, the best way to make use of this tweak is on a system where you have intense background processes running, but where, when someone uses the console directly, they receive priority.

# `2000/2003` Permanently Setting Processor Affinity for an Application

| High |
|------|
| Moderate |
| Low |

In multiprocessor systems, "affinity" is the term used to describe the dedication of an application to a particular processor. Normally, a program will find affinity with whatever processor is most appropriate—if the program is multithreaded, it will spread its workload across all the available processors unless told otherwise. In some cases, an administrator will want to insure that a given process *always* runs on a given processor.

## Overview

Multiprocessor systems have gone from being exotic, closeted specimens of the high-end server world to halfway commonplace desktop machines. Among the power-gamer set, a multiprocessor box is a luxury, but far from a rarity. In the server room, meanwhile, a multiprocessor computer is more the rule than the exception.

---

## The Party Line                                        Company X

```
Generally, the only way to set processor affinity for an
application is to manually select its image name in Task
Manager, right-click it, and chose Set Affinity. In theory,
it would be possible to script a program launch with an
affinity-setting action afterwards, but there's an easier
way to make affinity permanent for any application image.
```

## *The Undocumented Solution*

*Interestingly enough, the way to do this in a more permanent fashion comes from Microsoft itself, but with very little fanfare. It's also not easy to come by.*

## What You'll Need

A utility called IMAGECFG.EXE, which ships in the \support\debug\i386 folder of the Windows NT 4.0 CD-ROM, as a native component to Windows 2000 Advanced Server, and is available in the Windows 2000 Server Resource Kit Supplement One (http://www.microsoft.com/mspress/books/4994.asp).

Here's how to use the tool:

1. From the command line, type **IMAGECFG –A** [*affinitymask*] [*applicationpath*], where *applicationpath* is the drive and path to the application image.

2. The *affinitymask* parameter specifies which CPU to use (from 0 to 31—that is, processor number 1–32), and is a hex expression of a binary value. For instance, if you want to bind an application to processor 2, that would be 100 in binary, or 0×4 in hex, as you can see in the following table.

| CPU ID | Bitmask in Hex |
|--------|----------------|
| 0 | 0×1 |
| 1 | 0×2 |
| 2 | 0×4 |
| 3 | 0×8 |

**NOTE**   Don't attempt to run IMAGECFG on a kernel-level binary, such as NTDLL.DLL, or a kernel-level device driver. This can trash your system and force a replacement of the corrupted component.

# 2000/2003 Setting Device Driver Affinity in a Multiprocessor System

High
Moderate
Low

When device drivers run in a multiprocessor system, the computer usually binds the device driver to whatever processor and interrupt is available. The processor with the lowest interrupt request priority (usually processor 1) serves the request for that interrupt, unless its interrupts are completely filled. It is possible, though, to override this behavior and direct interrupts for device drivers to a specific processor.

## Overview

As mentioned previously, most multiprocessor machines are configured rather passively by their administrators. There's not a lot of work or planning done with affinity, whether for programs or drivers; there's also a tendency to let the chips fall where they may (pardon the pun). But a little work can yield some major results.

## The Party Line                                    Company X

```
Microsoft has largely taken a lot of the pain of configuring
device drivers out of the hands of administrators. Windows
2000 and 2003 no longer require the user to select IRQs
for hardware—in fact, they openly prohibit it unless the
machine in question is explicitly lacking in support for
IRQ assignments under Plug and Play conventions. This has
made it easier to get a machine up and running, but a little
harder to tweak it.
```

# The Undocumented Solution

*Microsoft itself has offered up (again, quietly, with little or no fanfare) a tool for allowing an administrator to associate a device driver with a particular processor. This makes it possible to do some very elegant load-balancing—for instance, if you have multiple network adapters, or a network adapter and a disk controller, you can assign them to different processors to more effectively distribute the incoming workload.*

## What You'll Need

A kernel-level filter driver, named INTFILTR, which can be found at ftp://ftp.microsoft.com/bussys/winnt/winnt-public/tools/affinity/IntFiltr.zip. Be sure to read the documentation for the driver before attempting to use it, however.

Here's how to use the filter:

1. Install the filter, INTFILTR.SYS, by copying it to the %SystemRoot%\system32\drivers directory of the computer.
2. Double-click the INFILTR.REG file to install the Registry changes needed to implement the filter.
3. Run the INTFILTR.EXE application. Select a device from the Devices list (shown in Figure 2-4), and click Add Filter to turn on filtering for that particular device.
4. The Don't Restart Device When Making Changes check box is for setting affinity on devices which should not be stopped and restarted right now, such as a video driver.
5. Click Set Mask for the device to control which CPU to assign affinity to.
6. Click Done when finished.
7. Reboot to institute the changes.

2000/2003 # Disabling Last Access Time Stamp in NTFS

| High |
| Moderate |
| Low |

NTFS tracks many different types of metadata for files, much more so than FAT or FAT32. Some of this information pertains to permissions on files or objects; some of it is quota information; and some of it is lesser-used but still-useful metadata, such as the last time a given file was accessed.

**CHAPTER 2**

Hardware Tweaking

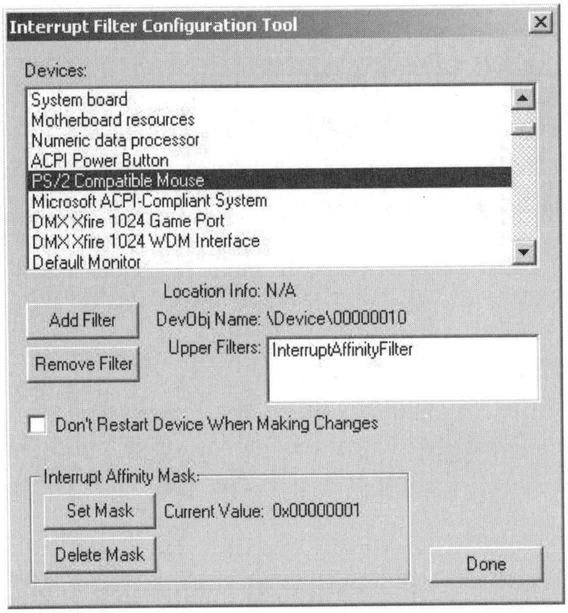

**Figure 2-4.** The Interrupt Filter Configuration Tool allows you to assign processor affinity to a specific driver.

## Overview

Any changes made to NTFS metadata require a certain amount of disk operations. Even though Windows has a good deal of intelligent disk caching, at some point things have to be written out to disk, and the less data that actually needs to be written, the faster things will move. To that end, there is a Registry entry that allows the user to disable the updating of the Last Access Time Stamp for NTFS.

By default, this function records the last time a given file was accessed in any form, whether for a read or write operation. Since there are many circumstances where this information is not terribly useful, it can be disabled.

## The Party Line                                    Company X

Microsoft does indeed mention disabling the Last Access Time Stamp in passing, but not as a performance-enhancing measure. In a way this is understandable, since this information is important for some people—for instance, information regarding file-repository servers. When Microsoft talks about it, it's only as a workaround for certain problems (such as in Article 150355, "Windows NT Nonresponsive During NTFS Directory Traversal," an NT 3.51/4.0 problem that appears to have been corrected with a service pack), almost never as a generic performance-enhancing trick.

## *The Undocumented Solution*

*Disabling the time stamp does speed up performance on NTFS partitions a bit, since it's one less thing that has to be written to disk. The one thing you need to keep in mind when doing this is whether or not that metadata is really important to you. If you can envision a case where it is, leave it on; if you can't, shut it off. You can always re-enable it later.*

*If you have many directories with thousands of files in them, the NTFS in-memory log buffer can be filled up very quickly by time stamp update operations, so turning this off is useful on systems with many files.*

## What You'll Need

A Registry editor, such as REGEDIT or REGEDT32

Be sure to reboot after following these steps:

1. Open the Registry Editor and navigate to the key HKEY_LOCAL_MACHINE\System\CurrentControlSet\Control\FileSystem.

2. Add a new DWORD value named **NtfsDisableLastAccessUpdate** and set it to **1**. (To re-enable the Last Access Time Stamp, set this value to 0 or delete the DWORD value completely.)

# 2000/2003 Disabling 8.3 Filename Generation in NTFS

For the sake of backwards compatibility, Windows maintains a store on each NTFS volume that contains a copy of all filenames on that volume, rendered in abbreviated

(DOS-style) 8.3 fashion. 8.3-style names have to be generated anew whenever a new file is created, an operation which takes a certain amount of overhead.

## Overview

If you have no DOS or Windows 3.*x* clients on your system, or if you're not using programs which require 8.3 filenames to work correctly (for example, 16-bit Windows or DOS command-line programs), you can disable 8.3 filename creation and gain back some speed.

---

# The Party Line                    `Company X`

```
Microsoft points out several things about this trick which
are worth keeping in mind. First off, as mentioned earlier,
you can't use this on a file system that is accessed by
any OS which only uses 8.3 filenames—DOS, Windows 3.x, or
Windows for Workgroups 3.x. Second, you should also be aware
that this trick does not remove existing 8.3 name stores—it
only stops the creation of new ones. So, any existing files
that have 8.3 names will continue to have 8.3 names, and any
files created after applying this hack will not.
```

---

## *The Undocumented Solution*

*There are a few other things which Microsoft does not point out—not directly, anyway—that are also worth keeping in mind. First, there are some 32-bit applications that will not install correctly unless 8.3 name creation is enabled. Microsoft's own Quicken 2003 is just such an application. Many servers may not rely on programs that need this enabled to install correctly, but it's best to be aware of it should problems arise.*

*Second, people have asked in the past how to remove the existing 8.3 namespace to free up room in the file system. There's no easy way to do this aside from moving all the files on a given volume off, disabling 8.3 name creation, reformatting the volume, and copying the files back in. An existing volume with a lot of files on it might gain back a few megabytes from doing this, but whether or not that little return is worth the investment of effort is up to the user. In theory, this might also lessen the amount of*

*NTFS directory structure fragmentation, but reformatting and recopying the disk's*
*contents would likely do that anyway.*

## What You'll Need

A Registry editor, such as REGEDIT or REGEDT32

Here are the steps for disabling 8.3 filename generation in NTFS:

1. Open your Registry editor and navigate to HKEY_LOCAL_MACHINE\
   SYSTEM\CurrentControlSet\Control\FileSystem.
2. Change the value of the subkey NtfsDisable8dot3NameCreation to **1**.

`2000/2003` # Changing Cluster Sizes in NTFS Volumes

When a partition is first formatted with NTFS, Windows uses a default cluster size that
is determined by the size of the partition. Most disk sizes these days will force a cluster
size of 4K, which is the largest default cluster size available. However, it is possible to
force a larger cluster size—up to 256K—by supplying options to the FORMAT command.

## Overview

Most users stay with the default cluster size, but larger cluster sizes can be used to gain
some performance increases and reduce the overhead required by the file system on
that volume. This has to be done when the drive is first formatted, for the most part
(see later in this section for more on that).

Larger cluster sizes work best on volumes where the files are rarely smaller than
the cluster size itself. 4K is chosen as the default cluster size for most volumes because
few files fall below the 4K threshold. A drive with a 64K cluster size, however, would
only benefit from having this if the vast majority of files were 64K or larger. Otherwise,
the amount of wasted cluster space would seriously offset any gains in performance.
This sort of waste is referred to as "slack space," since Windows only allocates a cluster
to one particular file at a time even if that cluster is not completely used.

## The Party Line                                    `Company X`

```
Microsoft discusses formatting a drive with a cluster size
other than the default, or one larger than 4K, and mentions
a point worth considering: application compatibility. For
instance, some setup programs use the cluster size to
```

compute available free space, and aren't aware that cluster
sizes can change. Because of this, they may report a lack
of free space where there's plenty to be had. A non-standard
cluster size also makes NTFS on-disk compression impossible;
anything other than a 4K cluster size disables NTFS
compression on that volume automatically.
Also, when you format a partition using the GUI formatting
tools, the cluster sizes only range from 512 bytes to 4K;
no other, larger options are given. They *are* available, just
not through the GUI. These options can only be performed
through a CLI FORMAT command.

## *The Undocumented Solution*

*The best approach to using a non-standard cluster size is to use it only on* **data** *volumes rather than any place where applications are being installed, and where NTFS compression is not going to be used.*

One good example of this would be a video-editing workstation. If you're storing your video clips all on one volume, and no clip is smaller than 64K, you can gain back some disk overhead and increase throughput slightly by formatting the storage partition with 64K clusters. Another good example would be an enterprise-level database server, where the database files can be gigabytes in size.

Another point Microsoft does not mention is that changing cluster sizes can have unexpected consequences for third-party disk utilities. There are some which are large-cluster aware, and others that can even perform on-the-fly cluster-size conversions, but a drive that is formatted with large clusters should be backed up a little more attentively than other partitions. (Non-standard clusters also cannot be defragmented by the built-in defragmentation tool, although in this case a third-party tool may be able to do so.)

> **NOTE**    Breaking a disk into more than two partitions is usually a waste of disk space. NTFS handles large partitions and large disks far more robustly than FAT or FAT32. If you want to partition a disk to segregate your operating system and your data, it's worth doing since you do get some benefit by having the two kept separate. More than two partitions will often make things even slower, since the drive head has to do that much more movement to transverse partitions. Also, never convert an existing FAT32 partition to NTFS if you can help it; if possible, format the partition as NTFS first and then move everything onto it.

## What You'll Need

The command-line FORMAT utility—you can't format a drive to a non-standard cluster size using the GUI-based format tools or the Disk Management snap-in.

Here's how to format using a nonstandard cluster size:

1. Prepare the partition in question. Any files on the drive will need to be moved off.

2. From the command line, type **FORMAT** [*volume*] **/A:**[*clustersize*], where *volume* is the drive letter for the volume and *clustersize* is the size of the cluster to use. *clustersize* can be 512, 1024, 2048, 4096 (the default), 8192, 16K, 32K, or 64K.

3. Provided the volume in question can support the format with that cluster size, the format will take place.

**NOTE**   Cluster sizes of 128K and 256K are supported on FAT16 and FAT32 volumes, but FAT is always less robust than NTFS when it comes to error correcting and recovery. If you're dealing with big files, it's probably smarter to use NTFS anyway.

2000/2003 ## Changing Master File Table Allocations for NTFS to Offset Fragmentation

The Master File Table in a newly created NTFS volume occupies a fixed percentage of the disk's space, referred to as the MFT Zone. As more files are added to that volume, the space allocated to the Zone may change, and if a great many files (thousands or tens of thousands) are added to a given volume, the MFT may grow quite a bit. Since the MFT does not shrink when files are deleted, this may cause it to fragment.

## Overview

As a way to pre-emptively guard against Master File Table fragmentation, it's possible to pre-allocate more space for the Master File Table by editing the Registry. This will cause all volumes mounted (not formatted) after the change to have a certain percentage of space dynamically pre-allocated.

## The Party Line                                    Company X

The default allocation zone for the Master File Table is
12.5 percent of free disk space. This percentage can be

CHAPTER
2

Hardware Tweaking

changed, although Microsoft recommends the defaults for most types of systems. By this, Microsoft means a computer without an extraordinarily high number of files per volume—as well as machines where large numbers of files are not being created and then destroyed.

There is some controversy about the fact that the MFT does not shrink. In NTFS5, the MFT Zone is a way of providing a certain amount of overhead for the MFT to expand without fragmenting. When files are deleted and new ones created, their empty entries in the MFT are re-used. If the entire MFT Zone is not eaten up in this fashion, then the next time the volume in question is mounted, the Zone starts at the end of the actual size of the MFT. Also, remember that this zone is *not* "off limits" to conventional files. If the system needs to put files there, it will.

## *The Undocumented Solution*

*If you're confronted with either of the two preceding scenarios, then raising the initial allocation for the MFT may help speed things up a bit. Keep in mind that this allocation is going to be perpetually top-heavy: once space is allocated, it's not freed up, so bear this in mind. (Note that the Zone is not the total space actually allocated to the MFT, but rather the space reserved for the MFT to expand into.)*

*Also, this option cannot be set on a volume-by-volume basis. Once it's set, it affects all volumes on a given system. If you only have one major volume, then this is moot, but for systems with multiple partitions, it needs to be considered as a possible reason not to do this (since what works for one partition may not work for another).*

*Finally, editing the Registry does not allow you to specify the exact size or even the ratio of MFT allocation to volume size. You are only allowed to set the MFT zone to one of four predefined sizes (defined by a DWORD which is, appropriately enough, 1 through 4). These values are not documented because they may be revised from service pack to service pack. The best thing to do is experiment by changing the setting from "1" to "2" and seeing if that has a positive impact on the allocation and deallocation of file space.*

## What You'll Need

A Registry editor, such as REGEDIT or REGEDT32

Follow these steps to change the allocation:

1. Fire up the Registry editor and navigate to HKEY_LOCAL_MACHINE\ System\CurrentControlSet\Control\FileSystem.
2. Create a new DWORD named **NtfsMftZoneReservation** and set it to **2,** initially (2 generally corresponds to 25 percent of the available free space).
3. Reboot.

## 2000/2003 Using a Third-Party Defragmentation Program

When files are created, deleted, and moved within a system, they become fragmented— the clusters that make up each file are no longer contiguous. If this happens enough, the system can slow down drastically. One common recommendation for a system administrator is to schedule regular disk defragmentation cycles.

## Overview

Starting with Windows 2000, Microsoft now ships a simple defragmentation tool— actually a scaled-down version of Executive Software's Diskeeper program—which allows defragmentation of conventional files and directories. It does not, however, defragment internal NTFS structures such as the Master File Table, nor does it defragment in-use files such as the swap file or the Registry.

## The Party Line                                    Company X

```
Microsoft itself strongly recommends using a defragmentation
tool regularly to enhance system performance. For basic
defragmentation needs—on a workstation, for instance—the
built-in defragmentation tool is acceptable. For a server,
however, it becomes far less adequate as time goes on. Since
the built-in defragger cannot handle many advanced functions
(such as defragmenting MFT space), a third-party defragger
is recommended for any machine that does more than casual
file serving.
```

## *The Undocumented Solution*

*While Microsoft does recommend a third-party defrag tool, they don't restrict themselves to saying which one to use. There are several choices for Windows servers, each with features peculiar to it, which may (or may not) grant a performance boost. The controversy over the specific advantages or disadvantages of some of these features is ongoing, and while there is a great deal of anecdotal evidence to favor the use of one or more of them, there is a lot less hard testing being done to determine their benefits (or downsides) than there really ought to be.*

One of the main features almost all of these programs boast is that they defragment and consolidate free space on a drive. I am still somewhat skeptical of the absolute value of this, since NTFS has a number of built-in measures to keep files from being fragmented (although they're far from perfect), and so having contiguous free space is often not as important. If a drive was big enough and there was enough on it, I would be willing to wager that the process of defragmenting would incur more overhead than the fragmentation itself—although I'd temper that by saying that's more likely to be the case if the administrator overscheduled defragging the drive.

To that end, here's a rundown of the major defragmentation programs and their benefits and deficits. Almost all of these programs are available in evaluation versions which run for 30 days or so, which should given an administrator enough time to determine their usefulness.

- **Executive Software's Diskeeper**    Shown in Figure 2-5, this is one of the most widely touted and famous disk defragmentation programs for Windows servers. Part of its fame comes from its existing synergy with Windows: the defragmenter shipped with Windows is a scaled-down version of Diskeeper. The full version of the product, which is in its 7.0 revision as of this writing, sports a number of features that makes it attractive to administrators: it can be pushed out across a network with relative ease to multiple machines; defragmentation cycles can be scheduled; the defrag algorithm copes far better with low disk space and is faster than the standard defragmenter in Windows; the program can be set to run only when the system is idling; and so on. Among the more useful features are a "Smart Scheduling" function which triggers defragmentation when a certain threshold of scattering is reached, and a "Frag Guard" technology which keeps the MFT and swap files from becoming fragmented. This is certainly the most robust and longest-lived defragmentation product for Windows servers, and probably the best place for an interested administrator to start looking. Diskeeper also has a "set it and forget it" function: Once a drive is configured, it can be defragmented on a regular schedule without user intervention.

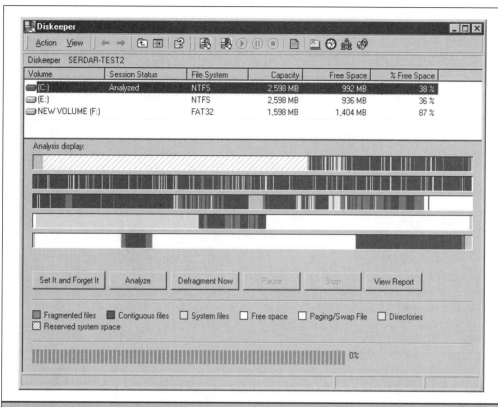

**Figure 2-5.**    The defragmentation tool included with Windows 2000 / 2003 is a stripped-down version of Executive Software's Diskeeper. The full version is far more robust.

- **Raxco's PerfectDisk**    Shown in Figure 2-6, this is a relatively new entry to the arena of defragmentation tools, and claims several features as its selling points. Like Diskeeper, PerfectDisk also defragments system files, although the truly immovable ones cannot be defragmented "live." Instead, they must be defragged at boot-time, before the GUI is loaded. The program's most widely touted feature is "SMART Placement" technology, which reorganizes the placement of files on the disk so that the most frequently accessed but least modified files are placed on the periphery of the disk, while those most commonly changed are placed closer to the center, around a contiguous block of free space. The benefits of this strategy may not be the same for all systems—for instance, if you're using a RAID array, what constitutes the "outside" and "inside" of the disk when dealing with cluster numbers may not correspond in any way to the physical organization of the disk. It has the benefit of being unique, however, and is certainly worth looking into as a creative solution to the problem of progressive file fragmentation.

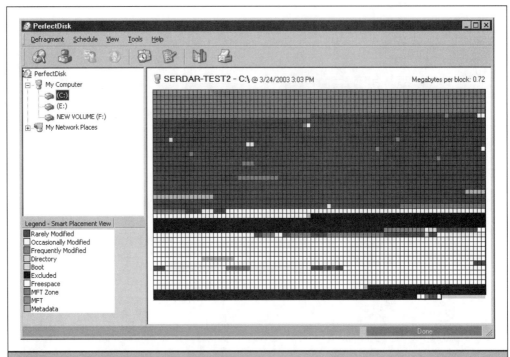

**Figure 2-6.**    PerfectDisk uses a patented disk-organization scheme to pre-emptively prevent fragmentation.

- **O&O Software's O&O Defrag**   Shown in Figure 2-7, this is the newest contender among these programs, and is in many ways quite competitive with the others. Its "Stealth" defragmentation mode reorganizes files only when the system is idle, and it features five separate strategies for defragmenting files: stealth, space (the standard defrag-and-push-everything-together strategy), defrag by filename, defrag by date (with the most recently used files placed "last") and defrag by last access. The last two modes will probably show the most benefit on systems with high traffic, although an administrator will need to evaluate that for themselves using real statistics rather than taking the programmer's word for it.

One good way to determine the efficacy of a defragmentation tool is to use live system statistics. For instance, a database system can be timed for a million-record random-access update using different defragmentation strategies to see whether or not organizing the database file according to date/time or free-space methods is more effective. This sort of testing can be time-consuming, but if you're building a system to last years, it's better to spend time now finding out what works than to put your faith in something that, in the long run, may be *less* effective than doing nothing.

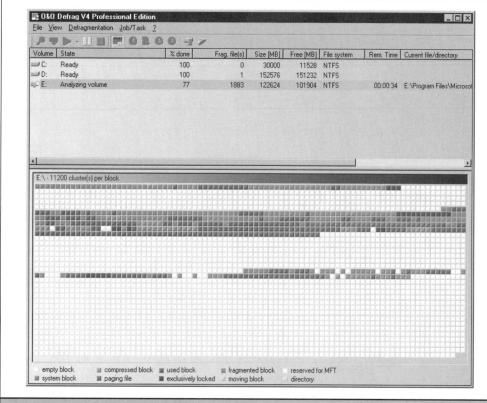

CHAPTER
2

Hardware Tweaking

**Figure 2-7.** O&O Defrag features five separate strategies for defragmenting files.

Last of all, it is possible to stick with the existing built-in defragmenter, even though Microsoft claims it can't be used to schedule defragmentation cycles. This is not entirely true, however, since it's possible to schedule a Visual Basic script that will run the defragmentation automatically.

The following code is a script that will do this. Copy it into a file named DEFRAG.VBS (the actual choice of filename is arbitrary, but it must have the .VBS extension) and using the Task Scheduler, schedule it to run at the intervals of your choosing. This script will work in both Windows 2000 and 2003.

```
set WshShell = CreateObject("WScript.Shell")
WshShell.Run "dfrg.msc"
WScript.Sleep 2000
While WshShell.AppActivate("Disk Defragmenter") = FALSE
wscript.sleep 1000
```

```
Wend
WshShell.AppActivate "Disk Defragmenter"
WScript.Sleep 500
WshShell.SendKeys "{TAB}{HOME}"
WScript.Sleep 501
WshShell.SendKeys "%A"
WScript.Sleep 502
WshShell.SendKeys "D"
While WshShell.AppActivate("Defragmentation Complete") = FALSE
wscript.sleep 5001
Wend
WshShell.AppActivate "Defragmentation Complete"
WScript.Sleep 503
WshShell.Sendkeys "{TAB}"
Wscript.Sleep 504
WshShell.Sendkeys "{ENTER}"
Wscript.Sleep 505
WshShell.AppActivate "Disk Defragmenter"
WScript.Sleep 700
WshShell.Sendkeys "%{F4}"
```

---

**NOTE**   For the best results with any disk defragmenter, keep at least 40 percent free space available. When there's less than 40 percent free space, the defragmenter takes much longer to move data around. Many defragmenters claim to work in as little as 5 percent free space, but the more you have free, the better. Also, defragmenters as a rule do not move data to other drives temporarily during the defrag process, so the free space needs to be on the drive in question.

---

# CHAPTER 3
## *Desktop and UI*

**In This Chapter:**

- [ ] Adding AutoComplete to the Command-Line Interface
- [ ] Adding a DOS Prompt / CLI Prompt Context Menu to Folders and Drives
- [ ] Customizing Explorer's Thumbnailing Settings
- [ ] Changing Start Menu Behavior
- [ ] Changing Taskbar Behavior
- [ ] Customizing the Windows OEM Options, Including Explorer Toolbar Bitmaps and Support Information
- [ ] Speeding Up Desktop Display Behaviors
- [ ] Setting ClearType Gamma Options
- [ ] Changing the Size of the Shell Icon Cache
- [ ] Enforcing Consistent Views of Folders and Windows in Explorer
- [ ] Setting a Password Grace Period for Screensavers
- [ ] Changing Directories for Temporary Internet Files
- [ ] Preventing Open Copies of Explorer from Restarting on Reboot

Most users think of a Windows server as something that sits in a back room somewhere, for the most part unseen and untouched. Administrators, on the other hand, deal with servers on a daily basis, or at least far more than non-administrative users.

On a basic aesthetic level, it makes sense to configure the Windows interface to be something you're comfortable with. If you spend a lot of time working with Windows, then the less eyestrain you suffer, the better. That's especially true if you're an administrator.

Another reason, not as widely discussed, is that changing the way Windows presents itself can sometimes give you a faster, more responsive machine. It won't overclock your CPU (not that you would want to, if you're running a production server!), but it will reduce the amount of lag time required for the system to animate things or create onscreen effects such as fades or rolling menus. They're pleasing to the eye at first, but after a while people would rather have menus and windows pop up immediately.

This chapter presents a number of ways to change the Windows interface, for the sake of greater speed or convenience. Not all of them may be to your taste or needs, but you can read them over and pick the ones most appropriate for you. Almost all of these changes bring with them little or no risk as well, so you can experiment freely (although you may want to do so in a non-administrator account!).

Microsoft has published an unsupported tool that allows you to make a number of these changes without having to delve into the Registry. Named Tweak UI, it was originally introduced in Windows 95, then later republished in Windows 2000 and Windows XP editions. It's still available, and is probably better than hacking the Registry directly—but there are a great many things it doesn't do. Also, it can be valuable to know how to manually change many of the settings it presents—in a piece of VBScript code, for instance, or in one's own programs. Tweak UI is available as part of the PowerToys for Windows XP download set, found at http://www.microsoft.com/windowsxp/pro/downloads/powertoys.asp.

A system builder who wants to deploy many of these changes at once can take advantage of some of the technologies in Windows to do that, either on existing systems or on newly built ones. Rather than re-insert everything tediously by hand, you can use one of the following methodologies:

- Create a .reg file which contains all the changes to be made, and merge it with a system build as part of a post-deployment procedure, or merge it with a system prior to imaging.

- Create an MSI file with the same changes and push it out to existing systems.

- Create a mandatory user profile with the changes in question (KnowledgeBase article 323368 explains how to do this for Windows 2000).

- Create a group policy configuration that includes these custom Registry settings. The way to do this is by creating administrative templates (.adm files) for the Group Policy Object Editor. An advantage to using group policies in this fashion is that the modifications are persistent. Because of this, you may want to choose your changes carefully. An example of such a file's structure and syntax can be found at http://msdn.microsoft.com/library/default.asp?url=/library/en-us/policy/policy/administrative_template_file_format.asp.

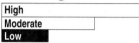

# Adding AutoComplete to the Command-Line Interface

| High |
|------|
| Moderate |
| Low |

Administrators love the command line. Nothing will probably ever completely replace it, and for good reason: it's sometimes just easier to type commands instead of working through the GUI to get to the right menu choices. To that end, the CLI—command-line interface—remains a continuing part of the Windows interface.

## Overview

Possibly because it's so ubiquitous, the Windows command line is also a little limited. It's been augmented and bolstered with each successive version of Windows, but at its core is the same CLI we've known, despite being under-documented and not as feature-rich out of the box as UNIX.

---

## The Party Line                    Company X

```
Microsoft doesn't aggressively document or promote
additional features for CLI users, which probably comes as
no big surprise. One of Windows' strengths is the classic
Windows GUI, which is favored heavily over the CLI when it
comes to features. As a result, the GUI winds up with most
of the interesting tweaks.
```

---

### *The Undocumented Solution*

*That said, there are augmentations to the CLI, not turned on by default, which can be quite useful. One of them is the AutoComplete feature.*

*Windows NT, 2000, and XP provide a feature at the command prompt (cmd.exe) known as AutoComplete. If this feature is activated, you can type a character followed*

CHAPTER
3

Desktop and UI

*by a special key, and Windows will try to automatically complete the command for you with the files or directories in the current directory—much in the same way that it tries to perform an AutoComplete for URLs in the Internet Explorer (IE) address bar. The system can be set to use different special keys for AutoCompleting files vs. AutoCompleting directories.*

*By default, this feature is only turned on for files, not folders, and the AutoComplete key for files isn't even documented: it's the TAB key. To edit it, you'll need to change the Registry entry that controls it.*

## What You'll Need

A Registry editor, such as REGEDIT or REGEDT32

Be sure to reboot after following these steps:

1. Open the Registry and navigate to HKEY_CURRENT_USER\Software\ Microsoft\Command Processor. If you want to make this change valid for all users, past, present and future, go instead to HKEY_LOCAL_MACHINE\Software\Microsoft\Command Processor.

2. Add or edit the REG_DWORD value named CompletionChar. This sets the completion keystroke for filenames.

3. Set CompletionChar to the hex value of the control character you want to use.

4. To set the completion keystroke for pathnames, add or edit a REG_DWORD named PathCompletionChar and set it to the hex value of the key code to use. See Table 3-1.

5. Reboot and test the AutoCompletion function in a CMD session.

| Keystroke | Hex Code |
|-----------|----------|
| CTRL-D | 04 |
| CTRL-F | 06 |
| BACKSPACE | 08 |
| TAB | 09 |

**Table 3-1.** Common AutoCompletion Keystrokes for the Command Line and Their Corresponding Hex Codes

2000/2003 # Adding a DOS Prompt / CLI Prompt Context Menu to Folders and Drives

| High |
| Moderate |
| **Low** |

Aside from extensions to the command line itself, other changes can be made to how the command line is invoked—for instance, through a right-click context menu.

## Overview

When a CLI prompt is launched (which is also generically referred to as a "DOS prompt," even though DOS does not exist in Windows 2000/2003), it usually opens in the Documents and Settings subfolder for the currently logged-in user. Most of the time, a user will want to do file operations in another folder, and anything that can spare users the trouble of having to manually change directories is usually worth it.

## The Party Line                                    Company X

Normally, the only way to launch a DOS prompt from the Windows interface is to either launch the Command Prompt shortcut in the Start menu, or to go to the Run box and type **CMD** to launch CMD.exe. It's possible to expand on this behavior, however—for instance, by creating a right-click context menu for any drive or folder that launches a CLI at that location.

## The Undocumented Solution

*Adding a right-click context menu to invoke the DOS prompt requires that you edit the Registry in two places.*

CHAPTER 3

Desktop and UI

## What You'll Need

A Registry editor, such as REGEDIT or REGEDT32

Make the following changes, in this order:

1.  Open the Registry and navigate to \HKEY_CLASSES_ROOT\Directory\Shell.

2.  Create a new subkey named DosHere if there isn't already one present.

3.  Edit the existing "(Default)" REG_SZ value in DosHere to read:

    ```
    Dos &Prompt Here
    ```

4.  Within DosHere, create a new subkey named Command.

5.  Edit the existing "(Default)" REG_SZ value under Command and set it to:

    ```
    E:\WINDOWS\System32\cmd.exe /k cd "%1"
    ```

6.  Navigate to \HKEY_CLASSES_ROOT\Directory\Shell.

7.  Create a new subkey named DosHere if there isn't already one present, and set its "(Default)" value as listed in step 3.

8.  Within DosHere, create a new subkey named Command.

9.  Set the "(Default)" entry within it to the same value listed in step 5.

10. Log off and back on again.

11. When you right-click files and folders, you should see the context menu for launching a DOS prompt shown here.

## Customizing Explorer's Thumbnailing Settings

Thumbnail View in Windows Explorer allows you to display the contents of a folder as a series of tiled thumbnail images. Any file format that can be understood by Explorer as being an image will show up in this mode. (Generally, any file that can be viewed in the Image Viewer is also visible as a thumbnail, but there may be exceptions. Some programs, such as Photoshop, save a thumbnail of the image as metadata.)

## Overview

While thumbnail mode is convenient, it's also slow—especially on machines that aren't very fast to begin with. Thumbnails are built and stored in a hidden file called THUMBS.DB, and are stored on a folder-by-folder basis: each folder has its own THUMBS.DB file.

Each time the folder is browsed anew, the THUMBS.DB file is re-created. Folders with a lot of images in them (several hundred or more) can take a long time to process. Worse, the process of rebuilding the thumbnails causes many of Explorer's other functions to grind to a crawl or stop completely!

## The Party Line                          Company X

To get around the slowness that using thumbnails can cause, a number of stock solutions are usually tossed around, such as storing less images per folder (which is actually a good idea anyway) or using a professional thumbnailing utility. For people who have no choice, however, or like the convenience that the built-in thumbnailer provides, there are some other answers. (If you *do* want to use a third-party product and are interested in disabling thumbnailing entirely, that's also possible; read on.)

## *The Undocumented Solution*

*There are three Registry entries that control thumbnailing: one to turn it on and two more to modify both the size and the quality of the generated images. Scaling back the size of the thumbnails or reducing the quality factor can often make the thumbnailing process go much faster, even on a folder with a great many images. Because the thumbnails are, by default, small (96 pixels maximum on a side), the quality doesn't need to be high in the first place, and so a good deal of processing power in creating the thumbnails is often expended for no good reason.*

## What You'll Need

A Registry editor, such as REGEDIT or REGEDT32

Be sure to log off and back on again after making these changes.

1. Open the Registry and navigate to HKEY_CURRENT_USER\Software\ Microsoft\Windows\CurrentVersion\Explorer\.

2. To change the size of the thumbnails, add a new REG_DWORD value named ThumbnailSize. Set it to the maximum size on a side, in pixels, that you want to use (in decimal).

3. To change the quality, add a new REG_DWORD named ThumbnailQuality, and set it to a number from 1 to 100 (again, decimal). Setting it to 1 produces quite satisfactory results; start there.

4. To disable thumbnailing entirely, navigate to the Advanced subkey of the current key and edit the value of DisableThumbnailCache. Set it to 1. If you've disabled thumbnailing, be sure to search your system for hidden files named THUMBS.DB and delete them to free up space.

5. Figure 3-1 shows a sample folder with an icon size of 128×128 pixels and a quality index of 1.

# Changing Start Menu Behavior

Windows 2003 contains several interface innovations ported from Windows XP. One of them is a redesigned version of the Start menu, with many context-sensitive functions that didn't appear before.

## Overview

Like the command line and Explorer, the Start menu is one of the few places Windows users spend a great deal of their time. There is a good deal of customizability available simply by right-clicking the Start button and selecting Properties.

# The Party Line                          Company X

```
However, a good deal of undocumented controls do exist for
the Start button, which are not exposed through the Properties
interface. As usual, Microsoft hasn't discussed many of these
options, if only because some of them may be reserved for
```

future uses which are not yet finalized. (This is actually one of the most common reasons for undocumented features in the UI remaining undocumented.)

# The Undocumented Solution

*What follows is a list of the most interesting and useful undocumented changes you can make to the Start menu.*

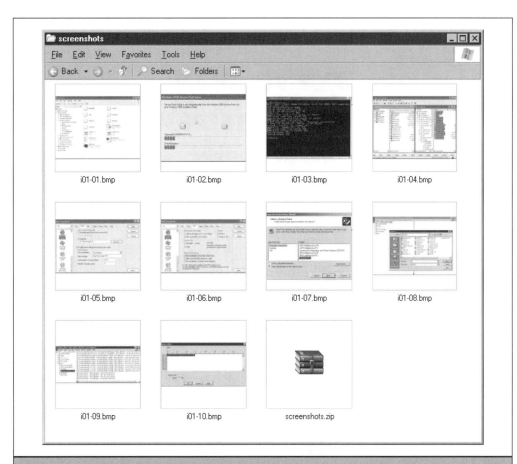

**Figure 3-1.**  A folder full of thumbnails at 128×128 pixels, with a quality setting of 1. It may not be that easy to see in this image, but most of the details have been preserved.

## What You'll Need

A Registry editor, such as REGEDIT or REGEDT32

Be sure to log off and back on again after completing the steps in each of the following sections.

To add a new Start menu entry just below the "Run" line:

1. Open the Registry and navigate to HKEY_CLASSES_ROOT\CLSID\{2559a1f6-21d7-11d4-bdaf-00c04f60b9f0}\Instance\InitPropertyBag.

2. Add a REG_SZ value named Param1, and set this to the command you want to execute when this command is run. This can be an executable or a valid URL.

3. Add a REG_SZ value named Command, and label it the way you would like it to appear on the Start menu. This command will be available for all users.

4. If you want to specify an icon for the image, open the DefaultIcon subkey (on the same level as the InitPropertyBag subkey) and set the "(Default)" value there to the path of an icon (whether in a valid icon file or in a .dll).

To set the number of items in the My Recent Documents list:

1. Navigate to HKEY_CURRENT_USER\Software\Microsoft\Windows\CurrentVersion\Policies\Explorer\.

2. Add a new REG_DWORD value named MaxRecentDocs and set the value to the number of documents you want to show in the list for the current user. If this key is deleted, the default is 15.

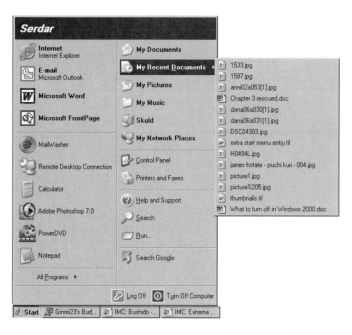

To force the Start menu to appear in its original (Windows 2000) format:

1. Navigate to HKEY_CURRENT_USER\Software\Microsoft\Windows\ CurrentVersion\Policies\Explorer\.

2. Add a new REG_DWORD value named NoSimpleStartMenu and set the value to 1. This will prevent the Start menu from appearing in its more advanced incarnation for the current user.

**NOTE** If you want to change the speed at which the Start submenus open, that's a global setting. See "Speeding Up Desktop Display Behaviors" later in this chapter.

CHAPTER 3

Desktop and UI

## 2003 Changing Taskbar Behavior

| High |
|------|
| Moderate |
| **Low** |

Like the Start menu, the taskbar in Windows 2003 Server has been redesigned with a host of new features drawn from Windows XP. Most of these features are behaviors that manifest themselves without user intervention, but which can benefit from a little tweaking.

## Overview

Most of the new taskbar functions deal with the way it handles massive numbers of open windows. If you have more than a certain number of similar windows open— such as multiple Internet Explorer sessions—the taskbar collapses them together into one entry to save space. Also new is the systemwide presence of balloon tips to call attention to certain taskbar functions, such as when a network connection fails or is established.

---

## The Party Line                                    Company X

```
Microsoft only allows for the outward customization of a
little of this functionality, and only through the standard
interface. Right-clicking an empty area of the taskbar to
bring up Properties allows you to make a few changes, but
a great many others have to be made manually.
```

---

## The Undocumented Solution

*Here is a set of the most useful under-the-hood changes you can make to the way the taskbar behaves.*

## What You'll Need

A Registry editor, such as REGEDIT or REGEDT32

Be sure to log off and then back on again after completing the steps in each of the following sections.

To change how the taskbar groups applications:

1. Open the Registry and navigate to HKEY_CURRENT_USER\Software\ Microsoft\Windows\CurrentVersion\Explorer\Advanced.

2. Add a new REG_DWORD value named TaskbarGroupSize and set its value according to the following chart:

| Behavior | Value |
|---|---|
| Group applications that have the largest number of oldest, opened windows first, and only when space is low | [Default behavior, no entry needed] |
| Group applications with the most windows open first, and only when space is low | 1 |
| Group applications with at least two windows open | 2 |
| Group applications with at least three windows open | 3 |
| Group applications with at least four windows open | 4 |

**NOTE**    This assumes that you have Taskbar Application Grouping turned on. To do this, right-click in an empty area of the taskbar, select Properties, and enable Group Similar Taskbar Buttons.

To change the behavior of a program in the taskbar that flashes to get the user's attention:

1. Open the Registry and navigate to HKEY_CURRENT_USER\Control Panel\ Desktop.

2. Edit the REG_DWORD value ForegroundFlashCount to the number of times an application should flash for attention in the toolbar. Setting this value to 0 means the application's icon will blink continuously until clicked.

3. To disable flashing entirely, edit the REG_DWORD value named ForegroundLockTimeout and set it to 0. To re-enable flashing, set the value to 200000 (decimal).

**NOTE**    This key also controls another behavior: the time period after user input during which the system will not allow an application to force itself into the background. It's set high (200 seconds, or 200,000 milliseconds), so that applications cannot jump into view and do things like interrupt your typing. This is especially useful if you use a program that throws a lot of windows onto the screen, such as AOL Instant Messenger.

To change the size of taskbar icons:

1. Open the Registry and navigate to HKEY_CURRENT_USER\Control Panel\ Desktop\WindowMetrics.

**CHAPTER 3**

Desktop and UI

2. Add a new REG_SZ value named MinWidth that describes the size of the taskbar in pixels, multiplied by –15.

To turn off balloon tips for items in the Notification Area:

1. Open the Registry and navigate to HKEY_CURRENT_USER\Software\ Microsoft\Windows\CurrentVersion\Explorer\Advanced.

2. Add a new REG_DWORD value named EnableBalloonTips and set its value to 0. Balloon tips like the one shown next will be disabled.

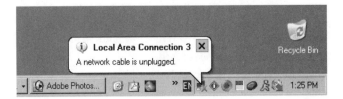

# Customizing the Windows OEM Options, Including Explorer Toolbar Bitmaps and Support Information

2000/2003

| High |
|------|
| Moderate |
| Low |

Many elements of the Windows interface can be customized by an OEM or PC manufacturer who wants to "personalize" their brand of PC. For instance, a Dell machine might sport the Dell logo on the desktop by default, or may come pre-shipped with an Internet provider that has "branded" Internet Explorer (IE) with their logos. All of these options are in fact available to the end user with a little work.

## Overview

Several OEM branding options are built into Windows, which make adding logos or customizations in certain designated areas quite easy. One common option among PC makers who customize Windows installations for their machines is to modify Explorer to add new bitmaps for the IE logo and the toolbar background bitmap. This includes the animated IE "swirling E" or "swirling flag" logo, which can also be changed. Another common branding option is to add manufacturer-specific support and equipment information to the General tab of the System Properties window.

## The Party Line

**Company X**

Most of the details on how to customize things like this are not offered up openly to end users by Microsoft. OEMs are often given far more detailed information on how to change such things, but even system administrators have to dig around a bit, and tools to make the job easier aren't bundled with Windows. Microsoft does offer the OEM Pre-Install Kit, available from their web site, but it requires registration to obtain and cannot be downloaded freely.

## *The Undocumented Solution*

*Customizing the presentation of IE and the support/manufacturer information in the General tab requires only that you have a Registry editor and a graphics editor.*

## What You'll Need

- A Registry editor, such as REGEDIT or REGEDT32
- A graphics editor, such as Photoshop or Paint
- A text editor, such as Notepad

Be sure to log off and back on again after following these steps:

1. Create the bitmap for an animated IE icon. This is the animation that appears when the browser loads pages. To do this, create a new bitmap that is 38 pixels wide, and 38 pixels times the number of frames in the animation tall. For instance, if you had an image that was 24 frames, then the bitmap would be 38×912 pixels. Save this image.

2. Create a copy of the 38-pixel-width image and reduce it to 22 pixels wide (but preserve the image proportions when doing so). Save this image as well, under a different filename.

3. Create the bitmap to appear behind the Explorer toolbar. This bitmap can be any size, but it should ideally be something that will show up easily behind the toolbar. (It's essentially a watermark-type image that is more wide than tall.)

**CHAPTER 3**

Desktop and UI

4. Open the Registry Editor and navigate to HKEY_CURRENT_USER\Software\ Microsoft\Internet Explorer\Toolbar.

5. Add or edit the existing REG_SZ value named BrandBitmap. Set this to the full path of the large bitmap you created.

6. Add or edit the existing REG_SZ value named SmBrandBitmap. Set this to the full path of the large bitmap you created.

7. Add or edit the existing REG_SZ value named BackBitmapIE5. Set this to the full path of the toolbar background bitmap you created.

8. Log off and back on again. The image shown next is a somewhat primitive example of a customized toolbar bitmap, although better artistic skills will probably produce better results!

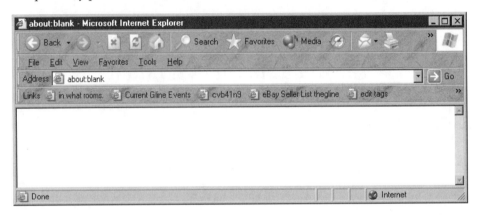

9. Go to the %SystemRoot%\System32 directory and edit the file OEMINFO.INI. OEMINFO.INI contains the following entries in its [General] section, which are left blank by default:

- **Manufacturer**   Set this to the name of the manufacturer or builder of the computer.

- **Model**   Set this to the specific make and model of the computer.

- **SubModel**   Optional setting that lets you specify a submodel for the computer.

- **SerialNo**   Optional setting that lets you provide the system's serial number, if needed.

- **OEM1, OEM2**   Other optional OEM information lines.

- **SupportURL**   Set this to the address of a web site, such as an intranet site, where support for this system can be obtained.

- **LocalFile**   Set this to the path of a local help file for this system.

10. In the [Support Information] section, you can insert multiple lines which can be used to provide additional support data. You can add as many lines as you want, in the format Line1=, Line2=, Line3=, and so on.

11. Create a "branding" bitmap for the General tab. This should be 180×114 pixels in size.

12. Save the picture as OEMLOGO.BMP in the same directory (%SystemRoot%\ System32). Here's an example of a customized General tab with a picture:

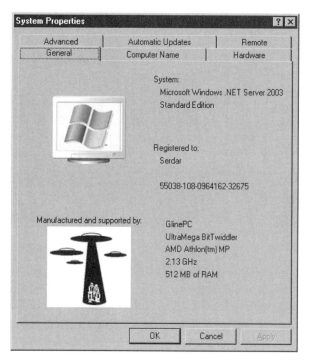

CHAPTER
3

Desktop and UI

## Speeding Up Desktop Display Behaviors

| High |
| Moderate |
| Low |

Certain elements of the Windows user interface—window animations or what Microsoft refers to as "visual feedback"—are designed to make the interface more coherent and sensible. For advanced users and administrators, however, they are often an annoyance, and they prefer to disable as many of them as possible.

## Overview

Windows 2000 Server has some elements of visual feedback turned on, but not others. Most of the visual feedback elements are disabled by default in Windows 2003 Server, so that the interface is minimally intrusive out of the box. This doesn't prevent such things from being reactivated, however, either by a user or by a program that insists on doing so.

---

# The Party Line                                    Company X

```
Microsoft does provide ways to turn off many examples of visual
feedback through the Display Properties page, but doesn't show
everything. Also, many aspects of the user interface's visual
feedback appear to be hardwired into the system, but can be
changed, even if Microsoft has not presented a way to do so
through Display Properties or other interfaces.
```

---

## *The Undocumented Solution*

*What follows is a list of many of the less-documented edits that can be performed on the user interface's visual feedback. Some programs can reactivate these behaviors, however, which might require an administrator to craft a script to reset them.*

## What You'll Need

A Registry editor, such as REGEDIT or REGEDT32

Be sure to log off and back on again after making any of these changes.

To change the reaction time for menus opening automatically when the mouse hovers over them:

1. Open the Registry and navigate to HKEY_CURRENT_USER\Control Panel\ Desktop.

2. Edit the REG_SZ value MenuShowDelay and set the value (normally 400) to the time to wait for a menu to open automatically when the mouse hovers over it, in milliseconds. Very low values for this will cause the menus to spring open whenever the mouse touches them. To force Windows to wait until the user clicks the mouse, set this to 65535.

To disable "smooth scrolling" in applications:

1. Navigate to HKEY_CURRENT_USER\Control Panel\Desktop.
2. Edit the REG_BINARY value SmoothScroll and set it to 00 00 00 00. Activating this option will cause application displays with scrollbars to scroll through them smoothly when the scrollbar is clicked, rather than jumping from one portion of a document to another. Turning it off speeds things up noticeably.
3. To turn scrolling back on, set SmoothScroll to 01 00 00 00.

**NOTE**   If SmoothScroll is not a REG_BINARY value, delete it and re-create it as one.

To turn off "window animations":

1. Navigate to HKEY_CURRENT_USER\Control Panel\Desktop\ WindowMetrics.
2. Set the MinAnimate REG_SZ value to 0. This will cause windows to no longer "fly" to and from the taskbar when they are minimized or maximized.

**CHAPTER 3**

**NOTE**   Some programs do this themselves without checking the Registry key, and do not allow this function to be turned off. Also, some other programs can reset this behavior without user intervention.

3. Set the MinAnimate REG_SZ value to 0. This will cause windows to no longer "fly" to and from the taskbar when they are minimized or maximized.

To turn off "menu animations" and "fade effects":

1. Navigate to HKEY_CURRENT_USER\Control Panel\Desktop.
2. Edit the UserPreferencesMask value. This is a binary value, and each of the properties in it have to be set using a bitmask. To do this, open Calculator in Hex mode, add up the values for each of the actions you want to enable from the table that follows, and then enter the results as the first two bytes of the UserPreferencesMask value. If you want to clear everything you see in this list, simply set both bytes to zero. The bitmask for each action is shown in Table 3-2.

To set Explorer to use "fast update":

1. Navigate to HKEY_LOCAL_MACHINE\SYSTEM\CurrentControlSet\ Control\Update.
2. Edit the REG_BINARY UpdateMode key and set it to 00 to enable Fast Update. To keep down the amount of disk "chatter," Explorer keeps an in-memory copy of the file system structure that it updates from time to time. While this uses up a little more memory, the gain in performance and responsiveness it provides is worth it.

**Desktop and UI**

| Action | Bitmask |
|--------|---------|
| Enable combo box animation | 0x0004 |
| Enable cursor shadow | 0x2000 |
| Enable list box animation | 0x0008 |
| Enable menu animation | 0x0002 |
| Enable menu fading | 0x0200 |
| Enable menu selection fading | 0x0400 |
| Enable mouse hot-tracking effects | 0x0080 |
| Enable tooltip animation | 0x0800 |
| Enable tooltip fade | 0x1000 |

**Table 3-2.**    Bitmasks to Use for Enabling Each Menu Action or Animation

To turn off Windows 2003 "balloon tips" systemwide:

1. Navigate to HKEY_CURRENT_USER\Software\Microsoft\Windows\
   CurrentVersion\Explorer\Advanced.
2. Edit the REG_DWORD value EnableBalloonTips and set it to 0. This disables
   the use of balloon-tip pop-ups for all programs that use it in Windows 2003,
   including Explorer and the shell.

# 2003 Setting ClearType Gamma Options

| High |
|------|
| Moderate |
| **Low** |

ClearType is Microsoft's special subpixel type-rendering technology, used to improve
the way typefaces render onscreen, especially on LCD screens. Its default settings are
not well-suited to all displays, however.

## Overview

ClearType was originally introduced for Windows XP, and is now part of Windows
Server 2003. However, it's disabled by default since it requires a little additional CPU.
Administrators who spend a good deal of time in front of the console, or who use
Windows Server 2003 on an LCD-panel monitor may want to turn it on for the sake
of eye comfort.

## The Party Line
**Company X**

Microsoft doesn't offer much in the way of out-of-the-box configurability for ClearType—it's either on or off, period. A diligent administrator will find that Microsoft did in fact publish utilities for setting ClearType controls, but it may just be easier to hack directly into the Registry and make the changes by hand.

## *The Undocumented Solution*

*By default, the gamma value—the scale of transition from dark to light—for ClearType is set to a value of 1400, which is a gamma of 1.4. ClearType allows gamma values of 1.0 to 2.2—darker to lighter, respectively. On some displays, lighter gamma values look more attractive, and so a little playing with the range of gamma controls is recommended.*

## What You'll Need

A Registry editor, such as REGEDIT or REGEDT32

Be sure to log off and on again after following these steps:

1. Make sure ClearType is turned on. Go to the Appearance tab in Desktop Properties, click Effects, check the box labeled Smooth Edges Of Screen Fonts, and then select ClearType from the drop-down list:

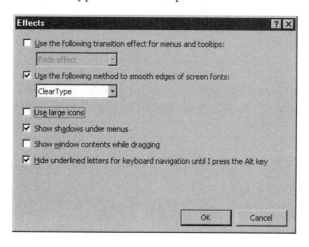

Desktop and UI

2. Open the Registry and navigate to HKEY_CURRENT_USER\Control Panel\ Desktop.

3. Add or edit the REG_DWORD value FontSmoothingGamma and set it to a value between 1000 and 2200. 1000 is the darkest possible value and 2200 is the lightest.

---

**NOTE**    Some conventional picture-tube monitors, such as those based on Sony Trinitron technology, can also look good with ClearType provided the gamma is set fairly high.

---

# 2000/2003 Changing the Size of the Shell Icon Cache

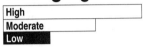

Icon images for objects are cached in a file called ShellIconCache. If this file exists, Windows reads the icon images from the cache instead of from the files themselves, which speeds things up. However, the size of the cache can sometimes be too small or even too big.

## Overview

Windows administrators are probably familiar with the disk chatter that takes place whenever a folder is opened. Most of this chatter, when it takes place, is Windows trying to find icons for each file. As it does so, the icon is cached in the ShellIconCache file for quick reference in the future. By default, the minimum value is 500 distinct icons, although a great many of those icons may be the system's, rather than icons for custom filetypes.

When the cache fills up, the oldest entries are purged, and if the cache is damaged or misread (which happens often), the wrong icons appear. This usually happens, again, for custom filetypes (such as document icons for installed programs).

---

## The Party Line                                    Company X

```
Microsoft makes little mention of the icon cache, and does
not provide any way to edit it directly. The only way to
deal with it, it would seem, is to delete the cache when
it becomes damaged or corrupted.
```

---

## *The Undocumented Solution*

*Fortunately, there is another way to deal with the problem of icon cache overflow: edit its Registry entry to make it larger, which will allow the file to need less maintenance.*

## What You'll Need

A Registry editor, such as REGEDIT or REGEDT32

Be sure to reboot after following these steps:

1. Open the Registry and navigate to HKEY_LOCAL_MACHINE\SOFTWARE\ Microsoft\Windows\CurrentVersion\Explorer.
2. Add a new REG_SZ key named Max Cached Icons (include the spaces) and set it to the number of icons you wish to keep in the cache. The more memory you have in your system, the larger this can be. Experiment with values from 2000 up.

CHAPTER
3

Desktop and UI

2000/2003 # Enforcing Consistent Views of Folders and Windows in Explorer

| High |
| Moderate |
| Low |

Many users are frustrated by what appears to be an inconsistency in the way Explorer handles the appearance of folders. Each folder normally retains its view settings—that is, the iconic or list view—so that when the folder is closed and re-opened later, the same view is presented again. However, on a system where the user is constantly opening many different folders, he may be frustrated to find that folders he set the view style for earlier have reverted back to the system default. Worse, there is no apparent reason for this.

## Overview

Windows maintains a circular list of each folder's settings in the Registry, *not* in the folder itself. This is why when you access a shared folder from two different machines, it shows up differently—each machine may have its own stored preferences for how to view that particular folder, and the folder itself holds none of that data. Such data includes not only the view style, but the size of the window, its onscreen position, and other details.

This cache of folder data is limited to around 400 entries, so that the newest entries overwrite the oldest. Because of this, a user who explores folders aggressively may burn through the 400-entry cache very quickly, and find that folders he explored earlier in the day suddenly don't look the same!

---

## The Party Line                                    Company X

```
Microsoft doesn't have any publicly exposed interface for
handling this problem, but they have built-in ways to manage
it under the hood—even if no direct way to edit it exists. A
value within the Registry holds the size of the folder settings
cache—or if it's undefined, it defaults to 400.
```

---

## The Undocumented Solution

*The solution, of course, is to raise the number of entries for the folder settings cache. Note that this value is set on a per-user basis, so it is possible to define it as being very low for users that don't log in locally a great deal.*

## What You'll Need

A Registry editor, such as REGEDIT or REGEDT32

Be sure to log off and on again after following these steps:

1. Open the Registry and navigate to HKEY_CURRENT_USER\Software\ Microsoft\Windows\Shell.
2. Add a new REG_DWORD value named BagMRU Size and set it to a value (decimal) that represents how many folders' worth of data to preserve.

# `2000/2003` Setting a Password Grace Period for Screensavers

| High |
|------|
| **Moderate** |
| Low |

Screensavers are often password-protected for security, although users who sometimes go idle at their keyboards for some time may find them annoying, since they require the user to log back in.

---

**NOTE**   This particular trick is being listed as a Risk Factor Moderate item because it can pose a potential security hazard. Don't use this tip in environments where physical access to the system is not tightly controlled (in other words, a locked door!), and security is paramount.

---

## Overview

In environments where security is not supreme, you can configure a "grace period" that allows the user to simply return to the desktop from the screensaver before the grace period has elapsed. By default, this is five seconds, but sometimes people's reactions are slower than that; they may need more time to remind the system they're still there without having to retype their password each time.

## The Party Line                                      Company X

```
Microsoft makes no mention of either the grace period or
its editability in the screensaver options listed in Display
Properties. Some individual screensavers may have an option
like this, but there's no information on how to do this
globally.
```

### The Undocumented Solution

*Normally, no Registry entry exists to specify the grace period, so to set it, it must be created.*

**CHAPTER
3**

Desktop and UI

## What You'll Need

A Registry editor, such as REGEDIT or REGEDT32

Be sure to reboot after following these steps.

1. Open the Registry and navigate to HKEY_LOCAL_MACHINE\SOFTWARE\Microsoft\Windows NT\CurrentVersion\Winlogon.

2. Add a new REG_DWORD value named ScreenSaverGracePeriod and set it for the grace period employed for all users, in seconds.

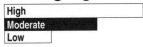

# Changing Directories for Temporary Internet Files

| High |
|---|
| **Moderate** |
| Low |

The temporary file folders for Windows' Internet access can become sprawling and cumbersome, and may be best moved to another place other than the user's documents directory.

## Overview

Windows maintains a folder called Temporary Internet Files, which is a repository for all the miscellaneous temporary files accumulated by Internet Explorer as well as any programs that use IE technology to access Internet objects or documents. By default, the size for this folder is set pretty high, but it's also placed in a location which can become burdensome—it's created as part of one's personal documents directory. A thoughtful system planner may not want that, and may instead wish to redirect the folder to another location—such as another physical drive or partition. This would increase parallelism and access speed, the same way that having the swapfile on another physical drive increases overall system speed.

---

## The Party Line                                  Company X

```
Microsoft does provide an interface for changing the location
of the temporary files folder. You can see this for yourself
in IE, by selecting Tools | Internet Options and clicking
the Settings button in Temporary Internet Files. However,
```

> an administrator may want to force this folder to appear
> in another place, perhaps as part of the standard system-
> configuration plan.

## *The Undocumented Solution*

*The cache paths are controlled by a set of Registry entries which are machinewide;*
*every account on the machine must use the same temporary folders. These Registry*
*entries can be set either by hand or in an automated fashion.*

## What You'll Need
A Registry editor, such as REGEDIT or REGEDT32

Be sure to reboot after following these steps.

1. Open the Registry and navigate to HKEY_LOCAL_MACHINESOFTWARE\
   Microsoft\Windows\CurrentVersion\Internet Settings\Cache\Paths\.
2. Under Paths are four subkeys named Path1 through Path4. In each of these
   keys is a REG_SZ value named CachePath. Modify each of these paths to point
   to a new set of cache folders. Note that each path entry must be to a different
   specific folder. The default setting is that they point to folders under a folder
   named Content.IE5.

To modify the settings for the current user:

1. Navigate to HKEY_CURRENT_USER\SOFTWARE\Microsoft\Windows\
   CurrentVersion\Explorer\User Shell Folders and modify the REG_SZ subkey
   named Cache.
2. Navigate to HKEY_CURRENT_USER\SOFTWARE\Microsoft\Windows\
   CurrentVersion\Explorer\Shell Folders and modify the REG_SZ subkey
   named Cache as well.
3. If you want to disable per-user caching entirely, navigate to HKEY_
   LOCAL_MACHINE\SOFTWARE\Microsoft\Windows\CurrentVersion\
   InternetSettings\Cache, create a BINARY value named User Profiles and
   set it to 00.

**CHAPTER 3**

Desktop and UI

# 2000/2003 Preventing Open Copies of Explorer from Restarting on Reboot

| High |
|------|
| Moderate |
| Low |

Explorer is set by default to reopen in its previous state when Windows is shut down or rebooted, but an administrator may want to defeat that behavior.

## Overview

When there are Explorer windows open—folders, drives, and so on—upon shutdown or logoff, Windows normally preserves the state of these open windows and restores them the next time the user logs in or the machine is brought back up. This includes the Control Panel, the Printers window, and other Explorer-derived windows. Some administrators may not want to preserve such behavior on the grounds that it might constitute a security risk.

---

## The Party Line                                    Company X

Microsoft provides no obvious way to prevent this from happening in Windows 2000. In Windows 2003, however, there *is* a setting that controls this in Explorer; it can be found by selecting Tools | Folder Options | View from an Explorer window, and clearing or checking the box named Restore Previous Folder Windows At Logon. By default, this is unchecked in Windows 2003, as shown in Figure 3-2. In Windows 2000, this option is enabled by default.

---

## *The Undocumented Solution*

*This setting can be modified through the Registry, either manually or as a scripted change.*

## What You'll Need

A Registry editor, such as REGEDIT or REGEDT32

Be sure to reboot after following these steps.

1. Open the Registry and navigate to HKEY_CURRENT_USER\Software\ Microsoft\Windows\CurrentVersion\Policies\Explorer.

2. Add or edit an entry for a REG_BINARY value named NoSaveSettings. Change its value to hexadecimal 1, so it appears as 01 00 00 00.

---

**NOTE**   It has been said that making this change will prevent you from placing new shortcuts on your desktop. This is not true, but it *will* prevent you from permanently repositioning desktop shortcuts and from adjusting the size and/or position of the taskbar. Bear this in mind before making this change.

---

**CHAPTER 3**

Desktop and UI

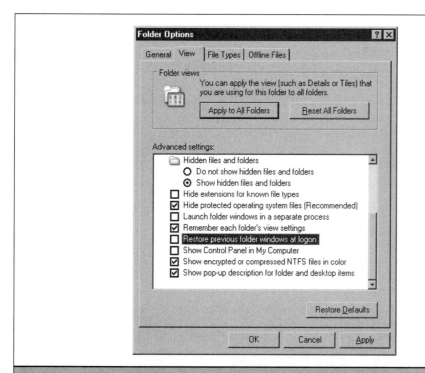

**Figure 3-2.**   The Restore Previous Folder Windows At Logon choice preserves the layout of the Explorer folders that are open when one logs off.

# CHAPTER 4
## *Memory*

**In This Chapter:**

- [ ] Disabling Kernel Paging to Disk
- [ ] Enabling Large System Cache
- [ ] Setting I/O Lock Pages
- [ ] Using Proper Pagefile Allocation Tactics
- [ ] Allocating Multiple Pagefiles to a Single Partition
- [ ] Running 16-Bit Applications in Discrete Memory Spaces
- [ ] Memory Defragmentation Examined
- [ ] Using Write-Back Instead of Write-Through Cache Behavior
- [ ] Increasing the Desktop Application Heap Size
- [ ] Setting the System Paged Pool Size
- [ ] Turning Off Unused Services to Free Up Memory
- [ ] Cutting Unneeded Processes in Terminal Server User Sessions

Memory comprises the final element in any computer's Holy Trinity, with CPU and hard storage being the other two. One of the most common suggestions for improving any system's performance, server, or workstations, is to add memory. Today, more is always better—especially since memory has become much cheaper over the past decade. To put things into perspective, my first PC, a 386/25, was upgraded to 4MB of RAM at a cost of over $100 a megabyte. Presently, $100 can buy 512MB or better, depending on where you shop and what brand or variety of memory you purchase.

Windows and many of the server applications that run on it are memory-hungry. They make heavy demands on available RAM and on available swap space. They also assume they are the only server product running on that particular machine, and are often hard-coded to lionize or monopolize as much memory as they possibly can. (This leads to one of the most common—and preposterous—scenarios, where a single application's memory footprint grows to an absurd size.) On top of that, many of Windows' own internal memory tunings are factory-set in ways that are self-managing and self-limiting, and are not exposed directly for editing by the administrator or end user.

This chapter focuses on tuning Windows 2000's and 2003's use of memory to produce the best possible performance. Some bits of advice are more conventional than others. For instance, most people know that adding more physical memory to any server gives it a boost. The question of how much and to what end, though, usually goes unspoken—and if a physical upgrade can be combined with other, intelligent performance tunings, they will go that much further. This not only includes OS-level tunings, but BIOS-level tunings often overlooked by administrators. (Note that the BIOS tunings described in this chapter may not be available on all systems.)

As with many other sections in this book, some of the advice discussed here is controversial or is widely seen as a quick fix to other problems, the importance of which has sometimes been overstated. In these cases, the fix and its appropriate relevance are described in detail along with recommendations about how to apply it and get useful results.

## 2000/2003 Disabling Kernel Paging to Disk

One of the more extreme ways Windows can save memory is by swapping out unused portions of the kernel to disk. In some cases, this may be desired; in others, it may be something to prevent.

### Overview

Portions of the Windows kernel, as well as kernel-mode drivers, are written in such a way that they can be swapped out to disk if the need arises. Usually this will only happen under extremely low memory conditions, but it is an insurance policy against system instability when memory overhead gets too tight.

On systems where there is an extremely large amount of RAM (512MB or more), the kernel may never be paged. For an extra performance kick, the administrator can force the machine never to page kernel memory to disk. This way, the entire kernel space remains consistently in memory—drivers, kernel code, everything—and there's no incurred overhead for swapping out the kernel.

A quick way to determine how much of the kernel is paged out is to fire up the Task Manager and look at the Kernel Memory section in the Performance tab. This measurement appears as two numbers: Paged and Nonpaged (see Figure 4-1). The Nonpaged memory counter is how much of the kernel must remain in memory at all times, while the Paged counter reflects how much of the kernel (and its memory space) can be swapped to disk. In the example shown here, the total amount of kernel memory is 11MB, with 6.8MB of it paged and 4.6MB nonpaged. This means at least 11MB—say, 16MB or so for safety—would need to remain consistently free if one were to disable kernel paging on this machine.

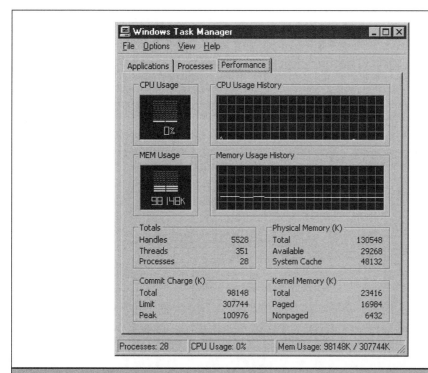

**Figure 4-1.**   The Paged and Nonpaged listings in the Task Manager describe how much kernel memory must remain "live" at all times and how much can be swapped out to disk.

The amount of installed RAM should not be the only guide to determine whether kernel paging is taking place. A system running SQL Server, IIS, or any other major server product would see a great deal of its memory eaten by that product. (Many Microsoft server products are designed to use as much available physical RAM as possible, a subject discussed in detail later in this chapter.) The preceding numbers are only an example and shouldn't be used as a hard guideline; the best way to learn how much kernel memory is used would be to run a performance counter trace against the kernel memory indices while the machine is experiencing a normal-to-heavy load and work from that.

---

# The Party Line                                            Company X

By default, any Windows 2000/2003 installation is set to allow the kernel to be paged out to disk. Microsoft doesn't have kernel paging available as a directly administrator-settable option, but it is possible to force paging on or off through a Registry setting. As you might imagine, Microsoft also has a caveat against doing this, as described in KnowledgeBase article 184419, since it can theoretically render a system unstable.

---

## *The Undocumented Solution*

*One important thing to keep in mind about this change: every process that runs uses a portion of kernel memory. If inactive kernel mode processes (such as sleeping threads) take up a fair amount of physical memory, the active applications will have their working memory sets cut back. This would wind up making things worse, so a change like this is going to have radically different effects on different systems.*

*Based on the experiments I've done, the best environments for this tweak are machines with a lot of physical memory, a decent-sized amount of memory overhead, and a consistently high amount of free RAM. Servers tend to fare better than workstations (that is to say, machines used for such a function, not which edition of Windows is installed on them), since workstations have a great deal more fluctuation in memory demand that is less predictable. On a server, the load can be to a fair degree predicted and accounted for (and even constrained), but on a workstation, if you open a 200MB Photoshop file, having kernel paging enabled suddenly comes in real handy!*

**NOTE** As mentioned earlier, this technique does not always work. Some machines may suffer a crash due to forcing a non-paged pool object into a paged-pool resource. If that happens, boot into Safe Mode and undo the changes immediately.

## What You'll Need

A Registry editor, such as REGEDIT or REGEDT32

Be sure to reboot after following these steps:

1. Open the Registry and navigate to HKEY_LOCAL_MACHINE\System\ CurrentControlSet\Control\Session Manager\Memory Management.
2. Add or edit the REG_DWORD value named DisablePagingExecutive. Set the value to **1** to disable paging of kernel memory. To allow paging of kernel memory, set the entry to **0**.

## 2000/2003 Enabling Large System Cache

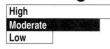

The Windows system cache is normally fixed to a specific size depending on your version of Windows, but it can be modified for either large- or small-memory footprints.

## Overview

The Windows file cache is a system-reserved section of physical memory that is not used by any applications or device drivers. Into this area the system places portions of code, which is "swapped" into this space in much the same manner as kernel or user code, or in the same way memory is "swapped" to disk when it's not needed.

As more programs open, the least-requested program code is migrated out of the file cache and into the swap file. This way the amount of active memory can be kept as high as possible without detracting from performance. Rather than swap unused code and memory directly to disk, it can be migrated in this fashion to keep a large, contiguous block of free memory available for launching applications quickly. The cache cannot be disabled, since it is an integral part of Windows memory management—and in fact, it shouldn't be, since it usually does its job very well!

## The Party Line                                    Company X

Microsoft has set the system cache to work in one of two sizes: large and small. The small cache is the default setting for Windows desktop operating systems, while the large setting is enabled by default in server-level operating systems.

## *The Undocumented Solution*

*If you are running Windows 2000 or 2003 Server, the large cache is enabled by default. However, if you want to force the system to use a small cache, which might be a good idea on servers that have relatively little RAM, you can set it to a small cache and put the same memory to more direct use.*

## What You'll Need

A Registry editor, such as REGEDIT or REGEDT32

Be sure to reboot after following these steps:

1.  Open the Registry and navigate to HKEY_LOCAL_MACHINE\System\ CurrentControlSet\Control\Session Manager\Memory Management.
2.  Add or edit the REG_DWORD value named LargeSystemCache. Set the value to **1** to use a large cache. To use the smaller cache, set it to **0**.

If you want to manipulate the size of the cache working set and get some immediate, direct control over its behavior (for instance, force it to flush out on demand), you can download a utility called *CacheSet* from the SysInternals site, at http://www.sysinternals.com/ntw2k/source/cacheset.shtml. With it, you can set the working minimum and maximum set sizes for the cache, and forcibly empty it on demand at the click of a button. They even provide the source code for free.

 ## Setting I/O Lock Pages

| High |
| Moderate |
| Low |

By changing the size of the system's I/O buffer, it is possible to improve system performance on machines with very active file systems.

## Overview

By default, the Windows file system manager locks a certain amount of RAM for file system operations. This means that a block of RAM is reserved exclusively for the file system, and that file operations are performed in memory in chunks of this size. By default, the lock amount is determined automatically by Windows, but is usually around 512K. This means that a 512K area of RAM has been set aside by the system for file I/O, and that the system fetches up to this much from the disk at one time.

512K is generally considered a very conservative size for this buffer, especially if you have a fast disk and disk controller. For that reason, systems with large amounts of RAM (even 256MB or more) can benefit from having the file cache expanded.

Generally, the more RAM you have, the bigger you can make the cache, and the more of a performance gain you can derive from it, especially if you have a very active file system. People who use their PCs for multimedia work, for instance, may see a substantial improvement in performance by doing this.

**CHAPTER 4**

Memory

## The Party Line                                    Company X

```
Microsoft doesn't allow direct editing of the cache size.
They assume, with some correctness, that not every system is
going to benefit from having a variable cache size, but with
the recent explosion of memory sizes, they may be playing it
far too conservative here. There is another argument as to
why they do not expose this function, which I discuss next.
```

## *The Undocumented Solution*

*To control the size of the cache directly, you can edit a Registry setting that lets you force the cache size as needed.*

## What You'll Need

A Registry editor, such as REGEDIT or REGEDT32

Be sure to reboot after following these steps:

1. Open the Registry and navigate to HKEY_LOCAL_MACHINE\System\ CurrentControlSet\Control\Session Manager\Memory Management.

2. Add or edit the REG_DWORD value named IoPageLockLimit.

Set the value according to the following table. Note that these are suggested values only, and that you may achieve better results by using larger or smaller numbers depending on your system load.

| Memory Size | IoPageLockLimit Setting (in Hex) |
|---|---|
| 128MB | 4000 |
| 256MB | 10000 |
| 512MB | 40000 |
| 1GB | 100000 |

One downside to using this is similar to the problems with disabling kernel paging. Use too large a file cache, and the rest of memory—memory you need for applications and data—gets crowded out, and once again system performance degrades rather than improves. (One of the ways this can happen by accident is if someone specifies the earlier value in decimal rather than hex, or vice versa.) The self-tuning mechanism that Windows uses for managing the cache size is usually well-suited to conventional use, so more is not always better.

However, if you are capable of experimenting with the computer in question, you may find that a system with a lot of disk activity—a database server, or a video editing workstation—benefits from having a consistently large cache. The rule of thumb here is: the bigger the size of the average file being worked with, the more a large file cache will be useful.

---

**NOTE**   Many Microsoft server-side applications *will not work correctly* if you change the size of the page lock limit. Because these programs make heavy use of raw I/O, changing the page lock size can disrupt their functioning. If you are running SQL Server, Exchange Server, or other similar MS server applications, test this thoroughly on a nonproduction system first.

---

**2000/2003** # Using Proper Pagefile Allocation Tactics

| High |
| Moderate |
| Low |

Aside from the amount of RAM in your system, the size and deployment of the Windows page file can be one of the most important ways to augment system performance.

## Overview

The exact way to set up the Windows page file has become another cause of disagreement among experts. Talk to five different experts, and you may get five different answers about the best ways to set things up. Because Windows depends so heavily on the page file, even on systems with a lot of memory, there's a lot of (justifiable) belief that how you set it up and how you allocate it will make a big difference in performance.

## The Party Line                    Company X

```
Microsoft gives very little, if any, direct information
about how big to set the pagefile or where to put it.
In Windows 2000 and 2003, the Virtual Memory window does
suggest a "recommended" size for the pagefile, but there
is no description of how this recommendation is derived.
What's more, multiple pagefiles can be placed on multiple
partitions, but again, there is no direct information
regarding which is the best strategy.
```

## *The Undocumented Solution*

*To understand what the best strategy for deploying a pagefile is, I need to discuss what the pagefile is for and how it's used.*

The standard version of Windows 2000 can directly access up to 4GB of physical memory, while Advanced Server can use 8GB and Datacenter Server can access 32GB. Windows 2003 Standard Edition can also access up to 4GB, while 2003 Enterprise Edition can access 32 and 2003 Datacenter Edition can use 64. The Itanium versions of Enterprise and Datacenter can use 64 and 512GB, respectively. The most important thing is that all of these OSes can access that much memory *directly*. Because of that, in Windows NT, 2000, and 2003, *all* system memory is considered virtual.

If you have 1GB of RAM, for instance, and another GB of swap space, programs will "see" 2GB of useable memory. A program can be written to be aware of what the virtual vs. physical memory allotments are (by gleaning that information from the statistics the OS keeps about the system), but programs are supposed to see all memory as being simply memory. Only the kernel and the memory manager know the truth.

Windows allocates memory in 4K chunks called *pages,* which is where the term "pagefile" comes from. Pages of data not currently in use are written out to disk to make room for other processes or data. Before an application can access any page of data, it has to be mapped into a section of physical memory first. In other words, it has to be copied back out from the pagefile into memory. Many people seem to labor under the delusion that the best thing to do with the pagefile is to make it as big as possible, which will yield the same results as having nearly unlimited memory. This is wrong. Page space is not a *substitute* for physical RAM, but an *adjunct* to it. The reason page space is not supposed to be much larger than the physical RAM on any given machine is because whatever goes *into* the page space also has to come *out* at some point. Page space is not infinite.

The more the system depends on page space rather than physical RAM for its operations, the slower things will get. So while it is possible to have a 128MB machine with a 512MB swapfile, it won't be anywhere near the same as having a 512MB machine, and should not be thought of as one. In short, never depend on paging files when you can use physical memory instead. If you are faced with the prospect of increasing your paging file size as a way to get around a physical memory limitation, look into upgrading your physical memory first.

The first thing to do when modifying your pagefile is to determine how much actual pagefile use is taking place. In Windows 2000, you can create a counter log to examine pagefile usage over an extended period of time (a few days, for instance), determine just how much of the pagefile is really being used—even under heavy loads—and plan from there. In Windows 2003, the Task Manager now has a Page File Usage graph in the Performance tab (in place of the Memory Usage graph), which can give you the same statistics at a glance.

Additional information can be gleaned from the Task Manager's Commit Charge pane in the Performance tab. The Total is the amount of memory currently committed for use in user space. The Limit value is the size of your physical RAM plus your currently allocated swap space, minus a bit for overhead. This is how much memory your system can have committed to use at any given time. The Peak value is how much the system has committed to use all at once since the system was booted.

If you find your swapfile is not being used to excess, then the default settings should be appropriate. In fact, if you discover the swapfile barely gets any use, you can probably cut it back significantly.

Place the pagefile on a drive separate from your operating system, and from your data if possible. Putting the pagefile on a drive with your data in a separate partition from your data is also possible, but again, you may take a performance hit from the drive head having to move across the partition boundary.

The exact size of the pagefile should be managed automatically *unless* you have confirmed through your statistics logging and analysis (see earlier reference) that the system is using a higher degree of pagefile than average. The system-managed size for a pagefile is generally the amount of physical memory in the system plus 1.5 times the same size. If more than 2GB of RAM is present in a system, the pagefile defaults to 2GB. This provides a safe margin for swap operations, although if you find the pagefile being eaten into a little more aggressively than normal, you can get away with raising that to twice the size of the physical RAM. More than that, however, and your system may simply be in need of more RAM. Windows 2003 includes an option to explicitly tell the system to manage the pagefile size automatically, as shown in Figure 4-2.

Set a *minimal* page file on your system drive—no more than a couple of megabytes. If there is a system crash/BSOD, this space can be used for dump information. You may have noticed that if you set the pagefile on your system drive to zero, you get a warning about this. The pagefile there doesn't have to be huge, especially if you're only doing a minimal dump (say, the 64K-sized variety) and not a full memory dump on crashes.

CHAPTER
4

Memory

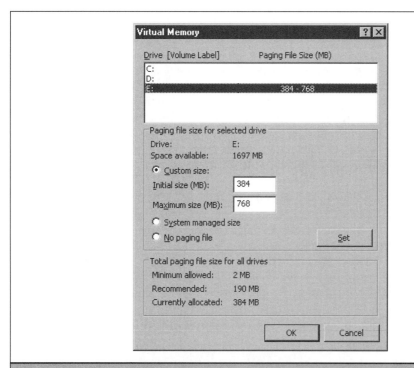

**Figure 4-2.**   Windows 2003's virtual memory management window sports a "system-managed size" selection that lets the OS decide how big to make the pagefile.

> **NOTE**   BackOffice Server requires a *minimum* of 256MB for any pagefile. If you are still running BackOffice, bear this in mind if you plan on applying this advice to older servers.

If you have a RAID array, organize your RAID volume to increase throughput to your pagefile. For instance, if you have a RAID array of four drives, two and two, you can use one pair of drives as the virtual disk for your OS and applications, and the second pair for your pagefile and data. This sort of thing can be difficult to do after a system is set up, so you may want to plan where everything will go before setting up a RAID array.

Don't place the pagefile on the same physical drive as your operating system. This is generally the first recommendation made to the burgeoning system administrator regarding where his pagefile should go. Placing the pagefile on the same drive as the OS will slow things down.

> **NOTE**   If you have absolutely no choice (for instance, if you're running 2000/2003 Server on a notebook or other machine with only one hard drive), you *can* get away with placing the pagefile in the same partition as the OS. This is not great, but it's still better than putting it in another partition. I explain why next.

Don't place the pagefile on the same physical drive as the operating system, *even if it's on a different partition*. In fact, this is even worse than placing the pagefile on the same partition as the OS because it takes extra time for the head to re-navigate across the drive into the other partition. I myself made this mistake many times in the past, because I believed that if the pagefile was placed on its own partition, it wouldn't get fragmented. The overhead from fragmentation is often minimal compared to the overhead from the head movements needed to traverse partition boundaries, and a newly-created pagefile will be placed in as contiguous a section of disk space as possible anyway. Also, if you have the pagefile set so that it is not re-created on each reboot, and if it is of a fixed size, it will not fragment heavily.

Don't place the pagefile on a software-created fault-tolerant drive or volume. Pagefiles do not need to be fault-tolerant, and the hit in performance due to the redundancy of a fault-tolerant drive will translate into a bottleneck for your whole system. If you're using a hardware RAID solution to perform fault tolerance, this is OK, since Windows will never know the difference.

Don't place the pagefile on a removable drive. This is generally not even possible, but if you are using some bizarre kernel-driver removable-drive controller that tricks the system into seeing such a thing as a fixed drive, don't try to put a pagefile there.

Don't place the pagefile on a network drive (see the earlier reference). Again, it's usually not even possible, but in the unlikely event someone finds a way to do it, the bottleneck from the network's throughput would kill whatever gain you would get from not having to store the pagefile locally.

 # Allocating Multiple Pagefiles to a Single Partition

| High |
|------|
| **Moderate** |
| Low |

In high-memory situations where it is not possible to assign more than one swapfile due to a small number of partitions in a system, it is possible to assign multiple swapfiles.

## Overview

The largest possible size for any *single* pagefile is 4GB, or 4095MB. If you have a *lot* of RAM in a system—as in Windows 2003's Enterprise and Datacenter editions, which can support up to 64 and 512GB of RAM, respectively—you can work around this limit by simply assigning multiple pagefiles to multiple partitions.

    If you don't have multiple partitions, you can do something even sneakier and trick Windows into inserting *multiple pagefiles on the same partition*—by placing them in different directories.

**CHAPTER 4**

---

## The Party Line                                      Company X

```
The user interface Microsoft provides for creating swapfiles
only allows you to create one per partition. However, the
internal structure for how pagefiles are defined in Windows
is flexible, but needs to be edited directly.
```

Memory

---

## *The Undocumented Solution*

*Bear in mind that putting multiple pagefiles on the same partition should only be used if you really need it. Also, the usage is in order of definition: when the first listed swapfile fills up, the others will be allocated in the order listed.*

## What You'll Need

A Registry editor, such as REGEDIT or REGEDT32

Be sure to reboot after following these steps:

1. Open the Registry and navigate to HKEY_LOCAL_MACHINE\System\ CurrentControlSet\Control\Session Manager\Memory Management.

2. Edit the PagingFiles value. This is a MULTI_SZ value, or a multistring value, so you can edit the value directly in the Registry editor in Windows 2003. In Windows 2000, use REGEDT32 (not REGEDIT) to edit this value directly.

3. Each paging file in the system will be listed on a separate line in this format:
   <path> <initial value> <maximum value>
   If you had a swapfile on your D: drive that started at 320MB and went up to 512, it would read:
   D:\pagefile.sys 320 512

Add new values as needed, with pathnames to different folders for each. The first pagefile should have its initial and maximum values the same; the others should start at 0 and work their way up.

# 2000/2003 Running 16-Bit Applications in Discrete Memory Spaces

| High |
|------|
| Moderate |
| Low |

By default, 32-bit applications are segregated in memory. The same thing can be done for 16-bit applications to increase their reliability.

## Overview

When Windows made the transition from 16-bit to 32-bit applications, Microsoft tried to retain backwards compatibility with 16-bit programs, without destabilizing things. Microsoft's approach to this in Windows NT and 2000 was to produce an emulation system, the NT Virtual DOS Machine or NTVDM, that would run 16-bit applications. An example of a program being run using an NTVDM session is shown in Figure 4-3. Even today there are still servers that run legacy 16-bit applications, either third-party applications or custom-written ones designed by people who may have left the company (or were independently contracted), so the NTVDM has become quite useful. Also, since the NT kernel does not allow direct hardware access, the only way to run 16-bit programs (which run in real mode) is to emulate them.

## The Party Line                                    Company X

```
Normally, one copy of the NTVDM runs on a given machine. All
16-bit applications run on it at once. It is possible, however,
to run each 16-bit application with its own copy of NTVDM.
```

## *The Undocumented Solution*

*Running multiple NTDVM sessions requires more memory, since a separate copy of the emulation engine has to run for each program. The upside is that it increases the reliability of each individual process. If one 16-bit process crashes, the others will continue to run in their own separate memory spaces. (If you have all the 16-bit applications in one memory space, one of them crashing may take the rest down as well.)*

## What You'll Need

A Registry editor, such as REGEDIT or REGEDT32

**CHAPTER 4**

Memory

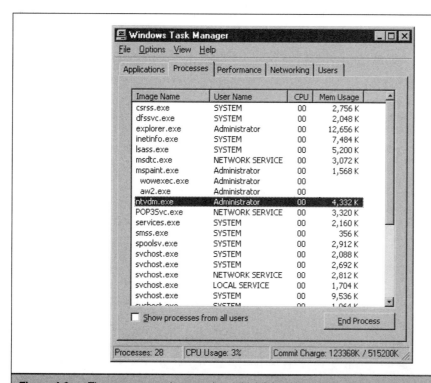

**Figure 4-3.**    The process, ntvdm.exe, shown highlighted, is running the aw2.exe 16-bit application in emulation mode.

Be sure to reboot after following these steps:

1. Open the Registry and navigate to HKEY_LOCAL_MACHINE\SYSTEM\ CurrentControlSet\Control\WOW.

2. Add or edit the REG_SZ value named DefaultSeparateVDM and set its value to **yes**.

3. Add or edit the REG_SZ value WowSize. This will control the size in megabytes of the memory space used to run 16-bit applications.

Another way to accomplish this with *individual* applications, rather than all at once, is to use the **START** command with the command **start /separate *<app-image>*** where *<app-image>* is the full path to the application image. You can also create a .PIF file for the application and check the Run In Separate Memory Space box, which does the same thing.

# Memory Defragmentation Examined

Hard drives and system memory have something in common—both are susceptible to performance degradation due to fragmentation. As with hard disks, there are utilities to defragment system memory, but they come with their own share of drawbacks.

## Overview

Windows does not, by default, keep user memory contiguous. Generally, if a program requests a block of memory, there must be a contiguous block of memory of that size already extant. If there isn't, the request will usually fail, even if enough memory *as a whole* exists in the system to satisfy that request. Programmers are especially familiar with this phenomenon, since special work is required to allocate large contiguous blocks of RAM. Part of the reason for this is to keep the amount of "garbage collection" activity to a minimum.

For most users, memory fragmentation isn't a big problem, but for server administrators, it can become a thorny issue. Clustering is one of the biggest casualties of memory fragmentation. One of the chief reasons Exchange 2000 can't take advantage of Windows 2000 clustering is due to this. Exchange 5.5 and 2000 both use a technology called *dynamic buffer allocation* to handle memory, which causes the memory "footprint" for the Exchange server process to reach what looks like ungainly heights to most people. This *is* by design, and it's a behavior that's echoed by other programs such as IIS and SQL Server, as detailed elsewhere in this chapter. Exchange does this to try and reach as much of an equilibrium as possible with other active processes, and to stake out as much memory as it can to keep as much data live in RAM as possible rather than swap it out to disk. A server running only Exchange, or IIS, or SQL Server, will see most of its free memory eaten by that particular process unless the administrator has taken steps under the hood to cut things back.

As far as clustering goes, the reason cluster state transitions (that is, failovers) don't work well on systems like this is because there is little or no contiguous memory available to mount the databases. On a small Exchange server with only a couple of hundred mailboxes, this isn't a big problem, but a machine with more than 1500 clients may be in trouble.

As I write this, Microsoft is working on ways to make clustering work better in high-load environments. In the meantime, the only practical solution for dealing with memory fragmentation problems in clustered systems seems to be "Think small"—or, depending on the load involved, using a memory defragmentation tool.

## *The Undocumented Solution*

*Memory defragmentation tools are programs that claim to be able to defragment user memory space. Most of these programs work similarly. They make a request for a large block of memory and then immediately dispose of it. This forces the system to run a garbage collection cycle it wouldn't normally perform, consolidating all the fragmented free space into a number of larger, contiguous blocks. By forcing such a large memory allocation, less-used .DLLs and programs will be swapped out to disk, making more room for programs that are running.*

Among third-party products that do this, and a good example for this discussion, is a program by Silicon Prairie Software named *MemTurbo II*. MemTurbo II uses the forced-allocation technique both on-demand and on a scheduled basis—the user can schedule memory to be "scrubbed" (their word) every so often, or when available memory plunges below a specified point. An example of the program in action can be seen in Figure 4-4. Interestingly enough, the program's documentation describes how a server scenario was what prompted its creation—that often the console would be nearly unusable because the shell and many of its components would routinely be paged out to disk in favor of the mail program running on the server. While the mail server would indeed run slower because of the memory-scrubbing operations, the user interface would respond faster.

If you have a server that is "headless" or "closeted"—in other words, it's been put in a server room somewhere and isn't interacted with except through Terminal Services—then the response time of the server desktop is going to be something of a nonissue. Using a memory defragmentation application that slows down the backend

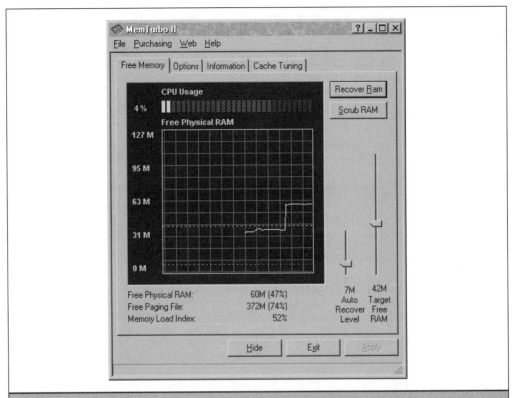

**Figure 4-4.**   MemTurbo II in action, recovering memory that has been lost to fragmentation.

defeats the real reason for running a server in the first place. However, if you are running Windows 2000/2003 Server not as a backend server, but as a desktop operating system so that programs like SQL Server can be used (for development, for instance), then the system's responsiveness to the user becomes more important.

Some questions remain about the validity of attempting to second-guess the Windows memory management system. In some extreme scenarios, forced flushing can help improve performance, but it is not always going to be beneficial, and frankly sometimes it can do more harm than good. One of the ways this happens is when the whole purpose of caching data in memory is defeated. If data is habitually cached by a certain process to accelerate performance, and then just as habitually flushed out by a memory defragmenter, the result will be a *slower* system, not a faster one. The system wastes time either re-caching the information or swapping it back into system memory. To be scrupulously honest, this negative behavior can be alleviated by tuning the aggressiveness of the defragmenter (to make it scrub memory less often or less deeply).

As there is no single magic number for good performance in such a scenario, getting it to work well involves a fair amount of experimentation. Whether an administrator is willing to spare the time and effort to do that, as opposed to allowing memory to manage itself, is a question he will have to answer for himself.

If the problem is that individual applications are being too aggressive in their memory usage, a better answer is to manage memory usage on an application-by-application basis. Some applications, such as SQL Server, allow the user to do this directly, through a user interface. Some, like Internet Information Server, need to have internal parameters edited through the Registry or Metabase to change their memory usage (which will be explored in a later chapter). Many applications have no user-settable memory management options at all and can only be constrained through the use of a product like the Windows System Resource Manager. The Windows System Resource Manager is a separate product, available as a free download from Microsoft, but only for Windows 2003 Server. It allows you to manage CPU and memory usage on a per-process or per-user basis, and supports scheduling and tracking of resource usage. This allows you to do tasks as diverse as running specific apps at specific times or creating billing reports for resource usage. Full information about the product and the downloadable binary can be found at http://www.microsoft.com/windowsserver2003/downloads/wsrm.mspx.

CHAPTER<br>4

Memory

## 2000/2003 Using Write-Back Instead of Write-Through Cache Behavior

Not all memory options in Windows are governed by the operating system. Some are governed by the system chipset, and as a result it's easy to overlook some key improvements to memory performance in the BIOS.

### Overview

Modern computers use caching to speed memory throughput, employing two cache-memory methods: write-back and write-through.

In write-back caching, data is written to the system's memory only when data is cycled out of the cache, either because of a flush operation or because the cache has filled up and the oldest data is moved out. Write-through caching has data written to main memory *at the same time* the data is cached, which is done so that the data written can be immediately available from the cache for other operations.

Generally, write-back caching yields better performance, since only one write operation at a time has to be performed rather than the two operations needed for write-through. There are a few situations where write-through is better, but they are mostly only useful for broad compatibility with operating systems, which is why such an option—choosing write-back vs. write-through cache behavior—is made available in BIOS to the end user.

## The Party Line **Company X**

```
Usually the only time Microsoft makes mention of
system-level caching is when it's referred to in the context
of debugging a Stop error or some other severe problem. As a
recommendation for system performance tuning, it's not
mentioned at all in their conventional documentation.
```

## *The Undocumented Solution*

*For the best cache performance in Windows 2000 and 2003, activate write-back caching. How this is done on your particular system will vary widely from computer to computer. Some systems use write-back caching only and do not allow for modification of cache settings through BIOS.*

There are reasons why write-through caching might be set by default on a system. A system's BIOS may be configured from the factory with write-through caching set, rather then write-back caching, simply as a way to insure compatibility with the broadest possible selection of software. Some operating systems may not install properly or may not run reliably if write-back caching is set, and so the default setting is for maximum compatibility. Some BIOSes—Award, for instance—have a "fail-safe" or "maximum compatibility" function which loads into the BIOS the most widely compatible presets for each BIOS setting. Write-through caching is sometimes set this way. If a system was being debugged from the BIOS on up and the administrator chose to use the fail-safe BIOS settings at one point, it might be easy to overlook write-through caching being set and not changed later.

## 2000/2003 Increasing the Desktop Application Heap Size

The desktop heap is a section of system memory reserved for application resources—windows, icons, and the desktop itself. Since it has a fixed size, it can be depleted if too many programs contend for it at once.

## Overview

The desktop application heap is one of many Windows' elements unknown to most users, yet it can affect their system performance adversely if exhausted. Symptoms of such depletion include

- Desktop or toolbar icons "blacking out" or vanishing entirely.

- Applications that simply vanish, or terminate without an error. This is one of the more common symptoms of heap exhaustion—an application that disappears from the desktop in mid-keystroke with no crash message and no error in the log. It's doubly confusing when this happens with a normally stable application.

- Opening a large file and having the system or application destabilize, when all other times it works fine.

# The Party Line

## Company X

In Windows NT 3.1, the default size of the desktop application heap was 3072K—an enormous amount of memory back then. (I'd bet this was part of the reason NT 3.1's memory requirements were, for the time, so piggish.) In Windows NT 3.5, the value was *decreased* to 512K, which actually improved performance, since it left more room for conventional applications to run without the cramp of a missing 3MB block of memory.

However, with the introduction of NT 4.0 and the subsequent explosion of cheap RAM, the picture changed once more. A larger heap was suddenly no longer an issue, and so the overall size of the heap was ramped back up to 3MB. In theory, this should be enough to support most common usage, but as people run more and more applications side-by-side, this may not prove to be the case. The problem gets worse if people use installations of Windows Server on a machine normally reserved for desktop use (which is sometimes required for running certain programs on the machine).

## *The Undocumented Solution*

*By editing the Registry, the size of the desktop heap can be changed.*

---

**NOTE** The application heap size should not be set to an exorbitantly high value. Since each process has the desktop heap mapped into its address space, increasing the application heap size to a very large value can cause the system to run much more slowly.

---

## What You'll Need

A Registry editor, such as REGEDIT or REGEDT32

Be sure to reboot after following these steps:

1. Open the Registry and navigate to HKEY_LOCAL_MACHINE\System\ CurrentControlSet\Control\Session Manager\SubSystems.
2. Edit the string named Windows.

Within that string is the SharedSection= value, followed by two numerical parameters separated by a comma. They usually appear like this:

SharedSection=1024,3072

The first of the two values is the shared heap that is common to all desktops, including the global handle table. This space is used to manage system windows, menus, icons, cursors, shared system settings, and many other things. This value should be left alone.

The second value is the size of the desktop heap for each *interactive* desktop (as opposed to non-interactive desktops, which is explained next). This is the value you want to edit. Try raising it by 256 (to 3328) to see if that stabilizes things.

The third value is used to control the heap for each desktop associated with *non-interactive* programs such as system services. This is set to 512 by default and generally does not need to be changed.

The total size of all the heaps must be less than 48MB.

## Setting the System Paged Pool Size

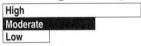

In Windows, the system paged pool is an area of physical memory that is reserved for system data or kernel code that can be written to disk when it is not in use. The size of the pool is generally managed automatically by Windows through internal algorithms, much in the same way the swapfile size is managed automatically. Under some conditions, the administrator may need to set the pool size manually.

## Overview

The size of the paged pool depends on several factors. In Windows 2000, a portion of the paged pool is reserved for holding the Registry, which makes the size of the paged pool and the Registry dependent on each other. The default maximum size for the Registry is 25 percent of the paged pool. Since the default size of the paged pool is 32MB, that makes the default maximum Registry size 8MB. The maximum amount of space the Registry can take up in the paged pool is 80 percent of the paged pool size. This size limit keeps the Registry from encroaching on space needed by active processes. (If a user attempts to force the maximum Registry size to more than 80 percent of the paged pool, the system will reset it to 80 percent.)

The actual size of the paged pool is usually determined by a Registry setting, which, by default, varies between editions of Windows. In Windows 2000, the maximum size of the paged pool is between 300 and 470MB, which sets the maximum size of the Registry between 240 and 376MB. If Windows 2000 is booted using the /3GB switch, the maximum paged pool size is fixed at 192MB, and the Registry is capped at 153MB.

Editing the Maximum Registry Size setting in the Virtual Memory section of the System Properties window sometimes changes the paged pool size so that the new Registry size can be accommodated, but this only happens if you really ramp up the maximum Registry size. When you set a Registry size limit, it limits *both* the paged pool size and the amount of disk space that can be used by the Registry, so it's generally a good idea to keep the Registry size as-is. Figure 4-5 shows how the Virtual Memory displays the current and maximum size for the Registry under the existing paged pool size configuration.

The finite size of the paged pool can be problematic. Under high loads, a Windows 2000 system will log errors that indicate the system paged pool has been exhausted. Under extremely heavy loads, the system can even grind to a halt with a Stop error, indicating the paged pool has been used up. This can happen for a variety of reasons, but one of the most common is that a great many file handles are open, and the system's memory manager cannot trim down the allocation of the paged pool fast enough to keep up.

**CHAPTER 4**

Memory

---

**NOTE**   In Windows 2003, the Registry is no longer constrained by the size of the paged pool. Instead, Registry data is mapped into the cache address space, which limits the maximum size of the Registry only by the amount of installed physical memory. Since Windows 2003 can now support up to 64GB of RAM, fewer problems arise from limited paged pool space (and Registry size) due to this new architecture.

---

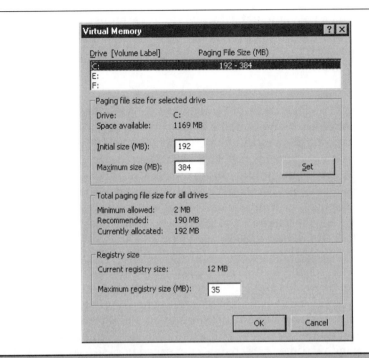

**Figure 4-5.** The Windows 2000 Virtual Memory window also lists the current and maximum size for the Registry. The maximum Registry size varies depending on the paged pool size.

# The Party Line                    Company X

Microsoft often pins the blame for exhausted paged pool resources on badly written drivers or programs. There's more than a little truth to this: Microsoft's own errors about the problem hint that one of the reasons for this may be a process that is leaking memory. (I know of at least one situation where Symantec Anti-Virus 8.0, Corporate Edition, turned out to be the culprit; the problem in that case was fixed by upgrading the program to a later revision.)
As one suggested fix for the problem, Microsoft suggests editing the Registry to increase the maximum paged pool size. This change is part of the solution quoted next, but even then it may only serve as a Band-Aid for a much deeper problem.

# *The Undocumented Solution*

*As a first step, the administrator can edit the Registry to increase the maximum size of the paged pool. This will at least keep the pool from being exhausted too quickly, and stave off a crash. Another solution is to use the Performance Monitor (also suggested by Microsoft, but less broadly) to profile processes suspected of being a memory leak. This way the offending process can be isolated and, if need be, removed.*

## What You'll Need

A Registry editor, such as REGEDIT or REGEDT32

Be sure to reboot after following these steps:

1. Open the Registry and navigate to HKEY_LOCAL_MACHINE\System\ CurrentControlSet\Control\Session Manager\Memory Management.

2. Add a new REG_DWORD value named **PoolUsageMaximum** and set the value to **40**. This will cause the Windows memory manager to begin trimming back the allocated paged pool memory when it reaches 40 percent of the total paged pool.

3. Edit the REG_DWORD value named PagedPoolSize and set the data to **0xFFFFFFFF** in Hex. This will allocate the maximum possible paged pool size for the physical memory installed in your computer.

To track the memory and pool usage for a process you suspect is causing a lack of pool resources:

1. Start the System Performance Monitor.

2. Select the Process object and add the following counters for that object: Handle Count, Pool Nonpaged Bytes, Pool Paged Bytes, and Private Bytes counters for the process in question.

3. Select the System object and add the Available Bytes counter. (The Private Bytes and Handle Count counters should be the first sign of trouble. If both counters increase without ever decreasing during the machine's uptime, then the process in question is leaking user memory.) An example of two processes having their resources tracked can be seen in Figure 4-6.

4. If the Pool Paged Bytes and Nonpaged Bytes counters also increase without decreasing, then the process in question is leaking kernel memory and should be taken offline immediately.

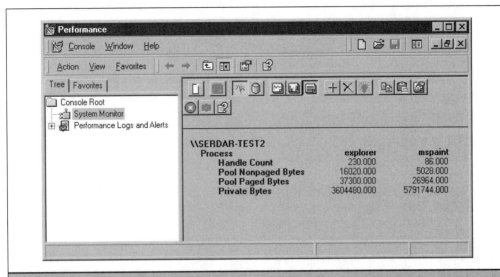

**Figure 4-6.** Two processes having their resources tracked in the Performance Monitor

The best way to monitor the use of the paged pool is to log the results to a file over a period of 24 hours and then analyze the log offline. Watching the changes that take place in the monitor "live" over a period of just a few minutes may be misleading.

A more advanced way to monitor the amount and allocation of paged pool resources is to use the poolmon.exe utility. The details for setting up and using poolmon can be found in KnowledgeBase article 177415.

---

**NOTE** Before using POOLMON, the administrator needs to enable "pool tagging," which allows allocations in the paged pool to be tagged with additional metadata for debugging. (The procedure for doing this is described in the article referenced earlier.) You do not need to enable pool tagging for Windows Server 2003 since it is *permanently enabled* there (and in later versions of Windows). It cannot be shut off, even by editing the Registry.

---

## 2000/2003 Turning Off Unused Services to Free Up Memory

Many system services that are used only intermittently or never at all can be shut off or disabled to save memory.

## Overview

Because system services run invisibly in the background, they aren't as obvious as applications that hog memory. What's more, a combination of several services that are running, but to no real purpose, can create a significant memory drain on a server— even if they are swapped out to disk.

## The Party Line

**Company X**

```
Microsoft takes the point of view that services should only
be disabled if there is a real overriding need—a stuck
service, for instance, or one which needs to be turned off
to prevent components from interacting badly. However, they
don't explicitly forbid shutting off certain services as a
way of saving memory, especially if those services are
rarely or never used.
```

**CHAPTER
4**

Memory

## *The Undocumented Solution*

*Listed here is a rundown of many common services that can be disabled with little or no side effects in both Windows 2000 and 2003. If a particular service only appears in one of the two operating systems, there will be a note to that effect. This list is not comprehensive of all services in Windows 2000/2003, but is limited to the services usually set to run by default when they may not have to be. One example of a service's properties can be seen in Figure 4-7.*

Before disabling any services, the prudent thing to do is to determine what, if any, dependencies exist for that service. (See Table 4-1.) To learn about a service's dependencies, double-click its entry in the Services management window and select the Dependencies tab. The bottom pane of the Dependencies tab lists what services depend on the one in question. If the window is grayed out, then the service can most

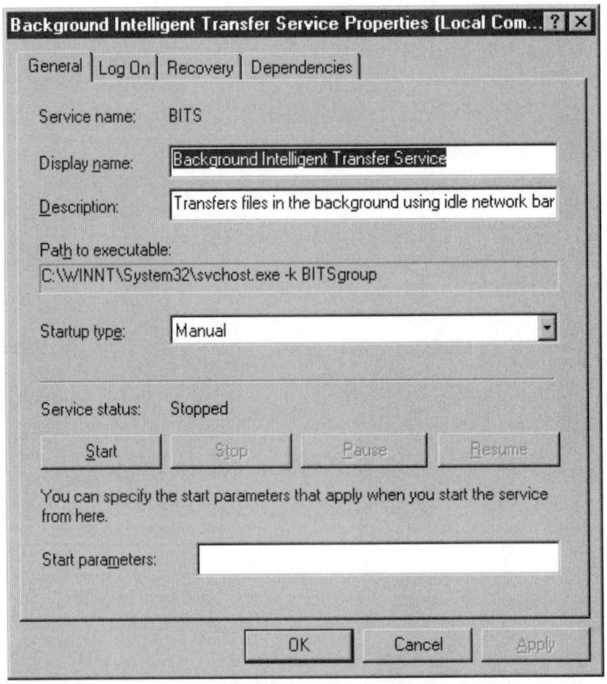

**Figure 4-7.**    The Background Intelligent Transfer Service shut off and set to manual

| Service Name | OS | Description | When to Disable? |
|---|---|---|---|
| Alerter | 2K/2K3 | Receives administrative alerts in a LAN | A common target for spammers now, so unless you are actually using administrative alerts in your network, disable along with the Messenger service |
| Automatic Updates | 2K/2K3 | Used by Windows Update to download and install published system component updates and service packs | Disabled automatically if you turn off Automatic Updates; in Windows 2000, from the Automatic Updates icon in the Control Panel; in Windows 2003, from the Automatic Updates tab in My Computer \| Properties |
| Background Intelligent Transfer Service | 2K/2K3 | Works with Windows Update to transfer data in the background as needed to the system | Disabled/enabled with Windows Update |

**Table 4-1.**    Services in Windows 2000 and 2003 that Can Be Disabled, and Under What Circumstances

| Service Name | OS | Description | When to Disable? |
|---|---|---|---|
| Computer Browser | 2K/2K3 | Maintains a list of all systems on the local network and provides it to any workstations which ask | Only one server per LAN should be running this; if you have multiple servers, turn Browser off on all but one to reduce NetBIOS "chatter" |
| DHCP Client | 2K/2K3 | Assigns IP addresses and DNS records to the local machine via DHCP | Only if DHCP is not being used |
| Distributed Link Tracking Client / Server | 2K/2K3 | Tracks linked files that are moved from one NTFS volume or system to another | When link tracking is not needed (which is generally often) |
| Error Reporting Service | 2K3 | Reports back error information on crashed applications to Microsoft | When extended error reporting is not needed |
| Indexing Service | 2K/2K3 | Indexes on-disk content for faster contextual searches | When text searches are not being performed |
| Print Spooler | 2K/2K3 | Manages print jobs for applications and the system, including virtual printer drivers (such as the Adobe Acrobat output driver) | When printing is not used |
| Remote Registry Service | 2K/2K3 | Allows the remote manipulation of the Registry on that machine | When remote Registry editing is not being performed—this is almost never done, so this service should be disabled |
| Task Scheduler | 2K/2K3 | Runs tasks automatically at a prescheduled time | When task scheduling is not in use |
| Wireless Zero Configuration | 2K3 | Automatically configures 802.11 networking | When wireless networks are not being used |

**Table 4-1.**   Services in Windows 2000 and 2003 that Can Be Disabled, and Under What Circumstances *(continued)*

CHAPTER 4

Memory

likely be stopped immediately without problems. An example of a service with no dependencies can be seen in Figure 4-8.

**NOTE**   The Dependencies window generally only lists *running* components, which depend on that service. If, in the future, you need to run a component that depends on a service which is turned off or disabled, you may get an error when the new service in question can't start because of this broken dependency. Be mindful when disabling services.

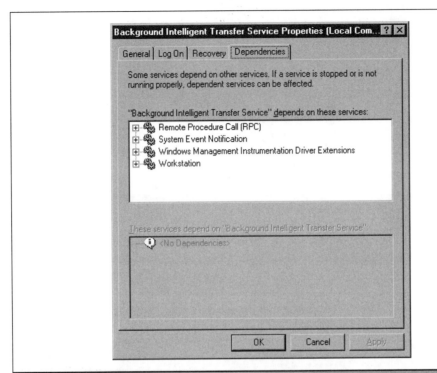

**Figure 4-8.** The Dependencies tab of the Background Intelligent Transfer Service. Since nothing else currently depends on this service, it can be disabled without any immediate problems.

## 2000/2003 Cutting Unneeded Processes in Terminal Server User Sessions

Windows 2000 systems used as Terminal Servers can experience memory consumption problems unknown to non-TS systems. One problem is when services or applications are loaded on a per-user basis rather than per-machine.

## Overview

Managing memory consumption on Windows servers used for Terminal Services requires a little more precision and finesse than on a conventional Windows server. What appears to be a memory leak may, in fact, be a subtler problem.

Imagine: If you have a server with 50 users logged on, each running one process that uses 0.25 percent of the processor time and 1MB of RAM, 12 percent of the CPU and 50MB of RAM will be eaten up before a single user application is launched. The more users log on, the worse things get, so the less programs each user runs by default, the better.

Services or programs that load in this fashion are not usually from any one source. Some come from Microsoft itself, while some are add-ons or enhancements from other manufacturers. For example, Citrix MetaFrame usually adds ICABAR (the onscreen administration toolbar) as a standard startup item for each user.

## The Party Line                                    Company X

Microsoft doesn't seem to have specific advice for avoiding redundant program images in this fashion. They do make the usual points about not running unneeded services on a per-machine basis, but not on an avoidable per-user basis.

## *The Undocumented Solution*

*A conscientious administrator should look into the contents of three Registry entries that govern which programs are loaded for each user. Two of them can be edited and then left alone, but the third may require more sophisticated intervention.*

## What You'll Need

A Registry editor, such as REGEDIT or REGEDT32

Be sure to reboot after following these steps:

1. Open the Registry and navigate to HKEY_LOCAL_MACHINE\Software\ Microsoft\WindowsNT\Current Version\Winlogon\Userinit.

2. This key usually contains %systemroot%\system32\userinit.exe, although it may harbor other entries delineated by commas. Remove the extra entries, but do not remove the entry for userinit.exe.

3. Navigate to HKEY_LOCAL_MACHINE\Software\Microsoft\Windows\ Current Version\Run.

CHAPTER
4

Memory

4.  If there is no Run subkey, then there's no need to change anything. If there is, inspect the subkeys within the Run subkey *carefully* and see if there are applications that do not absolutely have to be there. If so, delete them.

5.  To delete startup values for individual users not currently logged on, navigate to HKEY_USERS\<profile>\Software\Microsoft\Windows\Current Version\ Run (where <profile> is the GUID number for a given user). Edit as per step 4 earlier.

6.  If you don't want to edit out these entries entirely, you can block them from loading by using REGINI to restrict permissions on the subkey HKEY_ CURRENT_USER\Software\Microsoft\Windows\Current Version\Run. This way when the user logs in, no new keys (representing new programs) are copied into that subkey. To learn more about how to use REGINI, see KnowledgeBase document 237607.

# CHAPTER 5
## *Networking*

**In This Chapter:**

- ☐ Setting the Interframe Gap for Network Controllers
- ☐ Editing the TCP Window Size
- ☐ Editing TCP MTU Parameters
- ☐ Editing TCP TTL (Time-to-Live) Parameters
- ☐ Editing TCP Retransmission Parameters
- ☐ Limiting Incoming TCP Connections
- ☐ Editing TCP Keep-Alive Parameters
- ☐ Allowing Variant TCP/IP Database File Paths
- ☐ Editing Routing and Remote Access Queue Parameters
- ☐ Editing Other Routing and Remote Access Parameters
- ☐ Editing ARP Parameters
- ☐ Editing Alert and Network Error Parameters
- ☐ Editing IPX/SPX Error Parameters
- ☐ Editing NWNBLink Parameters
- ☐ Improving File- and Printer-Sharing Performance

☐ Changing Mailslot Behavior for Windows Networking

☐ Modifying PPTP Behavior

☐ Increasing PPTP and L2TP Connections

☐ Modifying NetBT Behavior

☐ Enabling 802.1x Support In Windows 2000

☐ Modifying DNS Caching Timeouts

☐ Modifying AFD Parameters

☐ Disabling Persistent Connections to Network Resources

☐ Switching from DHCP to a Static Address Without Rebooting

☐ Minimizing the Risk of Name Hijacking on a Network

☐ Cleaning Up Residual Registry Entries Left After Deleting a Network Adapter

☐ Forcing a License Server for Terminal Services

☐ Changing the Listening Port for Terminal Services

Networking is one of the core reasons for running a computer as a server in the first place. File and print servers, web servers, database servers—whatever the application, the common denominator among all of them is that they send data across a network connection to remote hosts. Obviously, the faster the machine can fulfill such demands, the better, and out of this need has come a veritable cottage industry of hacking and tweaking network settings.

Most of these changes fall into the category of tweaking TCP/IP settings for faster response. This is only a part of the focus of this chapter, however, since TCP/IP is only one protocol among many (although it is the most widely-used) and only one factor among many. The first part of this chapter talks about networking hardware, both wired and wireless, and changes that can be made to them to improve both speed and security. The next section discusses protocols and network standards such as DNS, then covers tricks involving Internet Connection Sharing. I've also taken some time to discuss advanced file and printer sharing techniques, plus some tips involving multihomed and load-balancing servers.

Like many other settings in Windows, network settings tend to be self-tuning. Consequently, changing network settings can be a double-edged sword. On the one hand, it can make a good thing better, by removing problems due to obstinate default settings. On the other hand, it can make a bad thing worse, or turn something good into something bad.

Whether or not tweaking will work to your benefit depends on many things: what the server is being used for, whether it's on a LAN or a WAN (because of latency, topology, and media type, just to name a few things), what the traffic load is like, and many other factors. There is rarely, if ever, a single "magic bullet" tweak that instantly makes everything go faster. There are a few select tweaks that ought to be used in just about all environments, but they too need to be considered carefully.

Because of the sheer volume of possible changes and settings in this chapter, I've broken out a great many of them individually to explain the consequences of editing them. Some of them may be familiar, although I hope that by spelling out their importance in detail, I can show how changing some of them may be ineffectual or flat-out counterproductive. Context is everything.

There are literally dozens of programs that offer to tweak network settings, either alone or as part of a general nostrum of system tweaks. Because of the sheer number of such programs, I've elected not to go into great detail about them. Many of these applications duplicate each other's functions, and not all of them provide intelligible feedback about what you're changing and why, and what consequences it will have. If you are willing to experiment and find one that suits your needs, feel free to use it once you understand the nature of the changes you're making.

Finally, some of the settings quoted here are reprised in the interface for the network card driver itself. One of the rules of thumb about NICs is that any card under $25 isn't worth tweaking, but higher-end management adapters or server-level adapters may certainly benefit from a little patience and experimentation.

# 2000/2003 Setting the Interframe Gap for Network Controllers

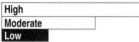

Modifying the interframe gap timing in local networks can decrease signal latency and boost bandwidth, but it isn't a stock change for all Windows machines, and it must be supported by the LAN hardware to work.

## Overview

The IEEE 802.3 Ethernet standard states that any Ethernet device that wants to transmit on the wire must wait until it senses 9.6 microseconds of silence. This 9.6-microsecond delay is the *interframe gap*, since it takes place between frames of data.

The original reason for setting the 9.6 microsecond gap time was to allow the last station that transmitted to switch from transmit to receive mode. This delay would allow the network interface to insure that it had not missed receiving a frame intended for it while changing from one mode to the next.

When the Ethernet standard was first developed, this interval was considered reasonable, but thanks to advances in network technology, 9.6 microseconds may be overly generous. In fact, it may be possible to increase performance, especially in 100-megabit full-duplex networks or faster, by tightening the interframe gap. A shorter gap time means that much less "dead time" on the wire, with that much more signal time available to each network interface. Also, too small a gap and the number of collisions between network signals goes up.

---

## The Party Line                                    Company X

```
Microsoft only recommends tuning the interframe gap if there
are explicit problems with high rates of collisions on
100-megabit networks, as described in KnowledgeBase article
315237, "High Rate of Collisions on 100-Megabit Networks."
With some care, however, tuning the interframe gap for local
networks can be done as a performance-enhancing measure as
well as a troubleshooting one—provided your network hardware
supports it.
```

---

## *The Undocumented Solution*

*Because the interframe gap is a hardware-level feature, changing the interframe gap will require making changes to the configuration of the network hardware in the computer. This is not something that every network card supports, and when it is supported, it is implemented differently.*

One good example of how this is executed with a particular manufacturer can be seen in Intel's Management Adapter network controllers. Because they are designed to work in a broad variety of settings, the Management Adapters are highly configurable and can be set to address a wide range of network conditions, including changing the interframe gap settings.

Among the options settable on the Management Adapters is a control labeled "Adaptive Interframe Spacing." Originally enabled by default, this option allows the adapter to tune the size of the interframe gap to reduce collisions. The card experiments with different frame gaps and determines the optimal size based on network conditions. In the last few years, however, this option has been disabled by default, since more people are now using switches rather than hubs, even in home networking environments. Switches work better with standard interframe gap timings, since they attempt to intelligently route packets rather than simply repeat the same signal across all ports. Some managed switches can be configured to work with a different interframe gap, but the vast majority of switches (especially the unmanaged, home-networking variety) will not be able to do so. Changing the gap settings with switches will probably not improve anything, and may only make things worse.

Another Intel option is "Adaptive Transmit Threshold," which controls underrun behavior. Generally, the network interface will begin to send a packet on the wire before it is completely copied from memory. If another device pre-empts the transfer process, then only part of the packet will be transmitted, which results in an underrun error. The interface does recover gracefully from an error like this, with the only side effect being a wasted partial packet sent across the wire. But if this transmission is successful, the latency for the transmission can be decreased and more data sent without increasing the window size. (See "Editing the TCP Window Size" for more on this subject.) The Adaptive Transmit Threshold indicator controls how many packets are buffered before they begin to be transmitted; the lower the number, the smaller the buffer, and the sooner the transmission begins.

**NOTE**    On some networks, the Adaptive Transmit Threshold needs to be set to a high number (200 or so) to prevent underrun problems. If you're experiencing a great many TX errors for no apparent reason, try setting this value. Intel also recommends not using a threshold below 200 on systems with multiple bus mastering cards or "machines with high latency."

Not every network card adheres to the 9.6 microsecond standard by default, either. Some are capable of switching faster, while some aren't. On a network with a variety of network adapters from different manufacturers (or even from the same manufacturer), you may notice a great deal of incompatibility. If you have a network where some cards are set to use the 9.6 standard (or are hardwired to do so) and some that use less, there is a chance that the cards with the longer gap time will lose data.

To sum up, the best way to take advantage of variable interframe gap timings is when you not only have the network interfaces to support it, but also hubs, switches and routers in your local network that support it. In truth, moving to switches alone over hubs (if you haven't done so already) may yield more of an improvement than changing the stated settings.

## 2000/2003 Editing the TCP Window Size

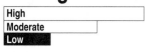

Of all the TCP/IP-based networking tweaks out there, editing the TCP receive window size is the one that generally produces the most immediate, dramatic, and useful increase in performance. However, it isn't a panacea, and it needs to be applied consistently among machines that use it.

CHAPTER
5

Networking

## Overview

In TCP/IP, the TCP receive window size parameter controls the amount of data that can be sent without an acknowledgment from the recipient. For instance, a window size of 4 kilobytes would mean that the sender would only be able to send 4 kilobytes of data before it would be required to stop and wait for an ACK packet from the recipient. If no ACK packet is received within a defined time, the packet is assumed lost and must be retransmitted. The larger the window, the more data can be transmitted at once without a break for an ACK, and the faster the network throughput.

TCP windows are primarily for congestion control. Wide area networks work across a diverse range of media and connection types, and each of those network segments has its own bottleneck controlling how fast data can be transferred. Many of Cisco's routers, for instance, support a maximum window size of 256 kilobytes, nowhere near what most operating systems are configured to use by default (including Windows 2000). Window sizing helps keep the throughput to a manageable level, but also allows it to be flexible as well.

With any TCP connection, there are two window sizes—one advertised by the sender and the other advertised by the receiver. The smaller of the two values takes precedence, but since you have no way of knowing if the other machine's TCP window is set to be large, it helps to have a large maximum window size. The key word here is "maximum," since the window size scales automatically depending on how the routers you are accessing are programmed. Setting your TCP window size to 64 kilobytes does not mean every TCP window is going to be that size; it simply means the packets can grow to that size if need be.

The default window size in Windows 2000 and 2003 is 8760 bytes, which is the industry-standard default for Ethernet. In LAN environments, this is considered to be a safe window size to use, but most recent (100-megabit or better) network hardware can almost certainly handle a far bigger window. If you have an intelligent or managed switch, the documentation for the product usually gives the maximum window size, and in some cases it can even be edited.

The one downside of using a big window size in a local network is that it becomes surpassingly easy to set the window too big and flood the switch's buffer with unrouted packets. This happens less so in a wide area network (WAN), because of the number of hops involved and the robustness of the switches used to carry the packets.

---

**NOTE** The TCP receive window size should *not* be confused with the MTU parameter, discussed later in this chapter. The MTU parameter controls IP *packet* size, and a single window can span multiple packets.

---

## The Party Line                    Company X

```
Microsoft does make mention of how to edit the TCP
window size via a Registry edit, along with a great many
other TCP parameters, but doesn't provide specific tuning
recommendations.
```

## *The Undocumented Solution*

*Because changing the receive window size is one of the most important things that can be done to enhance TCP performance, it needs to be discussed thoroughly.*

First of all, setting a big maximum window size can eat up memory on a machine that establishes a great many socket connections. Each socket connection requires a buffer the size of the negotiated window size, so if you have 100 connections open with a 64K negotiated window size each, that's 6400K in connection buffers *alone*. If this is a server that receives thousands of simultaneous connections and doesn't have a lot of RAM to burn, a large window size may choke the system.

Second, the window setting may not need to be edited depending on the type of connectivity to and from the server. If you are using Windows Server to run, for instance, SQL Server and IIS on a LAN—with no Internet or WAN connections; everything local—it's easier to assume that the window size of any connection is going to be the default of 8K, the Ethernet default. Since the latency in LANs is usually very low, changing the window size will not affect the throughput much in such an environment. The default settings will do. More than that and you might wind up needlessly saturating your switch (as described earlier).

There is a common formula for calculating the size of the window based on network conditions, which is called the *bandwidth delay product*, or BDP for short. This is the bandwidth of the slowest network segment in kilobits per second, multiplied by the average latency in milliseconds to the host, with the result multiplied by 1.5. For instance, a 56K dial-up connection for a home PC with an average latency of 200 milliseconds would be calculated as $56 \times 1500 \times 1.5 = 126,000$.

Obviously, the latency is going to vary a bit depending on the remote host, but since the 56K dial-up connection is the slowest element in the whole, the calculation is based from that. A faster link would be $800 \times 30 \times 1.5 = 36,000$. (Here, the value 800 represents a broadband link, such as cablemodem.) Connections with a low BDP can continue to use a small window size, to reduce the amount of memory usage, but they have the *option* of ramping up for added performance.

One approach to handling window size is to start off as aggressive as possible on either end and let the middle of the network—the switches and routers that do the vast majority of the work—handle the actual traffic control. Usually this approach involves setting the window size as high as possible and seeing how things go from there. In Windows 2000, the maximum window size can be enormous (1GB!), but setting the window to this size is probably counterproductive. On the whole, a receive window size from 32K to 64K seems to produce the best results. More than 64K causes the number of dropped packets in almost all WAN connections to increase significantly. Less than 32K doesn't yield a significant enough improvement in throughput.

Something else needs to be considered: the window size can be changed by many things, not least of which is the application using it. If you are using an application that has configurable network parameters, check to make sure it can take advantage of the maximum window size. If there are no explicit controls for this in the program, then it may be difficult to tell if it is using window scaling correctly. Also note that the destination computers on your local subnet need to be set to the same window size, meaning the setting should be approached globally if at all.

## What You'll Need

A Registry editor, such as REGEDIT or REGEDT32

Be sure to reboot after following these steps:

1. Open the Registry and navigate to HKEY_LOCAL_MACHINE\SYSTEM\ CurrentControlSet\Services\Tcpip\Parameters.
2. Add or edit the REG_DWORD value named TcpWindowSize. Set the value to the number of bytes for the maximum window size on the system.

# 2000/2003 Editing TCP MTU Parameters

Aside from adjusting the TCP Receive Window, the TCP Maximum Transmission Unit size is probably the most powerful and valuable adjustment that can be made to a network interface's default parameters.

## Overview

The Maximum Transmission Unit, or MTU, is a TCP/IP setting that dictates what the largest TCP/IP packet size will be, in bytes. (This is not the same as the *frame* size, which is used to control the transmission of the raw datagram that makes up the packet.) Packet sizes in some network environments are fixed: networks that use

Internet Connection Sharing (ICS) or Point-to-Point Protocol over Ethernet (PPPoE) employ an MTU size of 1492 or lower. The smallest possible MTU size is 68.

By default, Windows 2000 and 2003 both use an MTU size of 1500 bytes. Because this MTU size is a little on the high side, it can create packet fragmentation, which slows down the network. This is more of a problem for workstations than servers, but servers can still benefit from having the MTU modified depending on their network environment.

Every protocol has a different maximum MTU size by default. Ethernet is 1500 (hence the use of the 1500 MTU default for TCP/IP); X.25 is 576. The link layer for a network connection has to perform the MTU discovery and report that information back to the higher protocols.

---

**NOTE**  Some interface drivers, such as those for ATM network cards, report back an MTU higher than what would be expected for the network type. Windows will use this higher number as reported by the adapter even when it's larger than the normal MTU for that media. Because of this, forcing the MTU size may be required on a per-protocol basis.

---

**CHAPTER
5**

Networking

# The Party Line                          Company X

```
Microsoft does in fact discuss the use of the MTU setting in
a number of different scenarios, but only as a KnowledgeBase
article, and without exposing an interface to set the MTU
for any protocol directly. Some of Microsoft's discussions
of the subject are referenced in the sections that follow.
```

## *The Undocumented Solution*

*Several Registry entries govern the MTU size, both directly and indirectly. Aside from hardsetting the MTU, it's also possible to establish behaviors about the way the MTU is set when first attempting to contact a host. This may actually prove to be better than hardwiring the MTU to a specific value if you are deploying the server on a WAN; if you are using it in a LAN environment only, where network conditions almost never change, a fixed MTU setting may be the best place to start. Again, use this with care.*

## What You'll Need

A Registry editor, such as REGEDIT or REGEDT32

Be sure to reboot after following these steps:

1. Test for the proper MTU size. One way to do this in a given network is to use the PING command:

   PING –F –L <MTU> <target>

   <MTU> in this case refers to the MTU size you are trying to test for, and <target> is the target network object—usually your network gateway. Start with an MTU size of 1500. If PING responds with an error stating the data must be fragmented, lower the MTU until you find the highest possible number that works.

2. Open the Registry and navigate to HKEY_LOCAL_MACHINE\SYSTEM\ CurrentControlSet\Services\Tcpip\Parameters\Interfaces\<adapter ID>, where <adapter ID> is the GUID for the network adapter to make the changes to. If you're unsure which adapter is which, expand the adapter ID subkeys and look for the IPAddress or DhcpIPAddress entry, which should tell you which adapter is which.

3. Create a new DWORD value named **MTU**. The smallest possible value for MTU is 68. This particular MTU value will govern this adapter only.

4. Repeat as needed for any other network adapters.

One point that needs to be made clear is that remote networks—networks apart from your own internal LAN—have an MTU that is almost certainly different. If you are running a server that is open to public Internet access, then the server should be set to perform MTU discovery. MTU discovery allows the computer to determine the best possible MTU for all networks along the way to a particular remote host.

Normally, MTU discovery is enabled by default in Windows 2000 and 2003, but you may want to assess the impact of having it turned on or off. One of the downsides of the MTU discovery process is that it takes longer to establish a connection with a host. Sometimes the discovery process doesn't yield significantly better performance. Also, you may want to force MTU discovery off if you're running the server exclusively in a controlled LAN environment, where the MTU is consistently the same and discovery is not needed.

## What You'll Need

A Registry editor, such as REGEDIT or REGEDT32

Be sure to reboot after following these steps:

1. Open the Registry and navigate to HKEY_LOCAL_MACHINE\SYSTEM\ CurrentControlSet\Services\Tcpip\Parameters.

2. Create a DWORD value named EnablePMTUDiscovery. Set it to 1 to enable MTU discovery (the default); set it to 0 to disable it.

The discovery process involves sending a packet of data with the "Don't Fragment" bit set in the packet header. If the packet comes back with a "Host Unreachable" message, that means the MTU for that network is too high, and the TCP/IP stack responds by lowering the MTU for that particular network route.

If you explicitly disable MTU discovery, the default MTU size for *all* communications across remote networks is 576 bytes. This reduces the chances of packet fragmentation to zero, although it does affect remote network performance, since the MTU isn't optimal.

Another way to improve communication with remote hosts is to set detection for black hole routers. A *black hole router* is any router set not to return "Destination Host Unreachable" messages used by the MTU discovery process, making it hard to determine what the proper MTU is. Enabling black hole detection significantly increases the number of transmission retries for a given host (and makes initial communications with the host slow), so if you are only using a local network for a particular server, there is no real reason to enable this option there.

## What You'll Need

A Registry editor, such as REGEDIT or REGEDT32

Be sure to reboot after following these steps:

1. Open the Registry and navigate to HKEY_LOCAL_MACHINE\SYSTEM\ CurrentControlSet\Services\Tcpip\Parameters.

2. Create or edit a DWORD value named EnableDeadGWDetect. Set it to 1 to enable dead gateway detection; set it to 0 to disable it.

---

**NOTE** If you use Internet Connection Sharing or Network Address Translation in Windows 2000, the server will *not* perform MTU discovery on the public (that is, Internet) network interface. If the public interface's MTU is less than the local interface's MTU, the Windows server will omit packets without warning. This problem appears to have been addressed in Windows 2003, but Windows 2000 users will want to force the same MTU for each network interface by adding separate MTU entries. For the best results, set them *both* high (32K to 64K).

---

2000/2003 # Editing TCP TTL (Time-to-Live) Parameters

| High |
|------|
| Moderate |
| Low |

The default TTL (time-to-live) parameter in TCP/IP may simply be too small for effective routing on the Internet to certain locations. Increasing it can help stop timeouts, especially for servers trying to reach hosts that may be concealed by NAT schemes.

CHAPTER
5

Networking

## Overview

Each TCP/IP packet contains a parameter referred to as the time-to-live, or TTL. This value indicates how many times the packet can be forwarded before it expires. Normally, the TTL in Windows for TCP/IP packets is 32, but with networks growing more complicated (especially when NAT schemes come into play), the default TTL may no longer be enough to route a packet to its destination. As a result, many packets with a long round trip often timeout and are dropped, even though they do not have undue latency.

---

## The Party Line

**Company X**

Microsoft's documents only mention increasing the TTL in passing. Interestingly, one of their references is not even to the TTL setting as such, but to the way TTL is implemented in the command-line PING tool.

---

## *The Undocumented Solution*

*Increasing the default TTL in Windows is as easy as making a Registry edit. However, increasing the default TTL to above 32 doesn't always provide consistent results, although it does provide a level of insurance against timeouts. Some routers are programmed to cap any incoming packet's TTL at 32: if they receive a packet with a TTL above 32, they reset it to 32. Still, having a higher default TTL will at least insure that your packets have a slightly better chance of reaching their destination even if they are capped part of the way along.*

## What You'll Need

A Registry editor, such as REGEDIT or REGEDT32

Be sure to reboot after following these steps:

1. Open the Registry and navigate to HKEY_LOCAL_MACHINE\SYSTEM\
   CurrentControlSet\Services\Tcpip\Parameters.

2. Add a new DWORD value named DefaultTTL and set it to a range that is relevant to the network baseline. If you are aware that the routers in your subnet force a maximum TTL like 64, then set it to that; if not, try 256 and examine its effects.

# 2000/2003 Editing TCP Retransmission Parameters

| High |
|------|
| Moderate |
| Low |

Among the many other parameters explored in this chapter, the Windows TCP/IP stack has controls that govern its retransmission behavior. Unsuccessful send or connect operations can be retried up to a certain number of times before failing.

## Overview

On an exceptionally congested or convoluted network, the default timeout/retransmission parameters may be too small, and may fail even though the remote host is still reachable. To that end, it may be useful to edit the retransmission parameters.

The default wait time for a timeout value when trying to establish an outbound connection is 45 seconds, with four retries during that period. Conversely, on a highly reliable network, 45 seconds may be excessive, and an administrator may want to *decrease* the timeout value to one retry, the better to speed things up.

---

## The Party Line                                    Company X

```
Microsoft does in fact mention the timeout problem and the
listed solution in KnowledgeBase article 200770, but only
as a corrective for an NT 4.0 condition. It doesn't mention
reducing the number as a way of speeding things up on a
dependable connection.
```

---

### *The Undocumented Solution*

*Changing the retransmission parameters of TCP/IP involves editing two Registry entries that govern timeout behavior.*

## What You'll Need

A Registry editor, such as REGEDIT or REGEDT32

Be sure to reboot after following these steps:

1. Open the Registry and navigate to HKEY_LOCAL_MACHINE\SYSTEM\ CurrentControlSet\Services\Tcpip\Parameters.

2. Create a new DWORD value named TcpMaxConnectRetransmissions. This determines how many times the network stack will try to connect before aborting. The system will wait three seconds on the first attempt, six on the next, 12 on the third attempt, and so on until it runs out of attempts or until it makes a connection. The default value for TcpMaxConnectRetransmissions is 5, but raising it to 8 should help with any retransmission problems on flaky connections, and lowering it to 1 should help with networks that are highly reliable (such as local networks). Servers that perform their own outbound connections (such as servers that perform synchronization) will see the most benefit from this.

---

**NOTE**    If your server is a constant target for SYN flood attacks, you should reduce TcpMaxConnectRetransmissions to a small value (3 or less).

---

3. Create a new DWORD value named TcpMaxDataRetransmissions. This controls how many times the network stack will attempt to transmit a given data packet before aborting the connection. Unlike TcpMaxConnectRetransmissions, the original timeout value is based on the measured round-trip time of the connection, but like the previous entry, each successive retransmission time-out time is doubled. The default value here is also 5. Set it to 1 for high-quality networks, and to 8 for low-quality.

One of the other interesting and largely undocumented behaviors of the Windows network stack is how it handles Address Resolution Protocol (ARP) timeouts. ARP links IP addresses to MAC (Media Access Control) hardware addresses, and a TCP connection cannot be established unless there is an ARP resolution beforehand. When an ARP request takes place, it retries four times, doubling the timeout each time, and begins with a three-second timeout value—exactly the same way the TCP connection timeout works. Consequently, it can take up to 45 seconds for ARP requests to time out.

What's not widely discussed is that the TcpMaxConnectRetransmissions entry *also governs the number of ARP timeouts.* The two are not handled by separate Registry settings, although in theory they should be since ARP and TCP have nothing to do with each other. By setting the timeout for TCP connections, you also set the timeout for ARP, which is useful on local networks where there is very little latency and a high degree of dependability—and in a local network, odds are if ARP resolution isn't working, it's not because of poor network conditions. (More options for configuring ARP behavior are in the section "Editing ARP Parameters" later in this chapter.)

# Limiting Incoming TCP Connections

The number of incoming TCP connections can be limited without having to resort to a piece of third-party software or a firewall appliance.

## Overview

At some point, an administrator may consider configuring a public (or private) server to only accept a finite number of incoming TCP connections. There could be many reasons for this: any computer given direct access to the Internet risks being attacked more than ever, for instance, and limiting the number of connections is one possible way of preventing buffer overflow problems that result from attacks.

# The Party Line

**Company X**

```
Microsoft does have a Registry entry for controlling the
number of inbound TCP connections, but downplays it in favor
of using product-by-product control (for instance, if IIS is
being run, use the incoming-connection control in IIS instead).
```

## *The Undocumented Solution*

*There's a good deal of validity to Microsoft's stance about limiting incoming connections on a product-by-product basis. Setting a hard limit for incoming TCP connections isn't always predictable (which is one of the reasons why this tip is a Risk Factor 3 tip) and can break the functionality of some programs outright. That said, there may be cases where limiting inbound connections can be useful—for instance, in a diagnostic or experimental way.*

CHAPTER
5

Networking

## What You'll Need

A Registry editor, such as REGEDIT or REGEDT32

Be sure to reboot after following these steps:

1. Open the Registry and navigate to HKEY_LOCAL_MACHINE\SYSTEM\ CurrentControlSet\Services\Tcpip\Parameters.
2. Add a REG_DWORD value named TcpNumConnections and set it to the maximum number of inbound connections you want to support on that machine.

---

**NOTE**   Limiting inbound connections can cause real problems on Active Directory machines such as domain controllers and member servers. These machines depend on a large number of incoming connections and should not be changed in this fashion.

---

## 2000/2003 Editing TCP Keep-Alive Parameters

| High |
| Moderate |
| Low |

The Windows TCP stack transmits a "keep-alive" message at regular intervals to make sure remote servers have not disconnected.

## Overview

By default, the interval between keep-alives is two hours, which may be too long for some scenarios. Some network links do not use keep-alives as a way to gauge what links to drop and which to keep, and some can even be programmed to ignore them entirely.

---

# The Party Line                                    **Company X**

Microsoft makes mention of editing keep-alive parameters as a corrective to dropped connections, but not as a performance-enhancing method (for instance, a way of reducing interstitial network chatter, among other things).

---

## *The Undocumented Solution*

*Changing the keep-alive parameters of TCP/IP involves editing two Registry entries that control how keep-alives are sent.*

### What You'll Need

A Registry editor, such as REGEDIT or REGEDT32

Be sure to reboot after following these steps:

1. Open the Registry and navigate to HKEY_LOCAL_MACHINE\SYSTEM\ CurrentControlSet\Services\Tcpip\Parameters.

2. Add or edit the DWORD value KeepAliveTime. The default value is 7200000, which is two hours (measured in milliseconds). A shorter value, perhaps five to ten minutes, may be used. To disable keep-alives entirely, set this to zero.

---

**NOTE**   If you are using xDSL connections, setting the keep-alive time to a shorter interval (ten minutes instead of two hours) is a good way to keep the remote server from dropping the connection.

---

3. Add or edit the DWORD value KeepAliveInterval. This measures, in milliseconds, how long the system waits to retry a keep-alive packet if no acknowledgement is sent back. The default value is 1000, or 1 second. Setting this to a longer interval is a good way to adjust for slow network links.

4. Create a DWORD value named SessionKeepAlive. This governs how long, in seconds, to wait before sending a keep-alive packet on an active network connection. By default, this is 3600 seconds, or one hour. Set it to zero to turn off keep-alive transmissions when the network connection is alive.

## Allowing Variant TCP/IP Database File Paths

TCP/IP uses a number of text files for configuration—HOSTS and LMHOSTS, mainly—in addition to the usual Registry entries.

CHAPTER
5

Networking

## Overview

TCP/IP data files are usually kept in the folder \\*%SystemRoot%*\\System32\\Drivers\\ Etc. From the outside, it appears that this location is hardwired into the system and cannot be changed.

---

# The Party Line    `Company X`

Buried in the *Windows 2000 Resource Kit* is a passing reference to how the network stack finds its hosts files—through a Registry entry. It isn't expanded on much beyond that, so it's most likely one of the many bits of information Microsoft is not leaving to system administrators.

    Interestingly enough, a *programmer* can also change the database path. Within the MSDN library there is a reference to the WMI SetDatabasePath Method in Class Win32_NetworkAdapterConfiguration, which apparently does nothing more than change this Registry entry!

---

## *The Undocumented Solution*

*Nonprogrammers can always modify the Registry directly to change the database path. One possible use for this is to place the database files in a directory that is not part of the %SystemRoot% hierarchy, for modification by other applications or users.*

## What You'll Need

A Registry editor, such as REGEDIT or REGEDT32

Be sure to reboot after following these steps:

1. Open the Registry and navigate to HKEY_LOCAL_MACHINE\\SYSTEM\\ CurrentControlSet\\Services\\Tcpip\\Parameters.
2. Add or edit a REG_EXPAND_SZ value named DatabasePath. The default value is *%SystemRoot%*\\system32\\drivers\\etc. Set this to the path of your new database files location.

---

**NOTE** If you are going to include the system directory as part of the path, always use the variable *%SystemRoot%* to describe the system directory. Never use a hardcoded version of the system directory.

---

 # Editing Routing and Remote Access Queue Parameters

| High |
|------|
| **Moderate** |
| Low |

Both Windows 2000 and 2003 Server can function as routers between different networks using Routing and Remote Access (RRA). The default settings for how packets are queued for routing may not be enough for high-traffic WANs.

## Overview

When routing is enabled, the Windows TCP/IP stack enables its own built-in router cache and queue, which features a number of tunable parameters. Because these options are not exposed to the administrator, someone who is responsible for setting up an RRA server should be aware of them. If routing traffic is unusually heavy, a little tuning can improve performance with RRA.

---

**NOTE** Routing and Remote Access differs from Internet Connection Sharing in a couple of critical ways. One is the scope: ICS only supports up to ten client systems, while RRA can support up to a thousand (five thousand in Windows 2003 Server Enterprise Edition). RRA also provides secure tunneling and packet filtering, and can bridge connections between subnets (so that branch offices can share the same LAN resources as a local office). The question of which to use comes down to size. If you're using only a few machines, use ICS; if you have a lot of machines to manage, use RRA.

---

## The Party Line

**Company X**

```
Microsoft only mentions these parameters in the context of
bugfixes—for instance, to keep the forwarding buffer from
consuming all available kernel memory. (This is a legitimate
problem, as documented in KnowledgeBase article 221926, but
is limited to Windows NT 4.0.) Their standard claim about
TCP/IP being largely self-tuning holds true most of the
time, but it's worth discovering for yourself (if you can)
whether these changes will benefit you.
```

CHAPTER 5

Networking

## *The Undocumented Solution*

*The under-the-hood options for Routing and Remote Access are broken out across several Registry entries, discussed here in detail.*

## What You'll Need

A Registry editor, such as REGEDIT or REGEDT32

Be sure to reboot after following these steps:

1. Open the Registry and navigate to HKEY_LOCAL_MACHINE\SYSTEM\ CurrentControlSet\Services\Tcpip\Parameters.

2. Look for a key labeled IPEnableRouter, which should be set to 1 (Boolean). This key, which enables IP routing across networks through the computer in question, should be set automatically when RRA is installed. If it isn't set, and you are using RRA, set it to **1** (or add it and set it to **1** if it doesn't exist).

3. Create a new DWORD key named ForwardBufferMemory. The forward buffer in TCP/IP controls the amount of memory used for storing packet data to be forwarded. This memory space is called the *router packet queue*; too small a queue will cause packets to be dropped at random, and reduce the routing efficiency. Each data buffer in the queue is 256 bytes, so set ForwardBufferMemory to a value that is a multiple of 256. The default setting is 74,240 (290 buffers). ForwardBufferMemory should never be smaller than the size of your network's MTU. (See the section "Editing TCP MTU Parameters" for more information about the MTU.) A good way to figure the size of the buffer is to use 100 times the MTU size for a small network, and 150–200 times the buffer size for a larger one.

---

**NOTE**   The size of the routed *packets* (not the MTU) and the size of the buffers don't have anything to do with each other. A packet larger than 256 bytes will simply be stored in multiple buffers.

---

4. Create a new DWORD key named NumForwardPackets. This value controls the number of IP packet *headers* set aside for the router queue. As a way of saving space, the headers for the packets are buffered separately (since they can vary in size). As with the queue itself, if the system runs out of buffer space to store packet headers, it will drop headers from the queue, resulting in data loss. By default, Windows sets the size of the header queue to 50; the smallest size that should be assigned is the size of the ForwardBufferMemory entry divided by the largest IP packet size. If you set ForwardBufferMemory to 100

times the default MTU size (145,408), then NumForwardPackets should be set to at least 568. There is no reason other than wasted memory to set this number exceptionally high, though (1024 or more; 568 is probably the most realistic high number for moderate to heavy traffic).

5. Navigate to HKEY_LOCAL_MACHINE\CurrentControlSet\Services\ <adapter name>\ Parameters\Tcpip, where <adapter name> is the name of the network adapter used for Remote Access Services.

6. Create a new DWORD key named MaxForwardPending. This controls how many packets Windows forwards to a particular network at any given time. Multiple RAS connections that are fairly network-intensive may benefit from having this raised above the default setting of 20; try 40 to 200 depending on the network load. This setting needs to be created on an adapter-by-adapter basis, but it should only be set on interfaces that accept remote access connections.

CHAPTER
5

**NOTE** You can use this particular setting whether or not RRAS is installed. Many people have done this to create simple routers on Windows 2000 or even Windows XP.

**2000/2003** # Editing Other Routing and Remote Access Parameters

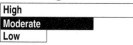

Aside from the queue parameters (which tend to affect RAS performance the most), there are a great number of other Routing and Remote Access parameters which are normally concealed from the end user or administrator.

Routing and Remote Access requires a higher degree of configuration than most other network services, which tend to be simply switched on. I've commented elsewhere in this chapter that File and Print Services tends to work the same way.

Networking

## The Party Line                              Company X

```
That said, Microsoft has seen fit to include some settings
in RAS not exposed through the administrative interface. A
good many of them are frankly not all that useful, or only
apply to client connections and not servers.
```

# *The Undocumented Solution*

*I've culled the most useful and server-related of the Routing and Remote Access Registry entries here. Some of them are only going to be useful to people who have a dial-up line (an increasing rarity, but still worth discussing here).*

## What You'll Need

A Registry editor, such as REGEDIT or REGEDT32

Be sure to reboot after following these steps:

1. Open the Registry and navigate to HKEY_LOCAL_MACHINE\SYSTEM\ CurrentControlSet\Services\ RasMan\Parameters.

2. Add or edit the DWORD NumberOfRings. This controls how many times an incoming call on a Unimodem device will ring before the server answers. If you share a data line for voice or fax, this is a useful parameter; it keeps the machine from prematurely picking up if you know that a call that rings $x$ times is a data call. The minimum is 1 and the maximum is 20.

3. Add or edit the DWORD Logging. When set to 1, this writes events to the system log indicating which users are logging onto RAS. If you use the system log as a way of auditing such things, this comes in handy.

4. Navigate to HKEY_LOCAL_MACHINE\System\CurrentControlSet\ Services\RasMan\PPP and add or edit the DWORD DefaultCallbackDelay. This measures, in seconds, how long RAS will wait before calling back to authenticate a remote user. If you have phone lines that don't disconnect immediately upon hanging up, this is useful, but if you have a very responsive phone exchange, you can lower the response time. The default is 12 seconds.

5. Add or edit the DWORD keys ForceEncryptedData and ForceEncryptedPassword. If you have non-Windows clients which are having trouble connecting to your RAS server, set both of these to 0 to see if that helps force clear-text authentication.

6. Navigate to HKEY_LOCAL_MACHINE\System\CurrentControlSet\ Services\RasMan\IPCP\ Parameters and add or edit the DWORD keys RequestVJCompression and AcceptVJCompression. Setting both of these to 0 disables VanJacobsen compression, or VJ compression, on the server. VJ compression confuses some dial-up clients, so shutting it off may alleviate this problem.

7. Navigate to HKEY_LOCAL_MACHINE\Software\Microsoft\Windows NT\ CurrentVersion\Winlogon and add or edit the DWORD KeepRasConnections.

Setting this to 1 will preserve RAS connections even when a person logs out (unless, of course, they explicitly disconnect). If you have a remote machine connected to your local LAN and multiple people use it, this is useful.

## 2000/2003 Editing ARP Parameters

Hosts on the same physical network must determine each other's physical addresses before they can communicate. TCP/IP uses a discrete protocol called ARP, or Address Resolution Protocol, to learn the physical address of a machine with a given IP address.

## Overview

Each ARP resolution made by a machine is stored on that machine in a cache table. The table has 50 entries by default but expands if needed; the size of the table is not editable. Any lookup that remains in the cache for more than two minutes without being used is purged. On local networks where addresses rarely ever change, two minutes is excessively small. Tuning the cache behavior, and the way ARP broadcasts are made, can improve network performance and reduce interstitial "chatter."

### The Party Line                              Company X

Most of the ARP parameter changes documented here are not described as performance enhancers by Microsoft, but are listed as fixes for extremely specific problems. That said, they can be used as performance enhancers—in the right circumstances.

**CHAPTER 5**

Networking

## *The Undocumented Solution*

*Changing ARP settings involves not only editing the Registry but performing a certain amount of research to determine the best tuning options.*

A note of additional caution is appropriate here. Some changes to ARP settings can make the network unusable if the administrator isn't careful; if ARP breaks, no machine on the network thus affected will be able to see any other machine and vice versa. Fixing the problem is often as simple as undoing the change in question, although sometimes the TCP/IP stacks of a machine thus changed might need to be rebuilt—but since even undoing the changes requires an investment of effort and time that many administrators would not appreciate, don't implement these changes wantonly.

## What You'll Need

A Registry editor, such as REGEDIT or REGEDT32

Be sure to reboot after following these steps:

1. On a machine that gets a representative amount of traffic on your network, open a CMD session and type **arp –s**. If you see a great many ARP entries in the cache and your network is primarily machines with static addresses that don't change often (or where the static addresses are assigned based on the machine's MAC address, as is sometimes the case), you can set the lifetime for cache entries high (60 minutes or more). If you know addresses change often (for instance, on machines with wireless adapters that are assigned and released frequently), you should continue to keep the cache lifetime low.

2. To change the cache lifetime, open the Registry and then navigate to HKEY_LOCAL_MACHINE\SYSTEM\CurrentControlSet\Services\Tcpip\ Parameters. Add or change the DWORD value ArpCacheLife and set it to the time, in seconds, that each entry lives in the cache when not in use.

3. Add or change the DWORD value ArpCacheMinReferencedLife. This value, in seconds, governs the maximum length of time any entry can remain in the cache, even if it is in use. Normally this is ten minutes, but you may want to raise it if you have a great many IPs that do not change; one hour is a good lifetime for such a network.

4. Add or change the DWORD value ArpRetryCount. This parameter indicates how many times the computer sends a "gratuitous" ARP—an announcement of its own IP address—when initializing. This is done to insure that the address is not already in use in the network, but if all systems in the LAN use a central DHCP server, three broadcasts is overkill. In fact, even one broadcast may not be needed at all; in LANs with DHCP, this can be disabled entirely. Set it to 1 to disable it; 0 means "use the default settings," which means it'll send three gratuitous ARPs.

5. Add or change the DWORD value ArpUseEtherSNAP, but only if you plan to use it. This value, when set to 1, forces TCP/IP to use 802.3 SNAP encoding for Ethernet instead of DIX Ethernet or Ethernet II encapsulation. This setting is somewhat dangerous, because if it is set, it must be used throughout *all* the machines in the local network; you cannot set it heterogeneously.

---

**NOTE** Do *not* use this on servers that provide connectivity for wireless networks, as they will no longer work correctly. 802.3 SNAP encapsulation does not work over 802.11.

---

## 2000/2003 Editing Alert and Network Error Parameters

| High |
|---|
| Moderate |
| Low |

Another way to reduce network chatter—or to increase the granularity of error reporting—is to change the limits on how quickly alerts and errors are reported.

### Overview

Windows 2000 and 2003 do not send alert messages across the network in real time. For one thing, to do so would be prohibitive from the computer's (or the OS's) point of view; for another, it would drive most administrators up a wall if they were bombarded with alerts in real time! To prevent both server and user congestion, the system checks for alerts every so often and then reports them only after that time has elapsed, or if the number of alerts is above a certain threshold.

Windows also keeps separate statistics for what percentage of network operations generate an error. If more than a certain defined percent of network errors takes place in a given span of time, then an error is reported.

---

## The Party Line                                    Company X

```
Microsoft makes little or no mention of how to tune alert
message time and percentage thresholds. This is something
of a shame, since tuning them can be useful for increasing
response time to problems. For instance, if you are working
in a situation where near-real-time monitoring of conditions
is useful, you can set the thresholds for alerts very low.
```

---

CHAPTER
5

Networking

## *The Undocumented Solution*

*Changing the thresholds for errors involves setting several Registry entries, most of which are not created by default.*

## What You'll Need

A Registry editor, such as REGEDIT or REGEDT32

Be sure to reboot after following these steps:

1. Open the Registry and navigate to the key HKEY_LOCAL_MACHINE\
   SYSTEM\CurrentControlSet\Services\LanmanServer\Parameters.

2. Add or edit the DWORD value AlertSched. This value controls how often the
   system polls for alerts, the default being five minutes. The maximum value is
   65535 minutes. To stop polling entirely, set this to 0, although the odds you will
   want to do that are probably zero as well.

3. Add or edit the DWORD value ErrorThreshold, which controls how many
   errors must be logged to trigger an alert before the AlertSched time elapses.
   The default is ten errors, and the maximum is 65535.

4. Add or edit the DWORD value NetworkErrorThreshold. This indicates the
   percent of failed network operations that will trigger an alert, again before the
   time indicated in AlertSched elapses. The default is 5 (5 percent) and the range
   is 1–100.

2000/2003 # Editing IPX/SPX Error Parameters

| High |
|---|
| Moderate |
| Low |

The non-routable IPX/SPX protocol still remains in use in many environments. Many
of its optional settings are hidden from the administrator or end user, however.

## Overview

The IPX/SPX protocol, originally devised for Novell NetWare but licensed for use by
Windows, is used for local network file and device sharing.

IPX/SPX stands in contrast to TCP/IP in many ways. For one, IPX/SPX is non-
routable. It only works on local networks, so some administrators find it a little easier
to configure—no messing around with subnet masks, for instance, and it is highly
self-configuring. IPX/SPX can be encapsulated over TCP/IP, too—for instance, when
point-to-point tunneling or virtual private networking is used.

Even though TCP/IP has elbowed it out in the majority of network environments,
there are still administrators who continue to use IPX/SPX for several reasons. One, a
Novell server may be in use, so backwards compatibility of some kind is needed. Some
like it because it provides security (because of its non-routability) and speed. And even
though it works well out-of-the-box, there are still many tunable settings for the
Windows IPX/SPX stack.

## The Party Line

**Company X**

Microsoft is apparently trying to phase out IPX/SPX and replace it entirely with TCP/IP. This is not a bad idea in the abstract, since IPX/SPX is not as widely supported as TCP/IP. That said, IPX/SPX support still exists in Windows, and remains in use. SQL Server, for instance, supports IPX/SPX as a standard transport for data connections. Despite this, word on how to tune or use IPX/SPX effectively is hard to come by.

## *The Undocumented Solution*

*Editing IPX/SPX behavior involves a number of Registry entries, not all of which are used in all circumstances. Some of them apply only to token-ring environments, rather than Ethernet, so read carefully before making changes.*

## What You'll Need
A Registry editor, such as REGEDIT or REGEDT32

Be sure to reboot after following these steps:

1. Open the Registry and navigate to the key HKEY_LOCAL_MACHINE\ System\CurrentControlSet\Services\NWLink\NetConfig\Driver01. The NWLink service controls IPX/SPX communications on an adapter-by-adapter basis, which is why the "Driver01" extension is needed.

2. Add or edit the DWORD value MakPktSize, which controls the maximum packet size for an IPX/SPX packet. If this value is set to 0 or is omitted, the NWLink driver picks up the packet size from the network environment itself. A nonzero value will be the size of the packet.

---

**NOTE**   One of the most common uses for changing this parameter is if you have two machines using different network media. Example: if you have a NetWare server connected to a Windows server via a Fiber Distributed Data Interface, you may find that file copy operations time out. Change the packet size to 1514 (from 4202) to fix this.

---

CHAPTER
5

Networking

3. Add or edit the DWORD value NetworkNumber, which determines the internal IPX network that interface is using. This is an eight-character hex value (for instance, 0000AA0E). Normally, this value doesn't need to be edited, but it helps to know where to change it internally if needed.

4. Add or edit the DWORD value PktType to select which of the five different network packet types are being used for that adapter (see Table 5-1). This can be changed using the GUI interface for the IPX/SPX protocol, but it's also useful to know how to change it under the hood if need be.

5. Add or edit the RipAgeTime DWORD value. For the sake of efficient routing, IPX maintains a Routing Information Protocol (RIP) cache in order to locate computers on a remote network. This entry tells IPX how long to wait before asking for an RIP update of any given address entry. Whenever a new RIP announcement is received for an entry already in the cache, the timer resets. To reduce the amount of routing chatter on the network, the RipAgeTime parameter can be moved up, even to its maximum of 65535, if most of the machines on the network remain running without being re-bound to a new address most of the time (that is, if they are not rebooted often). Sixty minutes is another good safe interval.

6. Add or edit the RipUsageTime DWORD value. This parameter tells IPX how long to wait, in minutes, before deleting an entry from the RIP cache. Again, if you want to reduce network chatter, it's possible to set this value to its maximum of 65535 on a network that rarely changes, but 60 is another good value.

---

**NOTE** The keys that relate to source-routing, described in Steps 7 through 10, are only for use with token-ring networks. They have *no effect* on any other network media.

---

7. Add or edit the SourceRouteBcast DWORD value. This (along with several other Registry keys described next) controls how IPX handles token-ring routing when transmitting a packet to the broadcast MAC address (FFFFFFFFFFFF hex). If SourceRouteBcast is set to 0, the packet is transmitted to the single-route

| Value | Packet Type |
|---|---|
| 0 | Ethernet II (default) |
| 1 | Ethernet 802.3 |
| 2 | Ethernet 802.2 |
| 3 | SNAP |
| 4 | Arcnet |

**Table 5-1.** List of Values and Corresponding Packet Types for the PktType Parameter

broadcast (0xC2, 0x70). If it's 1, the packet is transmitted to the all-routes broadcast (0x82, 0x70).

---

**NOTE**   Depending on the topology of your network, you can often create a big difference in your network overhead by choosing one variety of broadcast routing over the other, depending on how your ring bridges are set up. You will also need to change all the other IPX routing controls listed next to reflect your preferences, although they may not all need to be set the same way.

---

8. Add or edit the DWORD key SourceRouteDef. This affects broadcasts destined for machines not in the routing table. If the IPX driver finds the destination computer in the routing table, it uses that route. If it doesn't find a route, and the value of this key is 1, it uses single-route broadcasts; if 0, it uses all-routes broadcasts.

9. Add or edit the DWORD key SourceRouting. Set this to 1 to use source routing on token-ring networks. Setting it to 0 or eliminating the key entirely disables the use of source routing.

10. Add or edit the DWORD key SourceRouteMcast. If this is 0, or if the key does not exist, the IPX stack uses single-route broadcasts for multicast addresses; if 1, it uses all-routes broadcasts.

11. Navigate to the key HKEY_LOCAL_MACHINE\System\CurrentControlSet\ Services\NWLink\Parameters. The parameters listed next affect *all* network interfaces that use IPX/SPX and cannot be set on an interface-by-interface basis.

12. Add or edit the DWORD value WindowSize. Like the TcpWindowSize parameter for TCP/IP, this controls how many packets IPX/SPX can receive at a time. The default value is 4. On a highly reliable local connection, you can increase this value dramatically to increase throughput.

---

**NOTE**   If you are using a PPTP link into an IPX network, this may also speed things up, although it helps to increase the receive window size for the encapsulating protocol (TCP/IP, usually) if you haven't done so already.

---

13. Add or edit the RipCount DWORD value. This governs how many times RIP will try to find a route on a network before it gives up. If you are using IPX over a WAN connection, or if network traffic levels are normally quite high, increasing this value can help RIP find a route more reliably.

14. Add or edit the RipTimeout DWORD value. This value, calibrated in 500-millisecond intervals, dictates how long RIP has to wait before sending request packets for a particular route. Again, increasing the timeout on crowded networks or networks reached over WAN links can increase reliability. The default is 500 milliseconds, or 1.

**CHAPTER 5**

**Networking**

15. Add or edit the DWORD value ConnectionCount. This determines how many times SPX attempts to make a connection to a remote machine before returning a timeout error. The default is ten tries. Setting this to a higher value on a WAN can help avoid timeouts.

16. Add or edit the DWORD value ConnectionTimeout. This tells SPX how long to wait between sending connection probes, in increments of 500 milliseconds. The default is 2 (1 second). Increase this if you are trying to fight timeout problems on congested or WAN networks.

17. Add or edit the KeepAliveTimeout DWORD value. This indicates how many 500-millisecond intervals the network stack waits before sending a keep-alive packet to a remote station to verify that SPX is still working. Normally, this is set to 12 (6 seconds), but it can be raised much higher to reduce chatter on local networks.

18. Add or edit the KeepAliveCount DWORD value, which controls the number of keep-alive requests sent. Depending on how many connections you have that remain idle for long periods of time, you may want to ramp this up or down accordingly. Again, changing this may reduce network chatter.

## 2000/2003 Editing NWNBLink Parameters

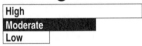

NWNBLink is a Microsoft-devised protocol that provides support for the Novell NetWare version of NetBIOS. It's usually found in environments where there is at least one Novell NetWare server running, although Microsoft-only systems can certainly make use of it themselves.

## Overview

NWNBLink has some advantages over IPX/SPX. For one, it's a routable protocol; it can be routed across multiple networks, and is usually used in multiserver or routed LAN environments instead of NetBEUI or IPX/SPX. Actually, NWNBLink requires IPX/SPX (or Microsoft's version of it, NWLink) to work properly, so it's not entirely correct to refer to it as a substitute for IPX/SPX.

---

## The Party Line                    Company X

As with IPX/SPX, NWNBlink parameters are hidden from administrative control. The protocol is apparently intended to be installed and used without a great deal of user intervention.

# The Undocumented Solution

*That said, Microsoft has built a number of Registry-editable parameters into NWNBLink for modifying a broad range of the protocol's behaviors.*

## What You'll Need

A Registry editor, such as REGEDIT or REGEDT32

Be sure to reboot after following these steps:

1. Open the Registry and navigate to the key HKEY_LOCAL_MACHINE\ System\CurrentControlSet\Services\NWNBLink\Parameters.

2. Add or edit the DWORD value Extensions. When this is set to 1, NWNBLink uses the Microsoft extensions for communicating with hosts as the default. If it communicates with a machine that uses the conventional Novell NetBIOS protocol, it falls back to the standard version instead of the extended version. If this is set to 0, the standard version is used as the default.

3. Add or edit the DWORD value AckDelayTime. This measures the length of time, in milliseconds, that is used when NWNBLink sends a delayed acknowledgment. The default delay is 250 milliseconds, so slower networks may benefit from having this ramped up slightly.

4. Add or edit the DWORD value AckWindow. This controls the number of frames received before an acknowledgment is sent. If you have machines on disparate network media (fast vs. slow), changing this value can increase the throughput: by receiving more frames before responding with an ACK, the slower machine can have slightly faster throughput. If both machines are on fast networks, set this to 0 for both.

5. Add or edit the DWORD value AckWindowThreshold. This value gauges in milliseconds whether it is required to send an automatic acknowledgment, based on the round-trip time for the conversation. If this value is set to 0, the AckWindow entry is used to determine the acknowledgment behavior instead. Normally, this is set to 500. On slower or wide area links, one second or more might be needed.

6. Add or edit the DWORD value EnablePiggyBackAck. Piggybacking acknowledgments is a way of saving throughput. When this is set to 1, ACKs can be piggybacked onto the end of a message. Set this to 0 and NWNBLink waits AckDelayTime milliseconds before sending an ACK. This will only work if you are using two-way NetBIOS traffic—in other words, if you are only generating but not responding to it, or vice versa, it won't work.

7.  Add or edit the DWORD value RcvWindowMax. This controls how many frames the receiver will handle at a time. A higher RcvWindowMax value—up from the default of 4—can increase throughput, much as it does with TCP/IP and IPX/SPX.

8.  Add or edit the DWORD value BroadcastTimeout. This controls (in 500-millisecond increments) the time Windows waits before sending find-name requests. Decreasing this value on a reliable network or one where NetBIOS names rarely change is a good way to decrease network broadcast chatter.

9.  Add or edit the DWORD value BroadcastCount. This controls how many times a particular broadcast is sent. Setting this to 1 will reduce chatter on high-speed networks, but this may need to be set to 3 or higher for slow or WAN-based links.

10. Add or edit the DWORD value Internet. This modifies the behavior of NWNBLink broadcast packets. If this is set to 1, NWNBLink sends Novell-style WAN packets, for use across WAN links. (If you're using either BroadcastCount or BroadcastTimeout, this must be set to 0 or removed completely.)

11. Add or edit the DWORD value ConnectionCount. This controls how many times Windows will send a connection probe using NWNBLink when a remote connection to a machine fails. The default is 5, but this can be set lower for better networks or higher for worse ones. On local networks with high reliability, set this to 1 to reduce chatter.

12. Add or edit the DWORD value ConnectionTimeout. This controls how long Windows will wait between sending probes. The value is measured in 500-millisecond intervals and defaults to 5, or 2.5 seconds. Again, you will want to ramp this down or up depending on your network media and conditions.

13. Add or edit the DWORD value InitialRetransmissionTime. This indicates how long, in 500-millisecond intervals, to wait before retransmitting dropped data. Set this to 2 to reduce traffic congestion; the default is 1.

14. Add or edit the DWORD value RetransmitMax, which controls how many times data is retransmitted before it considers the attempted network path to be bad. A slow or wide area network may need more tries. The default is 8; on a good network you can reduce this to 3 or even lower.

15. Add or edit the DWORD value KeepAliveCount, which governs how many times a keep-alive frame is sent. The default is 8, but can be set much lower on a good, reliable network.

16. Add or edit the DWORD value KeepAliveTimeout. This controls how often keep-alive frames are sent. The default is 60 (measured in 500-millisecond intervals). A better network doesn't need as many keep-alives.

> **NOTE** Many of these changes are going to be best suited for machines that have a good deal of older clients. Networks that still have Windows 95 or 98 clients (and I am surprised at how many of them still exist) may benefit the most from this.

# Improving File- and Printer-Sharing Performance

| High |
|------|
| **Moderate** |
| Low |

File and printer sharing are two of the most common duties performed by Windows servers. There is little in the way of external tunability for these settings, however, but a little work under the hood can yield a great deal of improvement.

## Overview

Most administrators don't do a lot of thinking about the performance of Windows file- and printer-sharing services: if it works, that's what matters. High traffic, bad organization, or slow network links can all cause problems with file and printer sharing, but so can leaving the file and printer sharing settings untuned, the better to take advantage of (or avoid problems with) local conditions.

---

## The Party Line                    `Company X`

```
Microsoft does provide some details about how to improve
Server service performance, but only in the context of
working around known bugs or other problems which don't fall
into the realm of regular operations.
```

---

### *The Undocumented Solution*

*Since a great deal of file- and printer-sharing configuration isn't exposed through the administrator interface, an administrator needs to edit the Registry to affect such changes.*

CHAPTER
5

Networking

## What You'll Need

A Registry editor, such as REGEDIT or REGEDT32

Be sure to reboot after following these steps:

1. Open the Registry and navigate to the key HKEY_LOCAL_MACHINE\ SYSTEM\CurrentControlSet\Services\lanmanserver\parameters.

2. Add or edit a DWORD value named MaxWorkItems. This allows you to change the number of receive buffers set aside by the server service. Receive buffers are used to store incoming data, so if the system runs out of receive buffers, no further data can be accepted until one of the buffers empties out. File-copy operations, for instance, would slow down drastically, or print jobs may be held up. For a heavily used server, set this value to 65535, which allocates the maximum number of buffers—about 4MB worth—into the system's non-paged pool memory.

---

**NOTE** Increasing the use of non-paged pool memory can destabilize some systems, as discussed in Chapter 4. Be careful with this setting.

---

3. Add or edit the DWORD value MaxRawWorkItems. This indicates the maximum number of raw receive buffers that the server can allocate. The best value to set this to is 512 or higher, which keeps the server from running out of raw receive buffers even under high loads.

4. Add or edit the DWORD value MaxFreeConnections. This value governs the number of free connection blocks maintained for each endpoint (that is, remote host). Set this to 100 to keep each endpoint from running out of connections, which will allow for mass parallel copy operations. Also add a DWORD named MinFreeConnections and set it to 32. This insures that at least that many connection blocks will be maintained for each endpoint. If you are logging a great many Event ID 2022 errors, setting this may be the first and quickest step towards resolving the issue.

5. Add or edit the DWORD value MaxMpxCt. This sets an upper bound, negotiated and finalized between the server and the endpoint, for how many concurrent outstanding network requests can exist between a client and a server. MaxMpxCt defines the upper bound for the current machine *as a server*. Normally, this value should be set to 125, and cannot be raised above that unless you are running Service Pack 1 or later for Windows 2000. (Windows 2003 does not have this limitation, of course.) If you are experiencing very high endpoint traffic—massive parallel copying operations, for instance—raising this is a good idea.

6. Add or edit the DWORD value MaxCmds. This sets an upper bound, negotiated and finalized between the server and the endpoint, for how many concurrent outstanding network requests can exist between a client and a server. MaxCmds defines the upper bound for the current machine *as a client*. The default is 50 and cannot be raised above that unless you are running Service Pack 1 or later (obviously this doesn't apply for Windows 2003). Again, if you have excessive endpoint traffic, as described earlier, raising this is a good idea.

---

**NOTE**    If you are using Windows 95 or Windows 98 clients with your server, *do not change these values*, since neither OS can function correctly if a larger value for either is negotiated during a network operation.

---

7. Examine the DWORD value EnableOplocks. If it doesn't exist, the default value is 0. If this value is set to 1, it disables the use of opportunistic locking on clients, which will place a greater strain on the server and increase the need for network work items (see elsewhere in this section for more on that). If you are losing data over a WAN when using Microsoft File and Print Services, you may need to disable oplocks to prevent data loss at the expense of some performance. Microsoft KnowledgeBase article 129202 explains opportunistic locking in detail and describes when this should be disabled. Generally, this is not changed unless you're experiencing extraordinary data loss in the way described.

8. Examine the DWORD value CachedOpenLimit. If it doesn't exist, the value is 5. This controls how many file handles are cached by the Server service, so that repeated open/close file operations can be buffered and therefore reused more efficiently. Sometimes this needs to be disabled or set to zero for compatibility. If you have noticed that under some circumstances a file being accessed across the network has a zero size, and access is being consistently denied, or you are seeing a great many unpredictable sharing violations, then setting this to 0 may help.

9. Examine but do not initially change the DWORD values MaxKeepSearch (default: 1800), MinKeepSearch (default: 480), and MaxGlobalOpenSearch (default: 4096). These values control how the results of directory searches are cached, so that search buffer memory can be reclaimed after a certain period of time. These values were originally created as a way to manage memory for MS-DOS or non-Win32 applications that did not automatically close searches after they were completed. If you are trying to conserve memory, you can lower MaxKeepSearch and MinKeepSearch to make them more conservative and thus dispose of search memory sooner. On the other hand, if directory search operations are timing out too soon or producing errors, you can raise these values. To satisfy more simultaneous searches, raise MaxGlobalOpenSearch to 16,000 (decimal); the maximum for this value is 65536.

10. One of a number of backward-compatibility values that can also be placed in this key is the DWORD EnableWFW311DirectIPX. This allows Word for Windows clients that run IPX to connect to the server with greater success. Set it to 1 to enable this.

11. Another backward-compatibility value for clients running direct-hosted IPX is the DWORD ConnectionlessAutoDisc, which measures in minutes how long a given client can idle before it is disconnected. The default is 15. If your clients are timing out too quickly, you can raise this value.

12. Add or edit the DWORD value AutoDisconnect. This value describes, in minutes, how long a given user's connection to the server is held open before it is disconnected. The default is 15 minutes.

---

**NOTE**  One of the ways AutoDisconnect is used—although this is not very scrupulous, if you ask me—is as a workaround for allowing more users to connect to a given server than would normally be allowed by the connection licensing. Usually this involves setting AutoDisconnect to some very low value, such as 1, to disconnect users immediately. Since most users connect and then remain idle, by disconnecting them much sooner the server can provide the illusion of being able to support more connections at once. For users who perform a lot of file-copying operations (or other things that require continuous connectivity), this trick won't work, but it *is* a way to allow slightly more user activity for less active users. I must emphasize that this cannot and should not be used as a way to get around Microsoft's per-connection licensing.

---

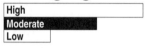

# Changing Mailslot Behavior for Windows Networking

There are six mechanisms used in Windows networking: named pipes, mailslots, NetBIOS, Windows Sockets, RPCs (Remote Procedure Calls), and Network Dynamic Data Exchange (NetDDE). Named pipes and mailslots were designed to provide backward compatibility with the old Microsoft LAN Manager products and applications, but have since taken on a life of their own. The Computer Browser Service, for locating machines on the local network, also uses mailslots.

## Overview

Named pipes and mailslots work as file systems, and if you dig around in the Windows driver set, you can actually find file system drivers for them (MSFS and NPFS). This type of behavior is borrowed from UNIX, where many devices are described as file systems to the OS, the user, and to applications, not only to give a consistent metaphor for programmability but also to allow the use of Windows' built-in file system security. Also, named pipes and mailslots can be used on a local machine without the overhead of channeling requests through the network stack. (This is why Microsoft and application gurus recommend using named pipes as the network protocol for a locally-running installation of SQL Server or Exchange Server: it's faster than using local TCP/IP and far more secure.)

Mailslots provide a form of connectionless or broadcast messaging, where delivery is not guaranteed but usually quite successful. Because of this, their usefulness is limited, and overusing mailslots can really bog a system down. They also cannot be used on WANs, and frankly shouldn't be, since they aren't designed for it and can't be used in a WAN without a lot of cumbersome piggybacking.

That said, mailslots still have their uses in an immediate or local fashion (much like named pipes), and there are a fair number of network applications that use mailslots (such as client-to-client messaging systems), even if only for discovery rather than actual data transmission. In a network environment where there is a fair reliance on mailslot-using applications, tuning mailslot behavior can pay off.

---

**NOTE** Mailslots work through UDP port 138. If you're configuring a firewall or router to pass mailslot messages, make sure this port is available.

---

## The Party Line
### Company X

```
Microsoft's documentation on mailslots is confined mostly to
bug workarounds for problems present in NT 4.0, rather than
performance improvements. That said, there are quite a few
tunable options for mailslots that are not openly documented
or made available through an administrative interface.
```

## *The Undocumented Solution*

*Mailslot behavior can be modified by editing the Registry. However, the effects of changing mailslot behavior may not be immediately obvious.*

## What You'll Need

A Registry editor, such as REGEDIT or REGEDT32

Be sure to reboot after following these steps:

1. Open the Registry and navigate to the key HKEY_LOCAL_MACHINE\ SYSTEM\CurrentControlSet\Services\Netlogon\parameters.

2. Edit or add the DWORD value MaximumMailslotMessages. This controls how much space Netlogon reserves for incoming mailslot messages. If the network is exceptionally busy, mailslot messages need to be queued and handled in the order they arrive; if there is not enough space to queue them, they will be discarded. Each message uses 1500 bytes of nonpaged pool memory, so if changing this value, you should set aside MaximumMailslotMessages×1500 bytes of nonpaged pool space for each mailslot message.

**NOTE** As with any other parameters that affect nonpaged pool memory, change this with care. Setting it too high can adversely affect system performance or even cause the system to crash.

3. Edit or add the DWORD value MaximumMailslotTimeout. This controls, in seconds, how long an individual mailslot message is valid. If an incoming message is older than the timeout value, it is discarded. On an exceptionally busy network, this value may need to be raised, since the default processing time is one second. Setting it to 10 should alleviate any problems in that regard.

4. Edit or add the DWORD value MailslotDuplicateTimeout. This controls filtering of duplicate mailslot messages. If the system receives one message, and then another exactly like it within the allotted timeout period, the duplicate is discarded. The default timeout is 2 seconds. Generally this does not need to be changed, although if many duplicate messages are showing up, the window can be increased to 5 seconds.

**NOTE** Changing the MailslotDuplicateTimeout parameter works only with the NETLOGON service. If you want to make *global* changes to this behavior, edit the same Registry entry in the key HKEY_LOCAL_MACHINE\System\CurrentControlSet\Services\msfs\parameters.

## 2000/2003 Modifying PPTP Behavior

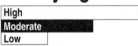

Point-to-Point Tunneling Protocol, or PPTP, allows the creation of virtual private networks across the Internet—thus permitting access to network resources that heretofore could only be accessed if those resources were in the same physical location as the network in question.

### Overview

Like many other network protocols, PPTP in Windows tends to be self-tuning. Aside from settings that control how PPTP handles encryption or handshaking, there are few obvious controls for modifying PPTP behavior. In cases where there are premature timeouts, for instance, it helps to modify the default timeout for PPTP connections to keep packets (and whole connections) from being dropped prematurely.

# The Party Line                    Company X

A lot of PPTP behavior is closed-ended and not intended to be modified. Microsoft's standard philosophy about self-tuning network stacks definitely applies here. However, since PPTP is at the whim of WAN conditions, a little tweaking of this variety can benefit most everyone.

## *The Undocumented Solution*

*Several Registry modifications are available for changing PPTP behavior and security. None of them, however, are available to the end user through an administrative interface.*

**CHAPTER
5**

**Networking**

## What You'll Need
A Registry editor, such as REGEDIT or REGEDT32

Be sure to reboot after following these steps:

1. Open the Registry and navigate to the key HKEY_LOCAL_MACHINE\ System\CurrentControlSet\Services\RasPPTPE\ Parameters\Configuration.

2. To add an additional level of authentication to PPTP, add the DWORD value AuthenticateIncomingCalls and set it to **1**, then add a MULTI_SZ value named PeerClientIPAddresses. Add into PeerClientIPAddresses the IP addresses of all the machines you will allow to access the system via PPTP, each address on a different line. Wildcards cannot be used.

3. To improve communication over flaky WAN links, navigate to the key HKEY_ LOCAL_MACHINE\System\CurrentControlSet\Services\Tcpip\Parameters. Add or change the DWORD value PPTPTcpMaxDataRetransmissions to **9**. This gives PPTP packets a better chance of getting through on slow networks.

4. To keep PPTP links from being dropped prematurely, navigate to HKEY_
   LOCAL_MACHINE\System\CurrentControlSet\Services\Raspptpe\
   Parameters\Configuration and then add or change the DWORD value
   InactivityIdleSeconds. This indicates how much time a link is held without
   activity; the default is 60 seconds, which for many PPTP links will be far too
   short. Setting it to 600 seconds (10 minutes) should do it. Then add or edit
   another DWORD, EchoReplyTimeoutSeconds, which measures the amount
   of time the server will wait for a reply after sending a request across the PPTP
   link. If no reply is received, the link is dropped. The default is 60 seconds, but
   increasing it to 120 should work.

## Increasing PPTP and L2TP Connections

| High |
|------|
| Moderate |
| Low |

---

**NOTE**   This tip has been reprinted from the JSI, Inc. web site (http://www.jsiinc.com), courtesy of
Jerold Schulman.

---

By default, a Windows RAS server supports a maximum of 1000 PPTP (Point-to-Point
Tunneling Protocol) and 1000 L2TP (Layer Two Tunneling Protocol) connections.
Servers that have to support a great many more connections than this will need to
change the maximum default settings. If you use the Routing and Remote Access snap-in
in the Administrative Tools folder, you can change these ports to support up to 16,383
PPTP connections and 30,000 L2TP connections.

---

## The Party Line                                    `Company X`

```
Microsoft doesn't discuss how to change these defaults
openly, and many administrators assume that the maximum of
1000 connections will always apply across the board for both
types of connections.
```

---

## *The Undocumented Solution*

*As it turns out, it is possible to raise these default limits by editing the Registry,*
*but the edits involved are buried fairly deep within.*

## What You'll Need

A Registry editor, such as REGEDIT or REGEDT32

Be sure to reboot after following these steps:

1. Open the Registry and navigate to the key HKEY_LOCAL_MACHINE\
   SYSTEM\CurrentControlSet\Control\Class\{4D36E972-E325-11CE-BFC1-
   08002BE10318}.

2. Expand each numbered subkey and look for the DriverDesc value name whose
   data value is WAN Miniport (L2TP). Double-click the MaxWanEndPoints value
   name of that subkey and set it, in decimal, to the maximum L2TP connections
   you want to allow.

3. Repeat Step 2 for PPTP. Look for the subkey with the DriverDesc value WAN
   Miniport (PPTP).

4. After rebooting, you should see these new values in the Ports Properties
   section of the Routing and Remote Access snap-in.

**CHAPTER 5**

## 2000/2003 Modifying NetBT Behavior

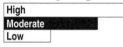

Since TCP/IP is now widely used as a standard for local networks, NetBT (NetBIOS
over TCP/IP) is one of the most common transports for Windows file and printer sharing.

## Overview

NetBIOS over TCP/IP is the most common way Windows file and print sharing is
accomplished in a LAN when the default setup parameters are used. When Windows
2003 is configured as a file- and printer-sharing device, for instance, NetBIOS is set up
over TCP/IP as the default protocol.

---

**NOTE**    If you have a server connected to the Internet, for instance, it is immensely important that
NetBIOS over TCP/IP be disabled over the outbound connection for security reasons. A publicly
available server with NetBIOS over TCP/IP running on its outbound connection can be attacked very
easily. The *one* exception to this rule is if you are using the Internet connection to run NetBIOS-based
management tools on the server, but even then, for the sake of security, it makes more sense to use a
PPTP connection to the server for this sort of thing rather than the public connection. Another option is
to run the management software on the server itself and use Remote Desktop / Terminal Services to
access it via a secured connection.

---

Networking

## The Party Line

Usually the configuration for NetBIOS over TCP/IP is little more than binding or unbinding it to a particular interface or network protocol. There's not much in the way of configuring NetBIOS behavior in detail, and Microsoft has concealed the methods for doing so even from administrators.

## *The Undocumented Solution*

*Without making too much noise about it, Microsoft has included several Registry entries for changing the behavior of NetBIOS over TCP/IP.*

### What You'll Need

A Registry editor, such as REGEDIT or REGEDT32

Be sure to reboot after following these steps:

1. Open the Registry and navigate to the key HKEY_LOCAL_MACHINE\ System\CurrentControlSet\Services\NetBt\Parameters.

2. Add or edit the DWORD value EnableLmhosts. When this is set to 1, NetBT uses the system's LMHOSTS file to resolve NetBIOS queries that cannot be resolved using WINS or broadcasts. If you have hostnames and addresses that almost never change, you can include them in the LMHOSTS file and thereby reduce the amount of WINS and broadcast "chatter" needed to resolve such names. This is the same as checking the Enable LMHOSTs Lookup check box in the WINS tab for advanced TCP/IP properties, but it may be useful to know how to modify this manually without going through the GUI.

3. Navigate to the key HKEY_LOCAL_MACHINE\System\CurrentControlSet\ Services\LanmanServer\Parameters and add or edit the REG_SZ key OptionalNames. This string value lets you specify a NetBIOS alias, or alternate NetBIOS name, for your computer. This is especially useful if you are changing the NetBIOS name for that computer at some point, but want to provide a degree of reverse compatibility.

---

**NOTE**    If you make this a REG_MULTI_SZ type key instead of a REG_SZ, you can provide multiple aliases, one on each line of the MULTI_SZ key.

---

4. Navigate to the key HKEY_LOCAL_MACHINE\System\CurrentControlSet\ Services\NetBt\Parameters and add or edit the DWORD value MaxDgram-Buffering. This controls the size of the NetBT datagram buffer, a pool of memory used to hold incoming NetBT datagrams. The default size is 128K (20000 hex), but on a very busy server you may need to raise it to 256K (40000 hex).

---

**NOTE**    If you log many instances of the error Netlogon Event ID 5701, the NetBT datagram buffer may be filling up too soon and need to be expanded as per the preceding tip.

---

5. Add or edit the DWORD BcastNameQueryCount, which controls how many times NetBIOS name query broadcasts are made on a LAN. The default is 3, but on a reliable network you can reduce this to 1.

6. Add or edit the DWORD BcastNameQueryTimeout, which is the timeout value for NetBIOS name query broadcasts. On a network that has a lot of burst traffic, increasing the timeout value *slightly* can reduce rebroadcasts, but turning it up too far will also increase delays against unreachable hosts. The default is 750 (milliseconds) and the minimum acceptable value is 100. Try increasing it to 1000.

7. Add or edit the DWORD value NodeType. This governs how the local machine registers and resolves NetBIOS names. This setting is actually more important on workstations than servers, but it is still useful if there are a number of servers in a network that communicate between each other. Set this value according to Table 5-2. If you are confident the WINS name server in the local network will be up continuously, you can set this to **2** and use that as the default value for other machines in the network as well. The default is 8. Any behavior that uses broadcasts only as a last resort or that disables them completely will cut down on the amount of NetBIOS query chatter on the network.

| Value | Node Behavior |
| --- | --- |
| 1 | Uses broadcasts only |
| 2 | Uses point-to-point name queries to a WINS server |
| 4 | Broadcasts first, then uses name server query if broadcast times out |
| 8 | Queries name server first, then broadcasts if query times out |

**Table 5-2.**    Node Types for NetBIOS, as Used by the NodeType Registry Entry

8. Add or edit the DWORD value BcastQueryTimeout. This limits the number of times NetBT broadcasts name resolution queries without receiving a response. The value is the interval, in milliseconds, between broadcasts. The default is 750. Raising the value will reduce the amount of broadcast chatter on the network, but if broadcasts are not being used (see Step 7 earlier) this setting will have no effect.

9. Add or edit the DWORD value LmhostsTimeout. This measures, in milliseconds, the timeout for a DNS query of LMHOSTS.

---

**NOTE**    Because the timeout timer for DNS queries is only granular to the length of the timeout, the timeout can be as long as twice the value of the timeout itself, depending on the conditions.

---

10. Add or edit the DWORD value CacheTimeout. This measures the length of time that NetBIOS lookups remain cached in the remote name table. The default is 600,000 milliseconds, or ten minutes. You may want to raise this considerably if you know that NetBIOS addresses rarely, if ever, change in your network.

11. Add or edit the DWORD value EnableProxyRegCheck. This defines whether or not the proxy name server sends a negative response to any broadcast name registration when that name is already registered with WINS. It also returns a negative response when the name is in the proxy's local name cache with a different IP address. Set this to 0 (disabled) if you use WINS and are having trouble changing IP addresses on certain machines. Set this to 1 if you are enforcing stricter-than-normal control over the use of IP addresses and NetBIOS names.

12. Add or edit the DWORD value NameServerPort to specify a port number other than the default WINS network port (UDP port 137) for name service information. This is useful if you are using some service other than WINS for name service lookups.

13. Add or edit the DWORD value InitialRefreshTimeout, which controls the initial refresh timeout (as the name implies!) used by the NetBT stack at name registration. The stack tries to contact the WINS servers after one-eighth of this interval has elapsed when it is first registering names. Once it has received a successful registration response, that response contains the new refresh interval to use. If you have a network where the NetBIOS names or assignments change rarely, you can set this value much higher, which reduces NetBIOS chatter. I have seen some recommendations set this as high as FFFFFFFF (hex), one-eighth of which is about 50 days!

14. Add or edit the DWORD value NameSrvQueryCount. This value controls the number of times NetBT queries the WINS server before receiving a response. The default is 3, but on a good, reliable network this can be set to 1 to reduce chatter.

15. Add or edit the DWORD value Timeout. This measures the time that NetBT waits before sending the next in a series of queries. The default is 1500 (milliseconds), or 1.5 seconds. You may want to increase this to reduce chatter or to improve performance on low-bandwidth networks.

16. Add or edit the DWORD value SessionKeepAlive. This is the interval in milliseconds that NetBT waits before sending keep-alive packets for a particular session. The default is 3,600,000 or 3600 seconds. Setting this to FFFFFFFF (hex) will disable keep-alives entirely.

---

**NOTE** Disabling keep-alives may cause remote links to drop unexpectedly. This setting should not be disabled unless you are actively discouraging the use of keep-alives—for instance, to reduce chatter.

---

17. Add or edit the DWORD value Size/Small/Medium/Large (yes, that includes the slashes!). This value governs the size of the name table used to store local and remote NetBIOS names. A system that acts as a proxy name server will want to use a larger cache size. A large cache would mean setting this value to 256; a small cache would be 16.

18. Add or edit the DWORD value BroadcastAddress. This value allows you to force NetBT to use a specific address for all broadcasts. Normally, NetBT broadcasts using the ones-broadcast address in a given net—for instance, for a network of 192.168.0.0 with a subnet mask of 255.255.0.0, the broadcast would be 192.168.255.255. If you set this parameter with a four-byte, little-endian encoded IP address, then all broadcasts go to that address from then on.

19. Add or edit the DWORD value RandomAdapter. This value is only useful for multihomed systems that practice load balancing. When set to 1, this value tells the system to randomly choose a network adapter to respond to an incoming NetBIOS query; normally the query is responded to on the network interface it was received on. Setting this to 0, or removing the key entirely, disables this feature.

20. Add or edit the DWORD value SingleResponse. This value is also only useful for multihomed systems that practice load balancing. When set to 1, the value tells NetBT to only supply an address from one of its bound interfaces in response to a NetBIOS name query. If this is set to 0 or removed, all bound interfaces are included in the name query response. (This way you can insist that traffic that starts on one interface remains on that interface.)

21. Add or edit the DWORD value RefreshOpCode. This forces NetBT to use a specific opcode, which is either 8 or 9. Microsoft uses 8 as the default, but some other implementations of NetBT, such as Ungermann-Bass, use 9. Normally, this should be 8, unless you are forcing compatibility with a non-Microsoft NetBT implementation.

# Enabling 802.1*x* Support In Windows 2000

| High |
|---|
| **Moderate** |
| Low |

While third-party products can provide support for 802.1*x* wireless security in Windows 2000, there is also a little-known first-party solution.

## Overview

Windows 2000, by default, does not contain support for the 802.1*x* wireless authentication protocol. Windows 2003 does, however, which makes using Windows 2003 for wireless networking a more comprehensive solution. But for administrators who must use Windows 2000, there is an answer.

---

## The Party Line                                    Company X

```
Microsoft has published a support package that adds 802.1x
support to Windows 2000. It's been very under-reported,
however, and so many administrators trying to provide 802.1x
support throughout their network don't know of its existence.
(A cynic might suggest that this is to further promote
replacing Windows 2000 Server with Windows 2003 Server.)
```

---

## *The Undocumented Solution*

*The fix for enabling 8021.x support in Windows 2000 is described in detail in Microsoft KnowledgeBase article Q313664. The quick link to downloading the package (for the English version of Windows 2000) is at http://www.microsoft.com/Downloads/ Release.asp?ReleaseID=45017.*

The fix supports IAS RADIUS authentication as well, but requires that Windows 2000 Service Pack 2 or later be present, as well as a number of other security-related patches. For the best possible results, the fix should only be installed on a machine that has the most recent service pack and security hotfixes.

A number of features native to Windows 2003's 802.1*x* support are not available in this fix. For one, Wireless Zero Configuration support doesn't exist; all wireless connections have to be set up by hand. Wireless configuration by Group Policy is also not supported, and only one wireless network adapter at a time will work. In short, the support is primitive, but functional, and people who are not in a position to upgrade to Windows 2003 but need 802.1*x* authentication should consider it.

# 2000/2003 Modifying DNS Caching Timeouts

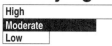

Windows 2000 and 2003 cache DNS queries, both for their own use and for the use of systems that rely on them as DNS lookup servers. This sort of behavior is seen most often when Windows Server is used as an Internet Connection Sharing gateway, and the client computers refer to the gateway as their DNS server.

## Overview

The most commonly used DNS queries will be reused often, so it makes sense to cache them for a long time. This reduces the amount of outbound DNS querying the server has to perform. On a busy network, this means that much less chatter. Since Windows 2000/2003 DNS also supports negative acknowledgments in DNS, that means negative as well as positive lookup responses are both cached. To improve performance, it makes sense to increase the DNS cache size and modify some of its default behaviors.

## The Party Line

### Company X

Microsoft notes that while it is possible to modify DNS caching behavior, they often recommend against it since it can have unpredictable results. A careful administrator, however, can greatly increase the speed and decrease the frequency of lookups with only a little work.

## The Undocumented Solution

*Modifying DNS caching involves both some Registry editing and some careful experimentation.*

CHAPTER
5

Networking

## What You'll Need

- A Registry editor, such as REGEDIT or REGEDT32
- The IPCONFIG command-line tool

Be sure to reboot after following these steps:

1. Open the Registry and navigate to the key HKEY_LOCAL_MACHINE\ System\CurrentControlSet\Services\DNSCache\Parameters.

2. Add or edit the DWORD value MaxCacheEntryTtlLimit in Windows 2000. In Windows 2003, add or edit the DWORD value MaxCacheTtl. (Note the difference.) Both of these keys use the same metric: they measure in seconds the default timeout for a positive lookup. In other words, if a DNS lookup is successful, the results are held in the system's DNS cache for this length of time. The default is 86400 seconds (or one 24-hour day), but on a very busy network you can raise this to a week or more with no ill effects.

3. Add or edit the DWORD value NegativeCacheTime in Windows 2000. In Windows 2003, add or edit the DWORD value MaxNegativeCacheTtl. Both keys measure, in seconds, the timeout for a failed DNS lookup. The default is 300 or five minutes. You may want to set this to be much lower, or disable negative lookup caching entirely if you have a great many spurious negative DNS lookups. Setting this to zero disables negative DNS caching.

4. Add or edit the DWORD CacheHashTableBucketSize. This controls the maximum number of columns used for the DNS lookup hash table. The default is 10, but on a very busy server you can raise this as high as 256 to accelerate DNS caching.

5. Add or edit the DWORD CacheHashTableSize, which controls the size of the cache itself. Again, on very busy networks, setting this higher than the default of 211 helps accelerate cache performance. Try a value of 16000 or more for high-demand environments.

6. Add or edit the DWORD MaxSOACacheEntryTtlLimit. This is the longest amount of time the cache holds SOA (start of authority) records. The default is 120 seconds, or two minutes. SOA records are not meant to be cached for long, since they are required for dynamic updates, but if you set this higher, you can often cheat a bit and get away with caching SOAs longer.

7. Add or edit the DWORD NetFailureCacheTime. This controls, in seconds, how long DNS holds off from attempting to resolve queries when a DNS lookup failure occurs. This keeps the system from getting tied up with repeated and unneeded timeouts when the remote DNS goes offline or becomes unreachable.

8. After rebooting, use the **IPCONFIG /DISPLAYDNS** command to check the contents of the resolver cache periodically.

---

**NOTE**   These parameters can also be applied on workstations as well, which also have their own local DNS cache.

---

# Modifying AFD Parameters

AFD.SYS is the kernel-mode driver in Windows used to provide support for applications employing Windows Sockets. AFD actually stands for "Ancillary Function Driver," and is kept separate from the actual Winsock libraries so that it can use the kernel's I/O manager. This allows sockets to be built using the file system, with all of its inherent security and interface behavior control. (You may remember Windows' handling of named pipes and mailslots works the same way!)

## Overview

Since AFD.SYS is a component unto itself, it has a great many undocumented or little-documented settings for modifying its behavior and performance. With a little care and some tweaking it's possible to change AFD.SYS's default behavior for the better, depending on your network and system conditions.

---

## The Party Line                                   Company X

Microsoft generally keeps mum about controls for kernel-level device drivers, and for good reason: change the wrong thing and you can create many more problems than you solve. But in the right hands, and with some care, those changes can be put to very good use.

---

## The Undocumented Solution

*Most of the Registry entries listed here do not exist and will need to be created when you implement them.*

## What You'll Need

A Registry editor, such as REGEDIT or REGEDT32

**CHAPTER 5**

Networking

Be sure to reboot after following these steps:

1. Open the Registry and navigate to the key HKEY_LOCAL_MACHINE\ System\CurrentControlSet\Services\AFD\Parameters.

2. Add the DWORD value DefaultReceiveWindow. This is the number of bytes that AFD buffers on a socket connection before using flow control. If you are using applications that normally deal with very large amounts of data, you can make this larger to buffer more data at once. Keep in mind that this will change the amount of nonpaged pool memory per socket used by the kernel. The default value is 8192; doubling this to 16384 is usually enough to cause an increase in performance.

---

**NOTE** Remember, increasing the use of nonpaged pool memory can destabilize the system if you overdo it.

---

3. Add the DWORD value DefaultSendWindow. Note that this is the same as DefaultReceiveWindow, but for sending rather than receiving. Again, setting this to a higher value will cause more nonpaged pool memory to be used, but will increase throughput for sockets. Set this to 16384 or higher.

4. Add the DWORD value DisableAddressSharing. If you are using legacy Windows NT 4.0 or earlier Windows 2000 applications that do not understand the socket option SO_EXCLUSIVEADDRUSE, set this to **1**. This forbids data theft from a socket by another process. Security-conscious administrators will want to set this.

5. Add the DWORD value DisableRawSecurity. This turns off checking for administrative privileges when using raw sockets. Usually you will want to set this to **0**, unless you have programs that cannot run for some reason as Administrator and that need to have raw socket access. If that's the case, set this to **1**.

6. Add the DWORD value DynamicBacklogGrowthDelta. This governs how many free connections to create when all sockets are used and more connections are needed. This option is not used much anymore, but may prove useful if you have a server that falls under high demand. Set it to a low value at first (4–8) and raise it tentatively to see if it has an effect on performance.

7. Add the DWORD value LargeBufferSize. This is the size for large buffers used by AFD and is set, by default, to 8192. Try setting it to 16384 or higher to affect throughput.

8. Add the DWORD value OverheadChargeGranularity. This controls how much overhead to charge for applications that appear to be performing an attack on the system's network stack. The value for this is always in powers of 2. Unless

you face a lot of attackers constantly or are doing stress testing, this won't need changing.

9. Add the DWORD value PriorityBoost. This describes how much of a priority boost, from 0–16, to give to a thread when it completes I/O. This can be used as a temporary remedy for application threads that aren't keeping up with I/O operations, or which are being shortchanged by the rest of the system's demands.

10. Add the DWORD value StandardAddressLength. This indicates the length of TDI addresses used. If an alternate transport protocol such as TP4 is used, you will need to increase this value to get a performance boost. For that reason, this value is almost never changed.

11. Add the DWORD value TransmitIoLength. This controls the size of I/O operations performed by the TransmitFile() function, and is usually one page of data. Changing this value is generally not recommended, unless you are experimenting with consistent sends of massive amounts of data (megabytes at a time).

12. Add the DWORD value TransmitWorker. This governs how AFD uses system threads. When set to 10 (hex), AFD uses system threads to do I/O for long data requests. (A long data request is anything more than two packet lengths.) Setting this to 20 (hex) causes AFD to execute everything in the context of the same thread. For systems that are constantly making long sends, setting this to 20 may improve performance since it reduces the number of context switches required. Systems that use advanced processors such as Pentium 4 or Itanium may not experience any advantage from single-threading sends, since they handle context switching very differently.

2000/2003

# Disabling Persistent Connections to Network Resources

Persistent connections can be used to map network shares to drive letters, but can be troublesome and slow when used in certain environments.

## Overview

Windows 2000 and 2003 have two ways of mapping drive letters to a network share: persistent connections and logon scripts. A persistent connection is created when a user maps a drive letter to a network drive and uses the Reconnect At Logon option. When this option is chosen, Windows remembers the mapping at the next logon and re-creates it automatically without user intervention. Removing this mapping can be done by simply right-clicking the mapped drive's icon in My Computer and selecting Disconnect.

The second way to letter-map a network connection is by using the **NET USE** command in a logon script. **NET USE** is slightly more flexible than using persistent connections, since a logon script can be easily edited, while persistent connections are a little more "buried" and harder to work with. Because of this, conflicts can arise between persistent connections and logon scripts, especially if logon scripts are created by an administrator. To map a network connection in a logon script without using a persistent connection, issue these commands:

- **NET USE /PERSISTENT:NO**
- **NET USE * /DELETE /Y**
- **NET USE** *<driveletter>* \\*<server>*\*<share>*

The first two lines are issued once in the logon script. The first disables the use of persistent connections for the session, and the second deletes any existing drive mappings to prevent conflicts. The third line can be repeated as many times as needed in the script, with each line mapping a different share to a different drive letter, where *<driveletter>* is the drive letter in question and \\*<server>*\*<share>* the UNC path to the share.

---

## The Party Line                                    Company X

```
Microsoft doesn't make specific recommendations about using
persistent connections versus scripts.
```

---

## *The Undocumented Solution*

*One way to insure that users cannot have their own drive mappings that interfere with logon scripts is to remotely disable persistent connections with a Registry edit on the machines in question. This can be done across many machines by making the changes in question on one machine, exporting the Registry keys, and calling them from a script in the logon script by using the **REGEDIT /S** command.*

## What You'll Need

A Registry editor, such as REGEDIT or REGEDT32

Be sure to reboot after following these steps:

1. Open the Registry and navigate to the key HKEY_CURRENT_USER\Software\ Microsoft\WindowsNT\CurrentVersion\Network\Persistent Connections.
2. Edit the SaveConnections value (a REG_SZ entry) and set it to **no.**
3. Navigate to the key HKEY_USERS\.DEFAULT\Software\Microsoft\ WindowsNT\CurrentVersion\Network\Persistent Connections.
4. Edit the SaveConnections value (a REG_SZ entry) and set it to **no.**

`2000/2003`
# Switching from DHCP to a Static Address Without Rebooting

**CHAPTER 5**

| High |
| Moderate |
| Low |

---

**NOTE**    Thanks to Jerry at jsiinc.com for the use of this tip.

---

Any changes to the way the IP address is configured in Windows 2000 often requires a reboot, but there are ways to circumvent this using the **NETSH** command.

## Overview

Windows 2000 can either use a predefined static IP address or an address derived from a DHCP server. However, to change from one to the other usually requires making the changes manually in the IP address configuration pages, and then rebooting. For machines that need to switch quickly between a static address and a dynamic one, this is troublesome.

Networking

---

# The Party Line

**Company X**

```
In Windows 2003 and Windows XP, Microsoft included the ability
to set a secondary, predefined IP address that Windows could
be switched to from either a primary "hard-wired" IP address
or from a DHCP address. However, Windows 2000 didn't (and
doesn't) have an easy way to do this.
```

## The Undocumented Solution

*It is possible to switch a Windows 2000 (and 2003) machine from static to dynamic and back without rebooting, by using nothing more than a batch file and the **NETSH** command. The **NETSH** command is included with Windows 2000 and does not need to be installed.*

*The user can create two batch files—one to switch the machine to DHCP addressing and another to switch it to static addressing. Each can be run as needed, as many times as needed, without rebooting.*

## What You'll Need

- The **NETSH** command (available in Windows 2000 and 2003)
- The ability to create command-line scripts

The batch file to switch Windows to DHCP should read

```
NETSH INTERFACE IP SET ADDRESS <interfacename> DHCP
```

where ***<interfacename>*** is the name of the network interface to make the change to. If you open the Network Connections icon in the Control Panel, you can see the names of each interface. Be sure to put the name of the interface in quotes. The default name for an Ethernet link would be "Local Area Connection."

The batch file to switch Windows to a fixed IP address should read

```
NETSH INTERFACE IP SET ADDRESS <interfacename> STATIC <ipaddr> <subnetmask>
NETSH INTERFACE IP SET ADDRESS <interfacename> GATEWAY = <gateway> GWMETRIC = <metric>
```

Here, *<ipaddr>* is the IP address, and *<subnetmask>* is the subnet mask to use for this connection. *<gateway>* is the address of the gateway server, and *<gwmetric>* is the interface metric to use (usually 1).

# 2000/2003 Minimizing the Risk of Name Hijacking on a Network

| High |
|------|
| Moderate |
| Low |

**NOTE** Thanks to Jerry at jsiinc.com for the use of this tip.

## Overview

Certain DHCP clients on a Windows 2000 DHCP server network can have the DHCP server perform Dynamic DNS registration on behalf of the client. This includes Windows 95 through Windows 98 Second Edition, Windows NT 3.51 or 4.0, many UNIX clients, and any Macintosh client.

An unscrupulous user could use the DHCP server to perform Dynamic DNS and overwrite the DNS records of another computer in the domain, hijacking its name and redirecting all traffic meant for it.

---

# The Party Line          Company X

```
Microsoft partly addresses this problem in Windows 2000
Service Pack 1 and later revisions of the OS (including
Windows 2003), but to fully protect against name hijacking,
a certain amount of additional work is needed.
```

CHAPTER
5

## The Undocumented Solution

*The solution is to have the DHCP service run in the context of another account that is not vulnerable to hijacking.*

Networking

## What You'll Need

- Administrator access to the server in question
- Windows 2000 Service Pack 1 or later if you are using Windows 2000 as your server

To prevent DNS hijacking through DHCP:

1. Do not install DNS and DHCP services on the same computer. This may not always be possible, but if it isn't, the rest of this tip should be followed closely.

2. Install Windows 2000 SP1 to take advantage of the ability to have the DHCP server impersonate an account to perform DNS registration. (The DHCP service runs under the domain controller's computer account and has Full Control of all DNS objects.)

3. Set up DNS to have Active Directory integrated zones, if you haven't already.

4. Set up a user account in Active Directory to perform the account impersonation mentioned in Step 2. This account can be named anything.

5. Use the **NETSH** command to implement DHCP server name impersonation for Dynamic DNS registration:

```
NETSH DHCP SERVER SET DNSCREDENTIALS <username> <domainname> <password>
```

6. The computer should respond with "Command Successfully Completed."

7. You must stop and restart the DHCP Server or reboot the computer for this to take effect.

8. To remove this impersonation, use the command:

```
NETSH DHCP SERVER DELETE DNSCREDENTIALS DHCPFULLFORCE
```

---

**NOTE**   Windows 2000 and 2003 also support secure DHCP server DDNS registration, which allows you to disable this behavior entirely and remote the risk at its root, but if that isn't feasible for some reason, you can use the preceding technique.

---

## 2000/2003 Cleaning Up Residual Registry Entries Left After Deleting a Network Adapter

Deleting a network component from Windows can sometimes leave "residue" that can interfere with the network stack and will need to be removed manually.

### Overview

Many network adapters ship from the manufacturer with not just a driver but a whole suite of client software. When the adapter is deleted, the Registry entries used by the adapter are not always automatically removed. This is usually the case if an uninstall application is used to remove the adapter's software. Sometimes the leftovers can cause the adapter to continue to appear in Network Properties.

Worse, this "ghost adapter" doesn't allow itself to be deleted. If you try to delete it, you may get the error "Component configuration option value missing in Registry." Since you have no way of knowing what the option is from this error, the only solution is to bulldoze out all of the relevant Registry entries for the adapter—by hand!

## The Party Line

Windows tries to automate the deletion of network adapters as much as possible, but obviously it's not possible to automate everything completely.

## *The Undocumented Solution*

*The only real solution is to manually remove the adapter information from the Registry, of course, which requires a certain amount of finesse and care.*

**CHAPTER 5**

## What You'll Need

A Registry editor, such as REGEDIT

To delete unwanted adapter information from the Registry:

1. Open the Registry and navigate to the key HKEY_LOCAL_MACHINE\ SYSTEM\CurrentControlSet\Services.

2. Look for a subkey under this key that features the name of the adapter or its manufacturer's name. The name of the adapter can often be somewhat cryptic, so look carefully.

3. If you find a key that looks likely, open it and look for a subkey named DisplayName, which contains a text description of the adapter.

4. If this *is* the correct key, delete the whole key, but make a note of the key name before doing so.

5. Navigate to HKEY_LOCAL_MACHINE\SYSTEM\CurrentControlSet\ Services\NWLinkIPX\NetConfig and look for subkeys here with the same name. Delete them as well.

6. Navigate to HKEY_LOCAL_MACHINE\SOFTWARE\Microsoft\ and look for similar key entries. Delete these, too.

7. Navigate to HKEY_LOCAL_MACHINE\SOFTWARE\MICROSOFT\ WindowsNT\CurrentVersion\NetworkCards and look for any similar key entries. Delete them.

8. Reboot the computer.

Networking

> **NOTE** If you don't want to actually delete the keys, you can always rename them. These can be changed back if necessary.

 **Forcing a License Server for Terminal Services**

High

**Moderate**

Low

In a network where Terminal Server licensing discovery is prone to failure, it may be necessary to force discovery of the licensing server.

> **NOTE** This tip does not apply to systems using Terminal Services for remote administration, since no licensing is needed for that.

## Overview

Windows 2000 servers that run Terminal Services also run a service called Terminal Services Licensing. The licensing service performs what is called *discovery*, where once it is launched it attempts to find a licensing server for Terminal Services by performing Remote Procedure Calls (RPCs) to every Windows 2000 domain controller it can find. Since licensing conditions can change at any time, the discovery process runs continually.

Any time Terminal Services Licensing discovery fails, an error with Event ID 1010 is written to the error log, with the description: "The terminal services could not locate a license server." Additional details are included.

Sometimes this can continue to happen even after you set a default licensing server for Terminal Services. This can persist if the location of the server changes, or if the original location wasn't valid to begin with, or if RPC calls to the server are not being honored for whatever reason.

> **NOTE** Since license discovery depends on RPC, one of the first things to check is if RPC is running on the target machine. If it isn't, proceed from there.

---

### The Party Line                                    Company X

```
Microsoft's main recommendation for a problem like this is
to check to see if RPC is running, as mentioned previously.
```

## *The Undocumented Solution*

*One way to get around the problem of discovery is to force the use of a particular license server by hard-assigning the name or address of the server to use in the Registry.*

**NOTE**   Think about whether to use an IP address or a network name to specify the license server. A network name may be slightly more reliable, since it may change less often than an IP address. However, it does require that NetBIOS be running between the machines in question.

## What You'll Need

A Registry editor, such as REGEDIT

To force a particular license server for Terminal Services:

1. Open the Registry on the computer running Terminal Services and navigate to the key HKEY_LOCAL_MACHINE\SYSTEM\CurrentControlSet\Services\TermService\Parameters.

2. Add or create a string (REG_SZ) value named DefaultLicenseServer. Set it to the network name or IP address of the license server to use.

**NOTE**   If you specify an IP address, this can be either a local machine or an Internet address, but you need to insure that the target machine is accessible via NetBIOS and RPC.

3. Reboot the Terminal Server.

When this Registry entry is implemented, the Terminal Server computer will not perform discovery for licenses. If no licenses are found at the address provided, it will still not search.

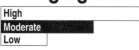

## Changing the Listening Port for Terminal Services

| High |
|---|
| Moderate |
| Low |

The network port for Terminal Services can be changed in the event TCP port 3389 is blocked or redirected.

## Overview

By default, Terminal Services listens and responds to communications on TCP port 3389. Remote Assistance in Windows XP uses port 3389 as well, since RA is simply a redeployment of the Terminal Services technology. If port 3389 is blocked by a firewall or is not available due to network security standards, Terminal Services will not work. Some organizations may pre-emptively block port 3389 as a way to prevent remote servers from being hacked, or as a way to prevent someone from setting up an unauthorized server inside the corporate firewall.

If another port besides 3389 is available, however, Terminal Services can be changed to use any other port not currently in use by a network service.

---

## The Party Line                          Company X

```
Microsoft doesn't recommend changing the value of the
listening port for Terminal Services, simply because port
3389 tends to be hard-wired into a variety of products—not
all of them made by Microsoft and not all of them easily
changeable. This is actually a very valid point and needs
to be kept in mind if you are using anything other than a
Terminal Server machine and a client (for instance, any
proxy software, and so on.
```

---

## *The Undocumented Solution*

*The port number for Terminal Services needs to be changed on both the client and server side, which involves editing the Registry on the server side and editing the connection information on the client side.*

## What You'll Need

- A Registry editor (for the server side)
- A plain-text editor (for the client side)

Follow these steps to change the port number for *all* Terminal Server connections on the server side:

1. On the Terminal Server system, open the Registry and navigate to HKEY_LOCAL_MACHINE\System\CurrentControlSet\Control\Terminal Server\WinStations\RDP-Tcp.

2. Edit the DWORD value PortNumber and set it to the network port number you wish to use. The default is 00000D3D (hex), or 3389.

Follow these steps to change the port number for a single Terminal Server connection on the server side:

1. On the Terminal Server system, open the Registry and navigate to HKEY_
   LOCAL_MACHINE\System\CurrentControlSet\Control\Terminal Server\
   WinStations\<connection>, where <connection> is the name of the connection
   to edit.

2. Edit the DWORD value PortNumber and set it to the network port number you
   wish to use. The default is 00000D3D (hex), or 3389.

---

**NOTE**    Terminal Server 4.0 does not completely implement the use of alternate ports, so it may not work correctly for such machines.

---

Follow these steps to change the port number for Terminal Server connections on the client side:

1. Open the Client Connection Manager on the client side and create a new
   connection to the server.

2. Export the connection to a file (it should save with a .CNS extension).

3. Edit the .CNS file using a text editor.

4. Change the line that reads

   ```
   Server Port=3389
   ```

   to match the port number used on the server side.

5. Save the connection once again and re-import it back into the connection
   manager to use it.

---

**NOTE**    If you are using the Terminal Server ActiveX client, it is hard-wired to use port 3389 and cannot be changed.

---

Follow these steps to change the port number if you are using the Remote Desktop Connection utility:

1. Open the Remote Desktop Connection application on the client side and create
   a new connection to the server.

2. Export the connection to a file (it should save with an .RDP extension).

3. Edit the .RDP file using a text editor.

4. Add a line at the top that reads

   ```
   server port:i:<portnumber>
   ```

   where *portnumber* is the port number used on the server side.

5. Save the connection once again and re-import it back into the Remote Desktop Connection program to use it.

# CHAPTER 6

## *Management*

**In This Chapter:**

- ☐ Migrating a Windows Installation to a Similar Computer
- ☐ Modifying NTBACKUP Behavior
- ☐ Backing Up and Restoring the Remote Storage Database
- ☐ Backing Up and Restoring IIS Installations
- ☐ Recovering the ASR Floppy from an ASR Backup Set
- ☐ Increasing GPO Logon Performance
- ☐ Troubleshooting Global Policy Object Behavior Using Logging and Tools
- ☐ Upgrading Windows 2000 Group Policies for Windows XP Professional Clients
- ☐ Repairing a Missing Default Domain Controller Policy on a Windows 2000 Server
- ☐ Performing Scripted Administrative Tasks on GPOs
- ☐ Cleaning Up Temporary Files in User Accounts
- ☐ Reinstalling TCP/IP in Windows 2003

Management is one of those catchall terms for computers. Depending on who you talk to, the definition can vary quite a bit, so to avoid confusion, I'm going to take the time here to describe exactly what we mean by "management"—and to that end, what this chapter will cover.

The way I see it, "management" is everything you do to a PC that doesn't involve setting it up or using it. This includes backups, preventative maintenance, policy and password control, security, and some forms of repair (including repairs to the preceding functions). I've also decided to discuss migrating Windows in this chapter, partly because migration is often done as part of other management tasks.

Policies are a fairly major Windows administration subject. As per the general theme of this book, I haven't tried to explain what they are or how they work or how to use them. I've limited my discussion of policies to behaviors that are either undocumented or not well understood. I've also set aside pages to cover policies as they relate to mixed environments—where Windows 2000 and Windows XP Professional machines coexist.

Another major subject covered in this chapter is backup operations—specifically, enhancements and tips that involve undocumented features or behaviors of the NTBACKUP tool and System State Backup function. This includes backing up and restoring such things as the Remote Storage database, or making offline backups of the IIS configuration.

## 2000/2003 Migrating a Windows Installation to a Similar Computer

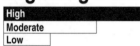

Moving a Windows installation from one machine to another is slightly complex, but some of Microsoft's own tools, in conjunction with a little ingenuity, can cover the distance.

### Overview

Administrators do not tend to think of Windows as being portable. Once installed on a given piece of hardware, Windows stays there until it is upgraded or until the machine itself is decommissioned. But the reality is different for many Windows machines, workstations, and servers. Often, administrators face the prospect of upgrading a Windows machine while preserving the Windows installation on board.

Sometimes this is the best way to go. Most administrators would rather migrate an existing Windows server with all of its user accounts, software, and tweaks than go through the agony of reinstalling everything anew on a brand-new computer. Client workstations are another story, since they are usually reimaged using a utility like Ghost or DriveImage. Servers, however, tend to be tougher to deal with since they are not usually created from a central repository of images (and in the case of domain controllers, they can't be!).

## The Party Line                                    Company X

```
Windows is designed to stay put on one system the vast majority
of the time. Microsoft does provide some details about cloning,
but moving an intact system to another hardware setup—software,
data, drivers, and all—is a step up from cloning.
```

## *The Undocumented Solution*

*Unfortunately, migrating a Windows installation from one machine to another isn't always a straightforward process. Like the proverbial cat-skinning, there's more than one way to do it.*

Here are three common methodologies for migrating Windows to new hardware:

- *Migration via system image.* This involves making an image of the contents of the system's hard drive—to tape, CD-R/W, DVD, a network repository, or directly to another hard drive—and using the image to re-create the system.

  This approach is probably the slowest of the three, since it involves copying everything twice—once to the image media, and then a second time to the target system. One major advantage to this method is safety: the copied image serves as a system backup, and the original system disk remains untouched. Another advantage is that any number of other systems can be produced from the original image, and further copies of that image can also be made. Finally, the type of media used is totally up to the administrator, although the imaging software may restrict one's choices. The most commonly used imaging program, Symantec Ghost, has a broad range of media choices; everything from CD-R to a network repository is supported. There's also Microsoft's own SYSPREP, which is covered in some detail later in this segment.

- *Migration via direct copying.* The hard drive for the target system is installed in the same machine as the source system, and a utility is used to copy the contents of the source drive to the target drive. The target drive is then placed in the target system and booted.

  This approach is slightly faster than system imaging—disk-to-disk copying is faster than copying to tape or another medium, because one, and only one, stage of copying is needed. The original disk also remains untouched, which is useful in the event the target drive turns out to be defective or some other disaster rears its head. Because of the speed and the convenience, this method is my own personal favorite. A number of inexpensive-to-free utilities for doing disk-to-disk imaging are out there, such as BootIt Next Generation (free) and the Western Digital Data Lifeguard Tools (free, but only usable with Western Digital drives). Note that there is a timeout required to bring the system down and insert the other disc, but this is generally less than the timeout required to image the system using a non-Windows tool.

- *Direct migration.* The hard drive for the source system is placed directly into the target system and booted.

  This is the fastest method, but it is also the riskiest. For one, if anything happens to the original drive or the Windows installation on it, the damage will be irreversible. However, there is a way to minimize the risk involved—by creating a separate hardware profile for the migration process.

Follow these steps to create a separate hardware profile:

1. Create a new hardware profile and boot into it. In both Windows 2000 and Windows 2003, right-click My Computer, select Properties, then the Hardware tab, then click the Hardware Profiles button to bring you to the window shown in Figure 6-1.

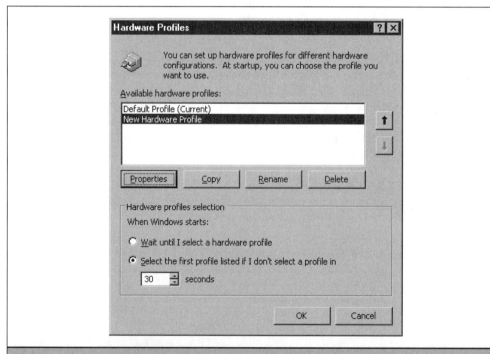

**Figure 6-1.** The Hardware Profiles menu in Windows 2000

2. Click Copy to create a new profile. Choose a name for it (it doesn't need to be unique, but it does need to identify the hardware profile for your sake), and then click OK on each window to close it out.

3. On your next reboot, you will be prompted to choose which hardware profile to use. Select the new one.

4. If the new system uses a different mass-storage controller driver than the one currently installed, install it using the manufacturer's installation procedure. This particular step can *sometimes* be omitted if the target system uses the default ATAPI/EIDE controller driver—for instance, if Windows is being moved to an IDE drive. If the existing system uses the same controller type, then you don't need to change this at all.

---

**NOTE**    Not all ATAPI/EIDE controllers are created equal, and not all of them will work correctly with the default ATAPI.SYS driver installed by Windows. Some of them require their own custom controller driver (such as controllers by Promise Technologies or VIA). However, most of them will work well enough to get through the migration process. The default driver may simply not support the more advanced features of that controller—the controller may default to PIO (programmed I/O) mode rather than UDMA (Ultra DMA) and may run more slowly. If the system seems to be unusually sluggish after the migration process, this is the most likely reason why.

---

5. Move the Windows installation to the new drive, or transplant the drive into the new system if you are using that strategy.

6. Boot on the new system, using the new hardware profile. If something goes wrong during the migration, you can put the drive back into the old machine (if you've chosen to move drives) and boot using the original profile. Any hardware changes will be recorded only to the second hardware profile.

7. Once Windows is up and running again on the new computer, the old hardware profile can be deleted.

The reason for this is simple: by confining any detected hardware changes to the alternate profile, it becomes much easier to recover from problems. If the new system refuses to boot, or boots but experiences problems, the hard drive can be restored to the original system and then Windows can be rebooted using the original hardware profile with little or no problems.

---

**NOTE**    Another suggested trick when performing this hardware-to-hardware migration is to switch the system HAL from ACPI to Standard PC, which ensures that it will work on a broader variety of hardware. When the migrated system is stable, it can be switched back to ACPI.

---

From what we've seen, all of these migration approaches have a common denominator. Windows often doesn't deal well with highly radical and sudden

**CHAPTER 6**

**Management**

changes in system configuration—doubly so now that Product Activation in Windows 2003 uses the hardware configuration as an indicator of whether or not the product has been licensed for that system.

To minimize the problems involved, the administrator doing the move should consider using the SYSPREP tool. SYSPREP is a Microsoft utility that prepares a Windows 2000 or 2003 system for cloning or imaging. Because of the way Windows 2000/2003 installations are uniquely identified, both in the software and the hardware, simply moving a Windows installation from one machine to another may not work. The main culprit is the system security ID, which cannot be easily replicated.

The system may become unbootable or may behave unpredictably. To make sure the transfer works, one way to handle it is by using SYSPREP to force Windows to redetect the hardware tree before physically moving the system. In other words, SYSPREP has to be run before any imaging, copying, or drive reinstallation takes place. Once it's run and the Windows installation is migrated to the new hardware, the system reboots, redetects the hardware in the system, re-activates if needed (in Windows 2003 only), and the administrator can continue where he left off.

---

**NOTE**   SYSPREP cannot be used to clone domain controllers, either for Windows 2000 Server or Windows 2003 Server. A cloned system must be a stand-alone server, or must be demoted to being a stand-alone server beforehand. Because this is difficult to implement practically, there are a couple of approaches to moving a domain controller. One of the easiest is to set up a new server and add it to Active Directory as a domain controller, then move the Operation Master and Global Catalog roles to the new machine and remove or demote the old one. This does not migrate installed software, however, which is one of the main reasons to migrate the installation to new hardware. Another trick is to use the "Disaster Recovery of Active Directory on Dissimilar Hardware" trick described in Microsoft KnowledgeBase article 263532.

---

One of the things SYSPREP does is change the SID, or security identifier, of the computer. The SID is an internal serial number generated by Windows 2000/2003 when it is first installed, and uniquely identifies that particular installation of Windows. Thus, since it's used to distinguish copies of Windows on a network (among other things), it is a bad idea to have more than one machine with the same SID unless you have a very specific reason for doing so—for instance, if you have software that relies on the SID for security.

SYSPREP removes the SID and configures Windows so that when it is next booted it regenerates the SID from scratch. SYSPREP can also force Windows to redetect an entirely new hardware configuration (except for maybe the mass-storage controller—needed to boot the system), which is what makes it important for administrators trying to migrate Windows.

SYSPREP 1.1 for Windows 2000 is available as a download at www.microsoft.com/windows2000/downloads/tools/sysprep/default.asp. For Windows 2003, SYSPREP 2.0 is included on the Windows 2003 installation CD-ROM. It is stored in the DEPLOY.CAB archive, found in the \SUPPORT\TOOLS directory.

---

**NOTE**   SYSPREP does not change access controls on Registry keys. If you try to view keys with accounts that were modified during SYSPREP, you may get an "Account unknown" error. If this happens, you may wind up breaking a lot of things unexpectedly, since many programs will fail if they are denied rights to certain Registry keys. The same applies to other objects with Registry referents such as printers and shares.

---

Even if the two machines are superficially identical, there are almost always enough differences between them that rebuilding the hardware tree is more or less mandatory when migrating to new hardware. For instance, if you are moving from a non-ACPI-compliant computer to one that is ACPI-compliant, the device tree has to be completely reconstructed. Non-ACPI machines don't enumerate devices the same way ACPI machines do. This re-enumeration is called a *mini-setup,* since it is essentially a stripped-down version of the setup process.

---

**NOTE**   Make sure absolutely nothing else is running before activating SYSPREP. This includes programs that are normally "idle" in the system tray. To be on the safe side, deactivate automatic startup for any programs that don't need it and reboot before imaging.

---

Here is a quick breakdown of the command-line options used with SYSPREP.

- **-pnp**   Used to force the redetection of hardware. Because this requires drivers being present, you'll need to have the CD-ROM handy on the target system, or modify the config files to point to a network share.

- **-reboot**   Automatically reboot after you're done. This is a good way to save time, but omitting it allows you the freedom to shut down the PC manually before migration.

- **-nosidgen**   Don't generate a SID. If you have software preloaded that depends on the SID for security, or you're having trouble with the cloning process, you may want to enable this.

- **-quiet**   No confirmation dialogs. Another speed option.

- **-factory** (only in SYSPREP 2.0)   Specifying the -factory switch will cause the system to reboot in a network-enabled state, adding customer data and new drivers specified in the answer file Winbom.ini. After the changes are made, SYSPREP is run again with the -reseal option. These two command-line options are normally only used for people working with mass-imaged machines rather than a single machine being moved, but they can be useful for other manually-added changes.

- **-activated** (only in SYSPREP 2.0)   This preserves a successful activation of the Windows installation.

**NOTE** You *cannot* use the -activated switch to activate a Windows 2003 installation and then move it to another machine. Windows 2003 *must* be re-activated on the target machine when it is moved. Also, you can only use SYSPREP three times on any given installation with the -activated switch. Finally, you can only store a prepped image of Windows 2003 for 30 days before the activation clock expires. These limitations make SYSPREP useless for pre-activating an installation. If you want to do that, you're better off obtaining a volume-licensed version of Windows 2003.

There are many more SYSPREP options available beyond the command line. For instance, if you are restoring the image on a system that has no local copy of the Windows 2000 drivers and want to point to a network share where drivers are located, you need to configure this manually. The administrator will need to create a SYSPREP.INF file—a plain text file with options in it—and place it in the directory with the SYSPREP executable before you run it. When you unpack SYSPREP, there is a sample SYSPREP file, named BothSysprep.ini, which you can customize as needed. Listed next are many of the common options (and the sections they are found in) that you may need to customize in order to use SYSPREP in a migration.

**NOTE** If you don't see any of these options in the file, you can simply add them manually using Notepad, one to a line.

## [Unattended]

- **InstallFilesPath**  Lets you specify a local drive or a network share where the Windows 2000 install files can be found.

- **OemPnPDriversPath**  Lets you specify a local drive or a network share where you have your OEM Plug-and-Play drivers.

**NOTE** As I hinted here, these two options are important if you're cloning out systems that need to detect new hardware, and you don't have local copies of the OS. If you're connecting to a network share that needs credentials, there's a way to specify them automatically in the following file.

- **OemSkipEula**  Set this to "Yes" to skip the license agreement screen. Most administrators will want to do this.

- **ExtendOemPartition**  Set this to 1 and it automatically extends the system partition to the size of the disk during reboot.

## [GUIUnattended]

- **OEMSkipWelcome**  Set to 1 to skip the welcome screen.

- **OEMSkipRegional**  Set to 1 to skip the regional options screen, such as which language locale to use.

## [Identification]

- **DomainAdmin**   Set this to the domain\username of an account with permission to add a computer account to a domain, such as household\w2kadmin. Use this only if you're reconnecting the machine to a domain.

- **DomainAdminPassword**   The password for the preceding account.

- **JoinDomain**   The domain to join (if any).

## [ProductKey]

- **ProductKey**   This lets you specify the Windows product key, to avoid having to retype this information on reboot, in the format
**ProductKey = "12345-ABCDE-12345-ABCDE-12345"**
This will allow Product Activation to be performed automatically, provided the machine in question has network connectivity.

## [SysprepMassStorage]

The SysprepMassStorage area allows you to identify mass storage device drivers that will be set up on the destination computer automatically. This is a convenient way to deposit mass-storage device drivers that will not be found on the source system. The syntax, however, is a little tricky, and setting up the entries for this section requires a little legwork.

# What You'll Need

- The device's .INF file, usually packaged with the driver

- A text editor, like Notepad, to make the appropriate changes to SYSPREP.INF

Here's how to add entries to SysprepMassStorage:

1. Find the hardware ID of the device in question from the .INF (_not_ .INI!) file for the device driver. The hardware ID usually looks like this:
PCI\VEN_1022&DEV_7007
The corresponding line in the .INF file will look like this:
%PCI\VEN_1022&DEV_7007.DeviceDesc%=AMDXP_Install,PCI\VEN_1022&DEV_7007

2. Copy the hardware ID and insert it into SYSPREP.INF with the following syntax:
<hardware ID> = "<path to driver inf>","<disk directory>","<disk description>","<disk tag>"
The <path to driver inf> is the full path and filename to the .INF file. This can be a subdirectory of the SYSPREP folder you've unpacked on that system.

CHAPTER 6

Management

The <disk directory> item is the name of the directory on the floppy disk provided by the third party that contains the copy of the mass-storage driver. This is important, since you may be prompted for a floppy-disk copy of the driver during setup. The <disk description> section is the description of the floppy disk as described in the TXTSETUP.OEM file provided by the third party, and <disk tag> is the disk tag for the floppy, again described in the TXTSETUP.OEM file.

A fully filled-in mass-storage reference would look something like this:
PCI\VEN_1077&DEV_1080 = "C:\Sysprep\qlogic\qlogic.inf",
 "\nt", "Qlogic Software Disk", "\qlogic"

3. Save the SYSPREP.INF file and make sure the appropriate drivers are available on the system itself. In Step 2, I noted that the drivers could be made available in a subsidiary of the SYSPREP folder, which is probably the easiest way to do it.

The $OEM$ directory can contain a file named cmdlines.txt, which allows you to specify additional commands to run at the conclusion of minisetup. These are all command-line commands, so you can run batch files, install additional applications after the image has been deployed, or whatever you like. You can gain a great deal of flexibility through creative use of $OEM$—if you've got drivers that need to be deployed on specific systems, for instance.

A full breakdown of the options and commands for SYSPREP is found in the REF.CHM file also included in the DEPLOY.CAB archive.

Finally, for some additional perspective, you may want to take a look at this article, "Using the System Preparation Tool on Dissimilar Computers" (Microsoft KnowledgeBase article 216915).

## 2000/2003 Modifying NTBACKUP Behavior

An administrator who relies on NTBACKUP for backup functions in Windows will want to know how to modify many of its apparently hard-wired behaviors.

## Overview

NTBACKUP, Windows 2000/2003's built-in backup program, is widely used by many administrators simply because it's free, easy to work with, and for the most part gets the job done. That said, it's also limited in its functionality, although it has some functions which are not directly documented and which can make working with the program a little easier.

# The Party Line

**Company X**

Since NTBACKUP is actually a stripped-down and rebranded version of a third-party product, Arcada/Veritas' Backup Exec, there are a number of undocumented extensions to the program that are not described by Microsoft in their documentation or their KnowledgeBase. This is not likely to change, either.

## *The Undocumented Solution*

*Many of NTBACKUP's default behaviors can be modified through a series of Registry edits that are not widely circulated.*

**CHAPTER 6**

Management

## What You'll Need

- A Registry editor
- The NTBACKUP tool, which should have been run at least once to set up its initial options in the Registry

To modify many of NTBACKUP's default behaviors:

1. Open the Registry and navigate to HKEY_CURRENT_USER\Software\ Microsoft\NTBackup\User Interface. (This affects the current user's settings only; the program cannot be modified on a global basis.)

2. Edit the REG_SZ value named Estimate Byte Count. Set this to **0** for faster backup starts; this disables NTBACKUP's enumeration of the total byte count for the backup, as shown here:

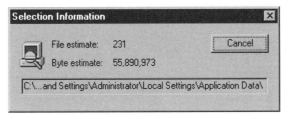

3. Edit the REG_SZ value named "Backup files inuse" (note that "inuse" is one word, exactly as printed). Set this to **1** to force NTBACKUP to use shadow

copying to back up files that are flagged as being in use, but are not themselves system files (such as open documents).

4. Edit the REG_SZ value named Remote Drive Backup. Set this to **1** to allow NTBACKUP to make backups of remote drives—drives exposed through a network share or mapped network path. Normally, this is not allowed.

5. Edit the REG_SZ value named Backup Catalogs. Set this to **1** to force NTBACKUP to back up all catalog files from your TEMP directory on each backup operation. (The catalog files will still be deleted when the backup operation is closed, but they will be saved to tape first.)

6. Edit the REG_SZ value named Skip Open Files. NTBACKUP attempts to open any non-system file for 30 seconds if it's being held open by another process. Change this value to **1** to force NTBACKUP to skip non-system files that are being held open.

---

**NOTE**   System files are, by default, copied using the shadow copy function, whenever a System State backup is being made.

---

7. Navigate to HKEY_CURRENT_USER\Software\Microsoft\NTBackup\ Hardware.

8. Add or edit the REG_SZ value Drive Settling Time (that's "settling", not "setting"!) as a type REG_SZ. The default value is 60 (seconds). Try setting it to 120 if the program times out waiting on your tape drives.

---

**NOTE**   Windows 2003 uses a different tape format for backup than Windows 2000 or Windows XP Professional. The Windows Server 2003 edition of NTBACKUP can allocate tape block sizes up to 64KB. NTBackup in Windows 2000 and Windows XP can only allocate block sizes of up to 32KB for tape. If Windows 2000 or Windows XP Professional try to read a tape with 64KB block sizes, they will report an error. There is no known way to force Windows 2003 to use 32KB block sizes on tape, but Microsoft has documented the problem in KnowledgeBase Article 821588 and should have a fix shortly.

---

# 2000/2003 Backing Up and Restoring the Remote Storage Database

| High |
|------|
| Moderate |
| Low |

The Remote Storage Service database contains information about remotely stored data. If you are setting up an entirely new Windows 2000 installation and you want remotely stored data to be available on the new system, you must restore the Remote Storage Service database on the new machine.

**NOTE**    Migrating or cloning a system will bring the database over automatically, so you don't need to do this on a machine that's been migrated or cloned.

## Overview

The Remote Storage database is one of the more esoteric components of Windows and yet it isn't discussed very widely. All metadata about data that has migrated into Remote Storage is kept here, but it is not generally accessible to the end user or administrator. This is apparently by design, since tampering with the Remote Storage database could make all remotely stored data unavailable.

## The Party Line                         Company X

Normally, if you make a System State backup or some other full-system image, the Remote Storage database is preserved. However, Microsoft doesn't describe how to back up the Remote Storage database independent of everything else.

## *The Undocumented Solution*

*As it turns out, the Remote Storage database can be manually restored, although it requires some work and isn't a simple one- or two-step process. Plan for some downtime when doing this, if you haven't done so already.*

## What You'll Need

- The Remote Storage Service, which should already be installed and running
- A tape drive or some other RSS-supported media
- A copy of the most recent backup media used for a Remote Storage action

To restore a copy of the Remote Storage database:

1. Right-click My Computer, select Manage, and open the Removable Storage snap-in. Under Media Pools, look in the Import Pool, which should be empty. If it isn't, don't panic; it simply means that there is a catalog there that does not reflect what you are going to restore. See Figure 6-2 for an example of where to look for the Import Pool.

CHAPTER
6

Management

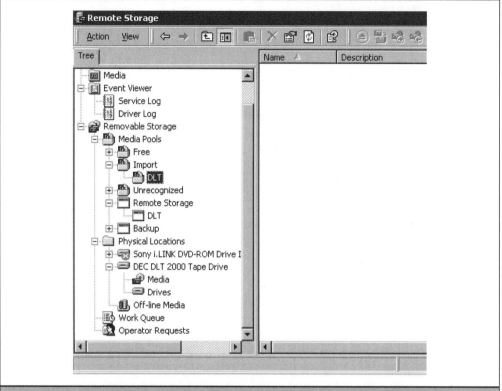

**Figure 6-2.**   The Import Pool in the Media Catalog, which here shows the presence of a DLT folder (which is empty)

2. Insert the most recent tape (or other media) used for remote storage. If the backup is on more than one piece of media (in other words, it spans two or more tapes or discs), catalog the media by moving them temporarily into the NTBackup media pool and checking the dates.

3. Move the media into the NTBackup media pool (usually named "Backup"). If there is no such pool, you can create one automatically by simply running NTBACKUP.

4. Launch NTBACKUP and catalog the media to find the last copy of the RSS database, which is stored in the *%systemroot%*\System32\RemoteStorage folder. Make sure you are getting the most up-to-date copies. This is critical; if you work from a less-than-recent piece of media, you'll have an incomplete database and you won't be able to get to everything in Remote Storage.

5. Select the most recent folders labeled NTMSData and RemoteStorage.

6. In the Restore Files To: box, select a new location and point to the drive that contains the *%systemroot%* folder.

7. Select Start Restore | Advanced, and then choose Restore Removable Storage Database. Click OK to go through each prompt.

8. Once the restore operation is finished, reboot.

9. Look in the Removable Storage Manager after rebooting and make sure all the databases have been restored. All the earlier media pools should exist, with all of their attendant media inside.

10. Check the Services snap-in to see that Remote Storage Engine, Remote Storage File, and Remote Storage Media are all stopped.

11. Look in the *%systemroot%*\system32\RemoteStorage\engdb folder (make sure you have Show Hidden Files/Folders and Show System Files turned on in Explorer, or you won't see anything). If there is anything in there, move it to another, temporary folder.

12. From the command line, type **RSTORE *%systemroot%*\system32\Remote Storage\engdb.bak.** This runs the RSTORE tool, which comes with the Remote Storage service to repair the Remote Storage database.

13. Restart the Remote Storage Engine, Remote Storage File, and Remote Storage Media services. Look in Remote Storage to make sure all the managed volumes listed there show up correctly. Then, test things out by restoring a few migrated files.

2000/2003 # Backing Up and Restoring IIS Installations

| High |
| Moderate |
| Low |

Internet Information Server's internal configuration can be backed up and restored locally, but it can also be backed up offline.

## Overview

When setting up Internet Information Server (IIS), an administrator will usually take great pains to tweak IIS so it runs just the way it's needed. This is true not only if there are a great many sites and virtual directories that need to be set up by hand, but also if IIS needs to be modified under the hood to run a certain way. If the IIS installation is lost and needs to be reconfigured from scratch, having a backup copy of the whole thing comes in handy.

CHAPTER
6

Management

---

## The Party Line

Microsoft has thoughtfully built into IIS a tool for backing up the current IIS configuration. The entire IIS configuration, including the Metabase (the Registry-like repository for data used by IIS), can be backed up and restored in this fashion. What's more, multiple backups can be made, so that an administrator can experiment with different configurations easily. What Microsoft didn't do, however, is provide the user with a direct way to back up that information *offline*.

## *The Undocumented Solution*

*Happily, saving IIS backup information offline isn't difficult. The data in the Metabase is saved to a file that can either be copied out by hand or copied using a backup utility of your choice.*

## What You'll Need
- The Internet Service Manager
- A safe place to back up the IIS directory data

To save the IIS backup information:

1. Back up the data directories for IIS themselves. This can be done in any manner you choose, and you usually don't have to take the site offline to do this, unless the contents of one of the directories in your web site are modified by the site's users. The reason for this is that it hardly helps to have a copy of the IIS site configuration information without also having a copy of the sites themselves, and the standard IIS config backup process doesn't back up site data.
2. Launch the Internet Service Manager.
3. Right-click the computer in question in the left-hand pane and select Backup/ Restore Configuration to produce the image shown in Figure 6-3.
4. Choose a descriptive name for the backup set. If you are performing a series of progressive changes on the site to see which work the best, make a small note

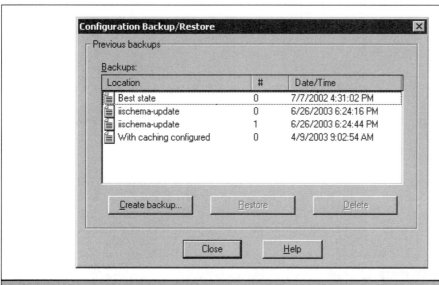

**Figure 6-3.**     Backups of IIS's configuration

here about what changes have been made, for instance. You don't need to specify the time and date since those are backed up automatically. Click OK.

**NOTE**     With IIS6, you can encrypt the contents of the backup by checking the box marked Encrypt Backup Using Password and then typing a password.

5. Shut down IIS. (This step is optional.)

6. Look in the *%systemroot%*\system32\inetsrv\MetaBack directory for a file with the name you chose and the extension .MD0. Copy that file and save it along with the backup of your site. In Windows 2003, there will be two files, one with the extension .MD0 and another with the extension .SC0; copy them both.

**NOTE**     These Metabase backups will only work on the same installation of Windows. They cannot be moved to another installation.

CHAPTER
6

Management

# [2003] Recovering the ASR Floppy from an ASR Backup Set

| High |
|---|
| Moderate |
| **Low** |

In Windows 2003 and Windows XP, the Automated System Recovery process creates a floppy disk that holds important system information, including Plug-and-Play device enumeration that may be needed to access the data in the accompanying backup setup.

## Overview

When an administrator runs NTBACKUP and creates an ASR (Automated System Recovery) backup set, the floppy disk that gets produced along with it is often the weakest link, so to speak. The floppy can be easily damaged, erased, or lost, and without it the ASR process cannot continue.

---

### The Party Line                                    Company X

```
Microsoft's standard dictate about the ASR floppy is that it
should be guarded carefully, but one of the things they
don't mention is that the contents of the floppy can in fact
be regenerated from the ASR backup set without a great deal
of work.
```

---

## *The Undocumented Solution*

*If you lose the ASR floppy, but still have the ASR backup set, you can mount the backup set on another computer and re-create the ASR disk without too much difficulty.*

## What You'll Need

- A newly formatted, blank floppy
- The ASR backup set
- The NTBACKUP utility

The steps to recover the floppy disk from an ASR backup set are as follows:

1. Start the NTBACKUP utility by typing **NTBACKUP** in the Run dialog from the Start button.

2. Insert your ASR backup media.

3. Select the Restore and Manage Media tab in NTBACKUP.

4. Select the media that contains your ASR backup from the media tree and expand it.

---

**NOTE**   If the media isn't present in the tree—in other words, if the media was backed up on a different system and this system's Media Manager does not have it—you will need to mount the media manually.

---

5. Open the *second instance* of the drive letter that contains the system files, and navigate down to the *%systemroot%*\Repair folder.

6. Select the files ASR.SIF and ASRPNP.SIF.

7. Set the Restore Files to: option to Single Folder and the Alternate Location option to the A: drive.

8. Click Start Restore. The ASR files should be copied out.

## 2003 Increasing GPO Logon Performance

One common complaint about Windows 2000 is that it can take a long time to start up or log in, especially on a domain that has Group Policies. Windows 2003 and XP Professional doesn't have this slowness, and a big part of the reason for that is the way the OSs behave by default when handling policies.

## Overview

Windows 2000 uses *synchronous* policy behavior at logon, meaning that each step of the policy is applied one at a time, with the server waiting for separate confirmation about each step.

Windows XP Professional, on the other hand, uses *asynchronous* policy behavior at logon. All steps of the policy are run at the same time, and the server doesn't hang around waiting for individual confirmation for each. This logs the user in much faster.

The downside of this behavior is that events are not processed in the order you might expect them to be, such as folder redirection and software installation. Folder redirection, for instance, might be critical to a program that runs later in the logon. What's more, a user may have to restart or log on up to *three* times to effect changes that require synchronous policies.

## The Party Line

Microsoft has several suggestions for reducing the time it takes to process GPOs. One is to combine as many GPOs as possible, or to filter their application by user group. Another, which is documented but little-discussed, is to make Windows 2000 behave the same way as Windows XP Professional when it comes to processing group policies: asynchronously.

## *The Undocumented Solution*

*The trick to changing Windows 2000's logon behavior is easy enough: asynchronous (and synchronous) behavior is controlled through a policy itself. However, there are side effects. If your workstations require logon event processing to take place in a certain order, you will not want to do this. The same goes for any servers, of course, that are affected by this policy.*

*If, however, the order of logon events is not critical (for instance, if you don't do much drive mapping, or if you use UNC names for remote drives rather than rely on drive mappings), you ought to try this, since you will get a significant improvement in logon time and startup time for Windows 2000 without any real tradeoffs.*

## What You'll Need

- The Windows 2000 server where the policies are managed
- The Active Directory Management Console (which is included by default)

Here are the steps to follow to change to asynchronous GPO behavior for Windows 2000:

1. Open the management console for Active Directory Users and Computers.
2. Right-click your domain, and then click Properties.
3. Under the Group Policy tab, select the GPO you want to edit and then select Configure.

4. Expand the tree to Computer Configuration | Administrative Templates | System | Group Policy.

5. In the Policy pane, double-click Apply Group Policy For Computers Asynchronously During Startup. Select Enabled.

6. Click Apply, and then click OK.

7. Double-click Apply Group Policy For Computers Asynchronously During Logon, and click Enabled.

8. Click Apply, and then click OK.

 # Troubleshooting Global Policy Object Behavior Using Logging and Tools

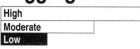

**NOTE**  Thanks to Darren Mar-Elia for the information in this section.

Global Policy Objects, or GPOs, are one way for administrators to constrain user and system behavior. Debugging and modifying them can be more complicated than it might initially appear.

## Overview

Microsoft provides a few tools for evaluating policies. The Resulting Set of Policy (RSoP) or GPO Results tool in Windows 2000, Windows XP Professional, and Windows Server 2003 is a good way to judge what effects a policy will have.

RSoP uses WMI to report what policy settings would be applied to a given workstation or user. If there are problems when an application of policy takes place, they're logged either to the Application Event Log on the target client or a log file on the server (in *%systemroot%*\debug\usermode\userenv.log). You can change the verbosity of these logs by editing the Registry key \HKLM\Software\Microsoft\ Windows NT\Diagnostics\RunDiagnosticLoggingGroupPolicy, a DWORD, and setting it to 1 for maximum verbosity.

**NOTE**  If for some reason you have disabled the WMI service on the target workstation or server (or something else has disabled it or is interfering with it), RSoP will not work for that machine.

*Management*

## The Party Line                              Company X

However, aside from using RSoP as a way to debug problems, there are some behaviors of GPOs that are not always spelled out by Microsoft, and which may have an impact on how well your system deals with policies.

## *The Undocumented Solution*

*Here are some additional reasons why GPOs may not be processed correctly, and some suggested ways to deal with them.*

*The way GPOs are processed* can be tricky and deceptive. GPOs are processed at boot time and when a user logs on. They are also processed at random intervals within 90-minute spans on member servers and workstations, and every five minutes on domain controllers.

What takes precedence over all of this, however, is whether or not something has *changed*. If a processing cycle listed earlier comes up for a particular GPO, but that GPO has not been changed, then nothing happens. Changes, not time elapsed, are what really trigger the processing of a GPO. You *can* force the processing of an unchanged GPO through an Administrative Template policy, but administrators shouldn't rely on this mechanism, since it also depends on whether or not the Active Directory–based GPO changes as well.

Because of this behavior, one good way to deal with GPOs that seem to be out of sync is to change an insignificant setting and then change it back again, which may force a refresh.

Another advantage to using this method is that the log will indicate if a *slow link* has been detected. Slow network links—dial-ups or even highly congested LANs—can foul up Policy processing, since certain policies are not processed by default if slow links are detected. This can also trip people up, since while the Event Log may report the policy was in fact processed, it doesn't seem to have taken effect.

To get around this, an administrator can edit the default slow-link threshold in the Local Computer Policy snap-in, in Computer Configuration | Administrative Templates | System | Group Policy, shown as Group Policy Slow Link Detection. This setting is calibrated in kilobits per second.

*Problems with DNS* can also cause GPO policy processing to go awry. GPO processing requires the SRV records used by LDAP (Active Directory is an implementation of LDAP, remember?). Try stopping and restarting the Netlogon service on your domain controllers to determine if SRV registration is taking place. If it still isn't working, something may be wrong with DNS.

# Upgrading Windows 2000 Group Policies for Windows XP Professional Clients

| High |
| Moderate |
| Low |

An out-of-the-box installation of Windows 2000 Server needs to be modified to use Windows XP Group Policies, which are not available in Windows 2000 by default.

## Overview

With Windows XP Professional starting to replace earlier versions of Windows in the workplace, many administrators have found that Windows XP Professional has a host of policies which don't exist in Windows 2000 Server and can't be administered.

---

# The Party Line    Company X

```
Microsoft is aware of this, and in fact has discussed the
problem (and a possible solution) in KnowledgeBase article
307900. The trick is to use the Windows XP policy settings
to upgrade the policies on the Windows 2000 server
(described next).
```

---

## The Undocumented Solution

*The exact process is simple enough, and is reproduced next, with some additional things an administrator needs to be aware of that Microsoft doesn't cover in their article.*

## What You'll Need

- A Windows XP Professional machine that has been joined to the Windows 2000 Server domain you are upgrading
- The domain administrator's logon information

CHAPTER
6

Management

Here's the process to upgrade the policy objects:

1. Log on to the Windows XP Professional workstation using the domain administrator's credentials. This particular (and previously undocumented) step is important, because it allows the XP user to traverse directories on the 2000 server.

2. From the Start | Run dialog, type **mmc** to open the Microsoft Management Console (MMC).

3. From the File menu in MMC, select Add/Remove Snap-In and add the stand-alone Group Policy Object, as shown in Figure 6-4.

4. When you are prompted to select a Group Policy Object, the local machine will initially be selected as the target object, as shown in Figure 6-5.

5. Click Browse and navigate to the server whose GPOs you want to upgrade.

6. Click Close and then OK to commit the changes.

7. Use a Windows XP Professional system with the domain administrator logon to manipulate the policy changes, since Windows 2000 will not be able to display the changed GPO objects. Windows 2003, on the other hand, is able to do so natively and doesn't need to be tweaked in this fashion.

**Figure 6-4.**   Adding the stand-alone Group Policy Object

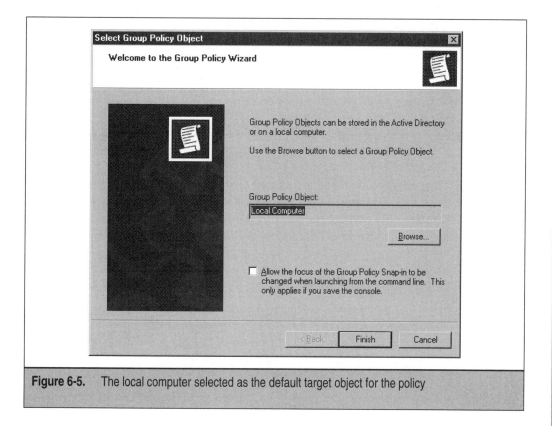

**Figure 6-5.**    The local computer selected as the default target object for the policy

 # Repairing a Missing Default Domain Controller Policy on a Windows 2000 Server

| High |
|------|
| Moderate |
| Low |

If a domain controller delivers errors whenever an administrator tries to edit or configure the domain policy, there is a good chance the domain policy has been destroyed, possibly by mistake.

## Overview

Missing policies can create a whole slew of bizarre behaviors. To find out if the default domain controller policy is in fact missing, look in the folder *%systemroot%*\SYSVOL\ domain\policies (where <*domaincontroller*> is the network name for your domain controller). Within that folder should be a directory starting with {31b2 (note the curly brace as part of the name), which indicates a GUID used to refer to the policy in question. If that folder is missing, then the default domain policy is also missing.

Another possible form of damage is a missing domain controller security policy, which is stored in the same location using a folder that begins with {6AC1. (Again, note the curly brace as part of the name.)

## The Party Line                          Company X

```
Microsoft's typical solution for a problem this deep-rooted
is to reinstall Windows, or to restore from a working System
State backup.
```

## *The Undocumented Solution*

*There is a roundabout way to reinstall the default domain policy, although it requires the presence of another domain controller from which to borrow the policy settings.*

## What You'll Need

- Another Windows Server that can be promoted to the status of a domain controller, or…

- Another existing stand-alone Windows domain controller

To rebuild the domain policies:

1.  Obtain access to or set up another Windows Server in the network.

2.  If you haven't already, run DCPROMO on that computer to promote it to the status of a domain controller. For the best results, make it a stand-alone domain.

3.  Once the new domain controller is up and running, go to the *%systemroot%\* SYSVOL\domain\policies directory on *that* machine, and look for the directory that begins with the GUID {31b2. (If you are repairing the domain controller security policy, look for {6AC1.) You can see an example of this in Figure 6-6.

4.  Make a copy of that directory and keep it somewhere safe.

5.  Demote the domain controller you just created.

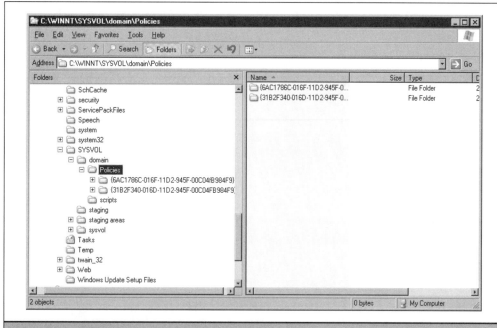

**Figure 6-6.**    The Policies directory with copies of the default domain and domain security policies

6. Copy the {31b2 (or {6AC1) directory into the Policies directory for your existing domain controller—whichever GUID matches the Object ID of the policy.

7. Reboot the domain controller.

---

**NOTE**    While this will provide you with a newly minted domain policy, a great many of the key policies in it will not be there and will not be correct. Take the time to walk through the default policy and set things up as they should be.

---

2000/2003 # Performing Scripted Administrative Tasks on GPOs

Group policies can be arcane and abstruse. Thus, sometimes the best way to explore them is outside the context of the Group Policy Management Console.

## Overview

The Microsoft Management Console application tends to be a one-size-fits-all approach to things, whether for Group Policies or just about anything else. It's designed mostly for top-down viewing, not allowing for advanced filtering and searching. For this reason it can be hard to analyze multiple group policies. There is also a great deal that the console doesn't do, or doesn't support directly—or maybe there are specific tasks you want to automate rather than do manually.

---

# The Party Line | Company X

```
Believe it or not, Microsoft has a solution for all of
this, albeit an enormously underreported one. After you
install the Group Policy Management Console, a whole slew of
administrative scripts are installed in the %programfiles%\
gpmc\scripts directory (where %programfiles% is the Program
Files directory for your system).
```

---

## The Undocumented Solution

*There are 32 sample scripts in the \scripts directory, which cover a broad variety of tasks: backing up an individual GPO, backing up the GPO in a domain, creating a copy of a GPO, creating a new GPO, creating a policy environment using an XML file, creating a GPO file that represents a policy environment, listing GPOs orphaned in SYSVOL, and many more. A full breakdown of the script samples can be found in the MSDN library, at http://msdn.microsoft.com/library/default.asp?url=/library/en-us/ gpmc/gpmc/group_policy_management_console_scripting_samples.asp.*

---

2000/2003 # Cleaning Up Temporary Files in User Accounts

| High |
| Moderate |
| Low |

On both workstations and servers, the TEMP directories for user accounts and the Windows installation can become cluttered with files that can cause program installations to fail, or create other bizarre behaviors.

## Overview

Windows maintains several folders for temporary files. One is a system-level folder, located in *%systemroot%*\TEMP. The other is in each user's Documents and Settings folder, in the path \Documents and Settings\<user>\Local Settings\Temp. Local Settings is a hidden folder, which makes this TEMP directory harder to find than normal.

Many different programs use the TEMP directories as dumping grounds for all sorts of digital trash. Installer applications usually unpack compressed files into these directories, for instance, and one of the common reasons an application install can fail is if files from another, totally unrelated program have left similarly named temp files there. The installer may balk at overwriting, and may instead fail, or even copy out the wrong information. For this reason, the TEMP directories need to be kept clear.

There's also the simple fact that, over time, this sort of accumulation becomes burdensome. While repairing a friend's computer, I found *over two gigabytes* of files in that user's TEMP folder. Deleting that mess cleared up almost all of the bizarre behaviors her machine had been exhibiting.

---

## The Party Line                        Company X

About the only acknowledgement Microsoft makes regarding the TEMP directory problem is through the use of one of their tools—the Disk Cleanup tool, which purges temporary files from many folders, but doesn't do the most consistent job of cleaning out the TEMP directory. The best way to do it, it seems, is by hand.

---

## *The Undocumented Solution*

*Many of the files in a given user's TEMP directory will be locked for exclusive access when that user is logged on. To get around this, use another account—one whose sole purpose is to purge other accounts.*

## What You'll Need

Administrative access on the computer in question

Here's the process for purging user's TEMP directories:

1. Create a new user account, preferably with a name and password that cannot be easily guessed, and give this account administrative privileges. I'll refer to this account as the "purge" account, henceforth.

2. Log off all other users and log on as the "purge" user.

3. Implement the following batch file command for each user whose directories you want to purge:
   **rd "<drive>:\Documents and Settings\<user>\Local Settings\TEMP" /S /Q**
   **md "<drive>:\Documents and Settings\<user>\Local Settings\TEMP"**

   For *<drive>*, substitute the drive letter where Documents and Settings is located; for *<user>* substitute the username. (You can look in the Documents and Settings folder to determine the exact name syntax.) Repeat this command as many times as needed in the batch file for each user.

4. You can now do one of two things. If you are inclined to do the purging manually, add this batch file into the "purge" user's Startup folder. If you wish, you can append a LOGOFF command to the file, so that the "purge" user is automatically logged back off when the command has finished running. This way, you can simply log in as the "purge" user periodically when you want to perform maintenance.

If you would rather perform the cleanups automatically, create a Scheduled Task for that batch file and run it in the context of the "purge" user account. Any logged-in user who has those files open will simply have them skipped over at the time of the purge. For that reason, you may want to schedule such cleanups to take place more than once a day.

# 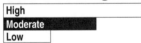 Reinstalling TCP/IP in Windows 2003

| High |
|------|
| **Moderate** |
| Low |

Because of changes to the way TCP/IP is handled in Windows 2003, it cannot be uninstalled and reinstalled in the conventional manner.

## Overview

Windows NT 4.0 and Windows 2000 listed TCP/IP as one protocol among many—it could be deinstalled and reinstalled like any other network component. In Windows 2003, however, that all changed: a curious administrator will find that the Uninstall button for TCP/IP in the Network Connection Properties window is dimmed and cannot be clicked. A surprising number of administrators attempt to deal with bizarre network problems by simply deinstalling and reinstalling all network components, without realizing that that doesn't always fix everything either for reasons described further in this section.

## The Party Line

### Company X

Microsoft rewrote the way TCP/IP works in Windows 2003 to be a core system component. Part of this was apparently for the sake of speed, since more network components are now handled through kernel-level drivers, but also to reflect a change in the philosophy behind the use of TCP/IP: it's not just *a* network component but *the* network component. If TCP/IP malfunctions in Windows 2003, an administrator may attempt to reinstall TCP/IP, only to find he can't.

## *The Undocumented Solution*

*The answer, as it turns out, is to use the NETSH tool to reconfigure the network stack. NETSH deletes and rewrites all IP-related Registry entries and refreshes the network stack as if it had been newly installed. (The affected keys, if you're curious, are HKEY_LOCAL_MACHINE\SYSTEM\CurrentControlSet\Services\Tcpip\ Parameters and HKEY_LOCAL_MACHINE\SYSTEM\CurrentControlSet\ Services\DHCP\Parameters.) Simply deinstalling network components does not always reset this information.*

To rebuild the network stack, issue the command,

```
netsh int ip reset <logfile>
```

where *<logfile>* is the path to a text file that will contain the results of the operation. The changes that take place will depend largely on what changes, if any, have been made to the TCP/IP stack. The machine will need to be rebooted after this change, however.

This technique also works for Windows 2000, and is in fact preferred to deinstalling and reinstalling TCP/IP "by hand."

---

**NOTE:**  If you've applied any of the tweaks or optimizations listed in this chapter, running this command will undo them and they will need to be recreated from scratch.

---

# CHAPTER 7

## *IIS and Active Directory*

**In This Chapter:**

Both Windows 2000 and 2003 come with IIS (5.0 and 6.0, respectively), and since it is one of the most commonly used components of Windows Server, some discussion of it is probably mandatory. I've listed a number of the most important tips for performance and functionality in IIS—editing the Registry and Metabase, for instance—and included a number of others that talk about some other advanced methodologies, such as installing IIS in a non-standard location. This chapter isn't meant to be a substitute for a complete book on the subject, of course, but it should give a good overview of some of the most common optimizations. In the same vein, I've detailed some techniques involving content caching, Active Directory, DNS, domain controller functions, and crash-logging ("Dr. Watson").

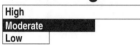

# Relocating the Default IIS Installation

| High |
|------|
| **Moderate** |
| Low |

IIS installs itself into a fixed location by default, but with some coaxing can be made to install itself in another, administrator-determined location.

## Overview

The support files for IIS—everything that is not actually installed in the Windows directory—are, by default, installed on the same partition as the operating system. Sometimes this is not the best place for these files, whether because of lack of space or simply the discretion of the administrator. Windows doesn't have any provision during setup indicating where to put the IIS files (the InetPub directories and their subsidiaries).

Sometimes an administrator will "inherit" an existing system that has IIS installed in a location that is troublesome (a system partition running out of space). It's also becoming common knowledge that not installing IIS in a predictable location is a way to defeat "blind" network attacks that assume the IIS directories are always in the same place. Because of these problems, many administrators are curious about how to change the default installation location for IIS.

---

## The Party Line                    Company X

```
Microsoft is not much help in this department; they provide
little or no information on how to relocate IIS from the
system partition.
```

## *The Undocumented Solution*

*The way to force IIS to install to a particular location is to script an unattended install for it. This necessitates a certain amount of downtime for IIS, and will also require that the administrator create an answer file (detailed next) to guide the installation.*

## What You'll Need

- A Registry editing tool
- The original Windows installation media, from which to re-install IIS
- Copies of the latest service pack for Windows and post-SP hotfixes, if any
- Notepad or another tool for creating a plain-text answer file
- Copies of any files needed to re-create the IIS installation that are not actually installed by Windows (for instance, the IIS directories you created)

Here are the steps to relocating IIS. Note that if IIS is not yet installed, you can skip any directions about backing up data.

1. Back up any files created by you to re-create your current IIS installation.

2. Make a note of the configuration settings used on each directory. You will probably not be able to back up and restore IIS's configuration information into the new installation.

3. Delete the Registry keys in HKEY_LOCAL_MACHINE\SOFTWARE\ Microsoft\Windows NT\CurrentVersion\Hotfix. This will keep the hotfix checking tool from misidentifying which hotfixes are in fact installed.

4. Uninstall IIS 5.0. This can be done simply by going to Add/Remove Software in the Control Panel and using the Add/Remove Windows Components option.

5. Once IIS is de-installed, delete the Registry keys in HKEY_LOCAL_MACHINE\ SOFTWARE\Microsoft\Windows NT\CurrentVersion\Hotfix. This is to insure that any hotfix auditing does not misidentify which hotfixes are currently installed in your system. You will need to reapply them after this is done.

6. Create an answer file for IIS. This is a simple text file named **iis5install.txt**, with the following contents:

```
[Components]
iis_common = on
iis_inetmgr = on
iis_www = on
```

```
iis_ftp = on
iis_htmla = on
[InternetServer]
PathFTPRoot="E:\InetPub\FTPRoot"
PathWWWRoot="E:\InetPub\wwwroot"
```

The path to the FTP and WWW root directories as listed here go to the E: drive, but you can edit this to point anywhere you need to.

7. Install IIS using the answer file by using the following command-line statement:

```
sysocmgr/i:%windir%\inf\sysoc.inf   /u:c:\iis5install.txt
```

This assumes that the answer file is in c:\iis5install.txt, but if it isn't, you can modify that to point to the answer file, wherever it is. Be sure to also substitute your current Windows install directory for the variable *%windir%*.

8. Keep the service pack files handy during the installation, as you may be prompted for them.

9. After the installation is finished, apply hotfixes and service packs as needed.

10. Re-create your content directories.

## 2000/2003 Caching IIS Content

| High |
| --- |
| Moderate |
| Low |

Caching is one of the common ways delivery of content is accelerated across the Internet, and especially the World Wide Web. Knowing how to take advantage of this feature with IIS can save you and your remote clients some bandwidth.

## Overview

Many ISPs with high-speed connectivity for their clients use content caching to cache images, static pages, or other documents that are not updated frequently. When a request is put out for the content, it is flagged by the cache. If no copy of the material currently exists in the cache, the cache forwards the request and then keeps a copy of the requested material when it comes back down the wire. Later, if other clients (or the same client) request the material again, the cache can do one of two things. It can check to see if the material has expired on the target server, and if so, obtain a fresh copy; otherwise, it will simply return a cached copy of the content to the requestor. Or, it can simply return the cached copy until its lifetime in the cache expires or it is cycled out of the cache by other, more widely demanded content. This is a bit of an oversimplification, but the idea behind caching is that it can reduce the total amount of traffic to remote hosts. Such caches are called *transparent cache servers*, since the user is almost never aware of their existence and doesn't need to modify his connectivity to use them (as he would for a proxy server).

Each HTTP request that is returned from a remote server can contain a line in its header that indicates its cache status. This is usually done with the [cache] header, which indicates when the content is due to expire. The cache can either honor this explicitly and not ask for a fresher copy of the file at all, or can simply ask the remote server if a fresher copy exists, depending on how it's configured. (Most of the time, the second behavior will prevail.)

## The Party Line                    Company X

```
Microsoft provides methods within IIS for automatic content
expiration, but many people have discovered that by themselves
they do not always work. The cache expiry information passed
by IIS is usually honored by Internet Explorer (and sometimes
not even that), but is not often honored by proxy servers or
transparent caches.
```

CHAPTER
7

## The Undocumented Solution

*The IIS administrator may need to specify other metadata in the HTTP headers in order to allow caching to behave as expected.*

IIS and Active Directory

## What You'll Need
The IIS Service Manager

Here is how to optimize IIS's handling of caching:

1. Organize your content so that cacheable content is aggregated into as few directories as possible. Use directory hierarchies: if you have several different kinds of images, all of which are cacheable, move them into subdirectories of a single /IMAGES directory.

2. Make decisions about the cache lifetime for each type of content. On the server I manage, there are two kinds of images, system-level and user-level. System-level images are things like menu items, sidebars, backgrounds, and other commonly used elements. User-level images are uploaded and maintained by users, and while they change more often than system-level images, they only change sporadically. To that end, I set a cache lifetime of one month for system-level images and one week for user images. Few caches may actually honor the full cache lifetime, but that is the absolute outer limit of the cache lifetime I wanted to use with such a setup.

3. Launch the IIS Service Manager.

4. Right-click the directory you want to set the cache lifetime for, and then select Properties.

5. Click the HTTP Headers tab, as shown in Figure 7-1.

6. Check the "Enable Content Expiration" box and set an interval for the content to expire after it is delivered. In the figure here, the time limit is 14 days.

---

**NOTE** When you set Content Expiration for a directory, all of its subdirectories inherit the same value unless you've specified otherwise for them individually. This is useful if you know all the subdirectories under one directory must have the same behavior, but if you want others inside it to behave differently, you must specify this explicitly.

---

7. If you want to insure that the content is *not* cached, employ the following steps; otherwise, simply click OK.

8. Check the Content Expiration box and select the Expire Immediately option.

9. Under the Custom HTTP Headers section, click Add.

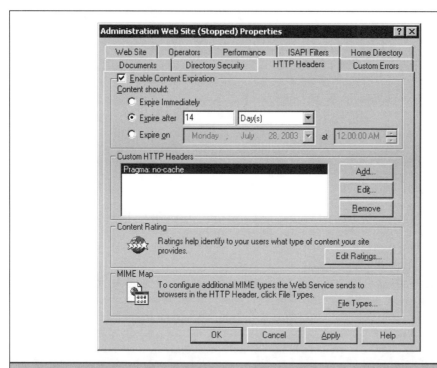

**Figure 7-1.** Setting the HTTP Headers tab for a particular site

10. Add a new custom HTTP header with the name **Pragma** and the value **no-cache**.

11. Add another custom HTTP header with the name **Cache-Control** and the value **private, no-store, no-cache, must-revalidate**.

12. Add another custom HTTP header with the name **Cache-Control** and the value **post-check=0, pre-check=0**.

---

**NOTE**  The reason all of this is needed is for compatibility with a broad variety of cache mechanisms that do not always honor the same statements in the same ways. **must-revalidate** appears to be used for flushing existing cache entries (as per RFC 2616), but may not always be needed. **private** tends to be the most consistently honored "don't cache this" statement, so sometimes you can get away with using only that and the **Pragma** declaration in your headers.

---

13. For ASP pages, you must also declare values for pages that do not have standard headers. At the top of ASP pages you want to expire immediately, use the **Response.Expires=-1** statement.

14. If you're using a Microsoft proxy server and want to ensure that the proxy does *not* cache ASP pages, use the statement **Response.cachecontrol="private"** at the top of the page. (Use **Response.cachecontrol="public"** if you *do* want to cache ASP pages at the proxy server, although you will probably not want to do this if you are using a lot of database-driven pages.)

---

**NOTE**  Another method for forcing a re-cache is to modify the URL of the retrieved object slightly. Many web sites do this, although it requires some programming expertise on the part of the web administrator to implement it reliably.

---

**CHAPTER 7**

**IIS and Active Directory**

## 2000/2003 Changing IIS Registry Settings

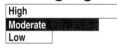

High
Moderate
Low

While many of IIS's most important settings are in the Metabase, the Registry still contains some key settings that can be tuned for the sake of performance.

### Overview

IIS, like many other software products, does not come configured "out of the box" for the best possible performance. An administrator almost inevitably has to tweak IIS to get the behavior desired for the particular site configuration used.

## The Party Line    Company X

Microsoft has written some good documentation about tuning
IIS for performance, namely the whitepaper "The Art and
Science of Web Server Tuning with Internet Information
Services 5.0" (available at http://www.microsoft.com/
windows2000/docs/WebSrvTnIIS.doc).

## *The Undocumented Solution*

*Microsoft's documentation on performance tuning is hardly complete. For one thing, there are several tunable settings that the document does not discuss. Also, the document has not been updated to reflect new settings available in IIS 6.0 and their behaviors there.*

What follows is a list of many of the most common performance-related Registry settings for IIS, with detailed information about their tunings.

## What You'll Need

A Registry editor

Perform the following steps:

1. Open the Registry and navigate to HKEY_LOCAL_MACHINE\SYSTEM\CurrentControlSet\Services\InetInfo\Parameters.

2. Examine the DWORD setting CacheSecurityDescriptor (default: one). This setting controls whether or not security descriptors are also cached along with a file when it is copied into the IIS file cache. If you are using Windows user-account authentication to control access to files, caching the security information saves the system a trip to determine the security information for the file. However, if security changes for a file on disk, and the file is still in the IIS cache, it is *not* updated with the new security information. If security information on pages changes constantly, or you want to change this behavior as part of an effort to tighten security sitewide, set this to 0 (disabled). If you don't use Windows authentication, or permissions change very infrequently on those files, leave this as 1.

3. Add the DWORD setting MemCacheSize. This controls the size of the memory buffer that IIS will use for its file cache. When this value isn't in the Registry, IIS, *by default*, assigns 50 percent of available RAM to the file cache.

This memory-assignment behavior is a big part of the reason why many administrators complain about the IIS process hogging far too much system memory or becoming "bloated." The blame for this problem has ranged from leaking processes to undisposed memory from ASP sessions. Since administrators have good reason to be worried about why a particular process is gobbling up so much memory, they want to know what can be done about it, especially if the machine that runs IIS is also hosting other servers, such as SQL Server (which can in itself be a memory hog if not throttled!).

If the "50-percent rule" is in use, every 60 seconds IIS calculates how much available memory there is and sets the cache to that size. If the cache is downsized, the oldest entries in the cache are cycled out to make room. If there are not enough cached objects to fill the cache, the cache will also be downsized to match. (This explains why the memory footprint for the IIS process starts off small and swells as usage goes up—the cache is simply filling up to meet demand.)

**CHAPTER
7**

**IIS and Active Directory**

Since IIS is often run on machines with other applications, throttling back the size of the cache can be useful, especially if you have a good handle on how much usage the site really gets. For instance, a site with only 12MB of total static content would not need a cache bigger than 12MB, and depending on how often and how much of that is accessed, the cache could even be half that size. Generally, the performance benefits of the file cache only show up when you are serving up a great many pages per second, so sites that experience a lower rate of traffic in general can also afford to have the cache slimmed down.

If you can afford to experiment with different values and use a load simulator, you may find out that a fix you didn't expect to do anything may have unexpectedly positive results, or that only a certain combination of settings helps. If you are trying to achieve a compromise for space vs. performance, especially when running other server processes, test "live"—in other words, run the other server during your testing as if you were using it for real.

**NOTE**  Some documentation lists this Registry entry as MemoryCacheSize rather than MemCacheSize.

4. Add or edit the DWORD setting ObjectCacheTTL (default: 30 seconds). This controls how long objects are held in the file cache. Any object not referenced for more than the defined time period will be dropped from the cache. Like MemCacheSize, this value is not included by default in the Registry and must be added manually.

Initially, this is set low to keep the system from caching a large number of volatile objects. If you have little memory to spare on your IIS server, you can leave this value as-is or even set it lower. Conversely, if you have a lot of memory, you can set this value higher, allowing more objects to be cached—

a good idea if you have a site with a great many different cacheable objects that are referenced constantly.

If you set this value to FFFFFFFF (hex), the "cache scavenger" is disabled. The cache scavenger is the process that goes through the cache and throws out anything whose lifetime has expired. Without it, the only way objects are removed from the cache is when there is no more room in the cache for a new object, thus forcing out the oldest-referenced one. If you have plenty of RAM and relatively static data, turning off the cache scavenger may actually be a good idea.

---

**NOTE** The object cache does not apply to ISAPI components or custom business objects called through Remote Data Services (any component that has to be registered using REGSRV32 or ClsIdView). It applies to documents in the web folders only.

---

5. Add or edit the DWORD setting PoolThreadLimit (default: two times the currently installed number of MB of RAM). This setting controls the maximum number of I/O worker threads that can be spawned in the INETINFO process.

   Since each inbound connection is tied to a single thread, this limits the number of simultaneous connections that can be made to the server at any given moment—although since the requests are, in theory, serviced immediately, any blocking caused by this effect is not normally noticeable.

   Each thread listens for a network request and handles it either by sending back a static file to the remote host or by passing the request to the appropriate ISAPI DLL or CGI that handles the file type. (ASP requests, for instance, are handled through an ISAPI DLL, not through the INETINFO process itself.)

   This value can never be larger than 256—although this does not mean that you can only have 256 inbound connections! If the system is getting blocked up even though you have 256 threads available, odds are there is a badly written ISAPI extension (for instance, one that requires synchronous processing) clogging up the works somewhere. A good ISAPI DLL will use its own thread pool for process queuing rather than tying up IIS worker threads. Incidentally, even on a fast system, 256 simultaneous threads will incur a fair amount of overhead due to the context switching involved in having that many threads open.

---

**NOTE** PoolThreadLimit restricts the thread count for *all* IIS services—HTTP, NNTP/SMTP, FTP, and everything else that runs as an IIS service. Bear this in mind when choosing a thread pool size.

---

Add or edit the DWORD setting MaxPoolThreads (default: four per processor). This controls the number of I/O worker threads to create per processor, for the sake of processing *static* files. PoolThreadLimit controls threads that manage

ISAPI requests *and* static files, so MaxPoolThreads can never be larger than the PoolThreadLimit.

The default setting of four is generally too low for a server that handles a large number of requests. This means the server can only process four CGI applications at once—far too small for someone using Perl or another CGI language, especially on a site where multiple scripts may need to run at once. Microsoft themselves recommend increasing this to 20, but not beyond that—more than 20 can create serious context-switching issues. Another possibility is to set the UsePoolThreadForCGI value to 0, but that can impact performance throughout the system if CGI requests are long-running (meaning it takes more than a few seconds to produce a given page).

6. Add or edit the DWORD value MaxCachedFileSize (default: 262,144). This controls the maximum size of a file that can be placed in the cache; no file larger than this will be cached. The bigger the site, the larger this value ought to be, especially if you have a dedicated IIS server with plenty of RAM.

7. Navigate to HKEY_LOCAL_MACHINE\SYSTEM\CurrentControlSet\Services\W3SVC\Parameters.

8. Add or edit the DWORD value UploadReadAhead (default: 48). This governs how much data in an HTTP POST action is pre-read by the server before passing it to the application handling the request. If you have a server with a generous amount of RAM and a lot of POST actions that are quite large (for instance, if people are uploading images through a form interface), you may want to increase this to something that is reflective of the size of the average upload. This entry is calibrated in kilobytes, so if you specify 32, it's 32K.

**NOTE**  In IIS 6.0, this has been converted to a Metabase entry with the same name.

## For IIS 6.0 Only

Navigate to HKEY_LOCAL_MACHINE\SYSTEM\CurrentControlSet\Services\ASP\Parameters and edit the DWORD value DisableLazyContentPropagation. This controls how IIS behaves when enough content is updated or changed at once to invalidate more than a certain amount of the in-memory template cache.

IIS has an internal limit for how much content can be updated in the document cache at once. If too much of the cached content is updated at one time, everything in the cache is invalidated, but if any of the invalidated documents are requested, IIS will serve up the expired documents from the cache until new copies can be compiled. Setting this value to 0 will cause IIS 6.0 to re-cache everything before serving any copies out of the cache at all. If you don't make a great many changes to documents, you can disable this behavior and have the most recent version of any page served.

**CHAPTER 7**

**IIS and Active Directory**

2000/2003 # Changing IIS Metabase Settings for Performance

| High |
|:---|
| **Moderate** |
| Low |

The Registry is not the only repository of settings that affect performance. IIS 5.0 and 6.0 also store many of their more commonly used and updated settings in the Metabase.

## Overview

The Metabase was created by Microsoft as a way to store settings for IIS that were updated or accessed more frequently than those in the Registry. As a rule, settings in the Registry are only read when a program or service is first started, to keep the amount of traffic to, and from, the Registry to a minimum.

In IIS 5.0, the Metabase is stored in a binary format that can only be read and written via a special utility, Metaedit.exe, which is not installed by default in Windows. It can be found in the \apps\metaedit directory of the Windows 2000 Resource Kit, or downloaded from http://download.microsoft.com/download/iis50/Utility/5.0/ NT45/EN-US/MtaEdt22.exe.

IIS 6.0 stores the Metabase as an XML file, which can be edited with any plain-text editing tool, although any edits need to be done carefully to make sure the integrity of the XML formatting isn't disrupted.

---

## The Party Line Company X

While Microsoft does give information about how to edit the Metabase and even gives some information (in the aforementioned whitepaper) about edit Metabase settings for performance tuning, the information is far from complete and doesn't include any details about Metabase settings new to IIS 6.0.

---

## *The Undocumented Solution*

*Listed here is a collection of suggested Metabase tunings for performance, both for IIS 5.0 and 6.0. Unless otherwise noted, each of these properties is available in both 5.0 and 6.0.*

Also, unless otherwise specified, each of these properties can be set in the following Metabase admin objects:

- IIsWebService (in /LM/W3SVC)
- IIsWebServer (in /LM/W3SVC/<servername>)
- IIsWebDirectory (in /LM/W3SVC/<servername>/ROOT/<directoryname>)
- IIsWebVirtualDir (in /LM/W3SVC/<servername>/ROOT/<virtualdirectory>/ <directoryname>).

## What You'll Need

A Metabase editor

Here are the settings to examine:

- **AspAllowSessionState** (default: true). When set to True, this value forces the use of session states on all ASP applications. Session states aren't used by all programmers, however, and tracking session states for each client requires that a cookie be placed on the client. Normally, the programmer can override the use of a session state on a per-page basis by using the statement <%@EnableSessionState= False%> at the top of the page. However, if session states are not being used at all on the site, turning them off sitewide can improve performance. Make sure that any future developers know that session states are disabled. (I have only met a few ASP programmers who ever bothered with the use of session states, and most of them found other mechanisms for doing the same things.)

- **AspBufferingLimit** (2003 only) (default: 4194304). This value sets the maximum size for the ASP output buffer, which is used to buffer output if response buffering is turned on (which it is by default). If the buffer fills up, the buffer is flushed and sent to the remote host. Set this to a smaller value if you want to automatically cause buffer-flushing at a specific size without using Reponse.Flush statements in ASP pages.

- **AspCalcLineNumber** (2003 only) (default: true). This controls whether or not the ASP processor calculates the line number of each executed line of code for the sake of error reporting. If you want to turn this off when you're not actually debugging anything, you can speed up processing a bit—just remember to turn it back on again if you need to track a problem.

- **AspExecuteInMTA** (2003 only) (default: 0). This value controls whether or not COM components for ASP threads are run in the multithreaded apartment model. If you have well-written third-party components that run as free-threaded or both-threaded, set this to **1** to enable multi-threading, which can enhance performance.

- **AspRequestQueueMax** (default: 3000). This property controls how many ASP requests are allowed to wait for processing in the queue. This was raised to 3000 from 500 in previous versions of IIS. If the queue fills up, the server responds with the infamous "HTTP 500 Server Too Busy" error (a common complaint about untweaked ASP servers). If the queue is filling up, the problem may be a process that is blocking the queue, rather than a queue that is too short.

- **AspThreadGateEnabled** (2000 only) (default: 0). When set to 1, IIS 5.0 changes the number of ASP worker threads in response to changing workloads, up to the value specified by AspProcessorThreadMax multiplied by the number of processors available to IIS. Enabling this value helps performance if you have radically varying workloads on your server. (IIS 6.0 no longer has this option as it manages the ASP thread pool automatically.)

- **AspQueueConnectionTestTime** (default: 3). If a request has been in the ASP queue for more than this number of seconds, the request is considered to be outdated and is discarded. This is to prevent impatient users from "hammering" a slow server and spawning dozens or possibly hundreds of requests that will never really be seen. If you have a server which bogs down a bit a times, you may want to lengthen this interval; you may even consider shortening it if your server is exceptionally speedy, and use the Response.IsClientConnected method in ASP pages to test whether or not someone is still connected.

- **MaxEndpointConnections** (default: 100) (IISWebService and IISWebServer only). This controls how many listening sockets can be aggregated on a specific network endpoint. If you have a server that has many clients who open multiple connections to the site and have many long-running pages, then leaving this at the default value is a good idea. Setting this lower will only allow that many simultaneous open connections to be made from any one network endpoint (and will restrict both usage and bandwidth).

- **ServerListenBacklog** (default: 5/40/200, depending on the ServerSize property) (IISWebService and IISWebServer only). This controls how many sockets can be queued, and works hand-in-hand with the MaxEndpointConnections property to determine the total number of pooled sockets. Whichever of the two properties is lower determines how many sockets will be pooled, up to a maximum of 1000. For the best results, set this to the same value as MaxEndpointConnections.

- **SMPAffinitized** (2003 only) (default: False) (only in /LM/W3SVC/AppPools/). This appears among other properties for a given application pool in the /LM/W3SVC/AppPools/DefaultAppPool hierarchy in the Metabase. When set to True for a particular application pool, that pool can be assigned to run on a specific CPU by setting a CPU bitmask in the SMPProcessorAffinityMask property. For instance, to set the process to use the third CPU in a four-CPU system, the bitmask would be 100 binary (third bit from the right), or four (in both hex and decimal).

# Compressing IIS Content

| High |
| :--- |
| **Moderate** |
| Low |

Compressing web server content can yield far higher throughput ratios at the cost of some CPU usage on both ends. However, IIS's default mechanisms for doing so are not always dependable.

## Overview

Most of what gets sent to a web browser is uncompressed 7-bit or 8-bit text and pre-compressed graphics. Obviously, the graphics can't be compressed any more than they already are, but the text often can. A web server that compresses its textual content for delivery can often save as much as 75 percent of the bandwidth normally used for delivering text.

Many web servers allow for some way to deliver compressed content to a web browser. This is usually done by using the *gzip* and *deflate* algorithms, as described in RFC 1952. IIS 5.0 and 6.0 also have provisions to deliver compressed content, both static and dynamic. Unfortunately, they're not very reliable.

---

## The Party Line                                    `Company X`

```
Microsoft's implementation of the gzip/deflate system
in IIS 5.0 has long been known to be problematic. Microsoft
has even acknowledged this in many different ways—consider
KnowledgeBase article 313712, where the first 2048 bytes
of a compressed page can go missing in a compressed page when
viewed with IIS 5.5 and 6.0. Unfortunately, the fix extended
in this case is only to the client and not the server.
(Another acknowledged bug (article 314307), "HTTP Compression
Does Not Work if Request File Name Extension Contains
Uppercase Characters" is also annoying but at least can be
worked around and was fixed in Windows 2000 Service Pack 3.)
```

---

IIS 6.0 has a more dependable compression system, although not everyone chooses to use it because it appears to be difficult to turn on. Some people elect to write their own on-the-fly compression algorithm using theASPX-based HttpModule filtering system. ASPX developer Ben Lowery has one such module (http://www.blowery.org/code/HttpCompressionModule_1.1.zip).

The bad news is that HttpModule appears to have some problems that make it difficult for third-party developers to create reliable compression plug-ins. If an ASPX developer requests something that calls Response.End, the ASPX filter is dropped from the output stream, which mangles the output. The same happens with Server.Transfer, which also triggers Response.End and drops the filter from the stream as well. (One workaround for this is to call Server.Execute rather than Response.End, or use tools that are authored entirely as ISAPI DLLs, since the code is detached from the ISAPI filter handling the request. The bad news is that this requires the author to write his code in C++ or Visual Basic and produce an ISAPI DLL—which is not a luxury everyone can afford.) In short, for those IIS 6.0 users who can't afford to code up an ISAPI DLL, the only real answer is to use IIS 6.0's built-in compression… provided they can turn it on.

### *The Undocumented Solution*

*Since IIS 5.0's own built-in page compression is not very dependable, the smart thing to do (for IIS 5.0) is to turn to third-party solutions that offer the same (or better) features. Some of these solutions also provide advanced content-caching, although features like that should be used at the discretion of the administrator—if you are using a database-driven site, for instance, it can be difficult to provide reliable content caching.*

XCache (http://www.xcache.com/) is one such product—it not only performs gzip/deflate but can also carry out intelligent caching of database content based on the administrator's preferences. CacheRight (http://www.port80software.com) intelligently implements all relevant HTTP 1.0 and 1.1 cache control headers including expires and cache-control, as well as max-age, public/private, and no-transform, and will work in as granular a fashion as needed (that is, sitewide, for specific directories, or only on specific files). PipeBoost (http://www.pipeboost.com) works with IIS 6.0 as well as previous versions of IIS, and can integrate closely with other ISAPI-driven content applications like ColdFusion and Akamizer.

IIS 6.0 does have more reliable page compression, but enabling it requires a little footwork on top of the normal set of directions from Microsoft. It can be found at http://www.microsoft.com/technet/treeview/default.asp?url=/technet/prodtechnol/windowsserver2003/proddocs/standard/qos_utilbandwdth.asp.

## What You'll Need

- The IIS administration tool
- A Metabase editing tool

Here are the steps for enabling content compression in IIS 6.0:

1. Open the IIS admin tool and right-click Web Service Extensions.

2. Choose "Add a new web service extension" and pick a name that identifies what you'll be doing ("HTTP Compression" should work fine).

3. Add the file \Windows\System32\inetsrv\gzip.dll as the extension itself, which is the ISAPI .DLL that performs gzip/deflate compression on content.

4. Change Set Extension Status to *Allowed*.

5. Click OK.

6. Shut down IIS by selecting Stop Internet Services from the All Tasks menu for the IIS MMC panel.

7. Make a backup of the Metabase, since you'll be editing it.

8. Open \Windows\System32\inetsrv\MetaBase.xml and search for IISCompressionScheme. Look for two elements under it—one for deflate and the other for gzip. Both elements have properties named HcFileExtensions and HcScriptFileExtensions. Each contains a space-delimited list of file extensions for content that can be compressed under each algorithm.

9. Add **aspx** to the list of extensions in HcScriptFileExtensions and **htm** and **html** in HcFileExtensions for both types. If you are using plain old **asp** as well, add that to HcScriptFileExtensions.

10. Restart IIS.

You can also register file extensions by using the ADSUTIL.VBS command-line script using this syntax:

```
cscript.exe adsutil.vbs
set W3Svc/Filters/Compression/GZIP/HcFileExtensions "htm" "html"
```

Obviously, all you need to do is change HcFileExtensions to HcScriptFileExtensions to register changes for that element, and also change the file extensions to match.

> **NOTE**  Compressing pages that build progressively with multiple buffer flushes over a long time, such as scrolling chat-room pages, may produce unpredictable results. Since the compression takes place in discrete blocks, the pages may no longer stream to the browser as they did before, or may break entirely.

## 2000/2003 Using Free Log Analysis Tools for IIS

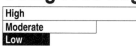

| High |
| Moderate |
| Low |

Many IIS administrators want to produce detailed log analysis reports for their web sites, but are stymied by how expensive many log analysis packages are. A program such as Webtrends can cost upwards of several hundred dollars, and might be overkill for many people.

## The Party Line

Neither Windows 2000 nor Windows 2003 comes with built-in web log analysis tools. There *was* such a tool, named Site Server Express, but Microsoft has since discontinued it.

## *The Undocumented Solution*

There are many third-party log analysis tools for Windows, although many of them are rather costly. One of the best and, interestingly enough, one of the cheapest (as in "free!") is a tool called Analog.

Analog has long been popular on Linux and UNIX, and a Win32 build of the program has also been around for some time—although it has not caught on as widely as it should with Windows administrators. As of this writing, it is at version 5.32, with a 5.90 beta in the works that permits XHTML and XML export, with a good deal of its code completely rewritten for speed.

One of the strengths of Analog is that it requires very little work to produce a broad range of sophisticated reports. The default output is highly informative and broken down into a broad range of common queries such as referrer URL, operating system and browser of remote host, data transferred, most requested pages, most requested objects, and so on. The program's other major strength is its massive customizability—almost every aspect of the output, from the formatting to the way stats are tabulated and weighted, can be changed. Reports can be flat or hierarchical, so that a referring-domain report can be broken out by subdomains, down to as many levels as you like. Also, the program caches statistics from previous runs to avoid excessive amounts of processing time on newer logs.

The program, including original source code and documentation (both online and off) can be downloaded at http://www.analog.cx. For an example of some Analog output, see http://www.statslab.cam.ac.uk/webstats/stats.html (the site for the Statistical Laboratory at Cambridge, in England), or examine Figure 7-2.

Another good, inexpensive log analyzer is WebLog Expert Lite (http://www .weblogexpert.com/lite.htm). This is a stripped-down version of a much larger product, but includes a decent number of reports and summaries in the free version. It doesn't have the same breadth of statistics that Analog does, however, but if the budget exists to ramp up to a more sophisticated product, consider this as a way of trying out WebLog Expert.

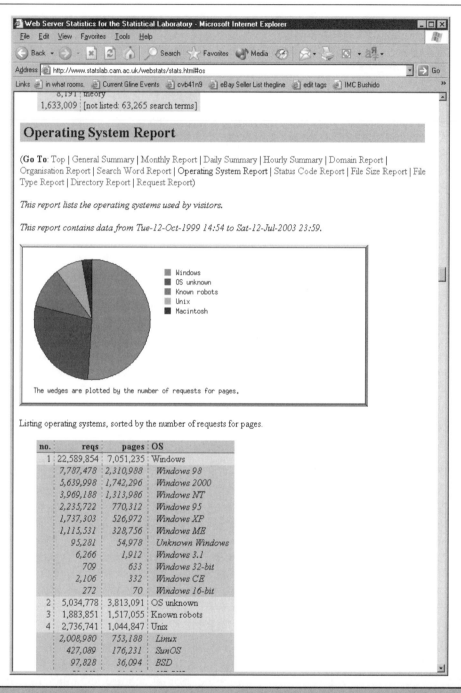

**Figure 7-2.** Sample output from Analog

 **Modifying Active Directory's Tombstone and Garbage Collection Lifetime**

| High |
|------|
| Moderate |
| Low |

Modifying the way Active Directory handles deleted objects can be used as a way to get out of a possible tight spot if you don't have a recent AD/System State backup.

## Overview

When an Active Directory object is deleted, it is converted into a "tombstone," a marker that indicates a deleted object. A tombstone remains in the system until Windows runs a garbage collection process and deletes all tombstones permanently.

Active Directory maintains two attributes that govern how deleted AD objects are handled. The first, tombstoneLifetime, describes how long deleted objects are maintained before they are removed by garbage collection. It defaults to 60 days. The second, garbageCollPeriod, indicates how often garbage collection runs, which defaults to 12 hours. The maximum garbage collection interval is one-third of the tombstone lifetime (in hours).

The tombstone lifetime should *always* be longer than the replication latency period, which is why the lifetime is initially set to 60 days. The reason for this is simple: when an object is deleted, the deletion needs to replicate to all the member servers before truly taking effect. When each server receives a replica of the tombstone, its lifetime is marked from the time of its original deletion, not the time it was received in replication. This way all the replicas of an object can expire across the network at the same time.

---

## The Party Line                                    Company X

```
Normally, Microsoft insists on leaving the tombstone lifetime
as is, and they're right for the most part. Changing the
tombstone lifetime in particular is something you should only
do in two instances: when first configuring Active Directory,
as a way to determine how aggressively the Active Directory
database should have garbage collection performed; and as a
last-ditch effort to perform disaster recovery.
```

---

If you have more than one Windows 2000 domain controller in your network, the best way to reproduce a damaged AD store is to replicate the store from the other domain controllers. However, if there are no other domain controllers in the network, the only way to restore AD is from a System State backup.

There's another hitch. If the backup is older than 60 days, Windows will not restore from it. Since the tombstone lifetime is, by default, 60 days, any backup older than that is assumed to have objects that have not been deleted, and will be rejected. For the same reason, if a domain controller is shut off or disconnected from the network for 60 days (or whatever the tombstone lifetime is), it must be reinstalled for the same reason.

Obviously, one good way to avoid all this is to make regular System State backups, but if you're stuck and need to restore the AD database from an older backup, this is one way to get around that restriction.

# The Undocumented Solution

*Changing the tombstone lifetime and garbage collection deletion period requires editing Active Directory config objects.*

**CHAPTER 7**

## What You'll Need

A tool for editing Active Directory. Here we will use the ADSIEDIT.MSC tool available in the /SUPPORT/TOOLS folder on the Windows 2000 CD-ROM. (The tool is installed by running setup.exe in that folder.)

To change the tombstone and garbage collection intervals:

1. Open Active Directory with the editing tool.
2. Expand the tree for the Configuration Container.
3. Expand the subtree CN=Configuration, then the subtree CN=Services, and then the subtree CN=Windows NT. This portion of the tree can be seen in Figure 7-3.
4. Right-click CN=Directory Service and select Properties.
5. In the Select A Property To View drop-down, choose tombstoneLifetime. Type the new value for the tombstone lifetime, in days, into the Edit Attribute text field, as shown in Figure 7-4. Click Set to apply the changes.
6. Select the property garbageCollPeriod and set it in the same manner. garbageCollPeriod is calibrated in hours, not days.
7. Click OK to close the Properties window. This will generally cause the database to shrink slightly.

IIS and Active Directory

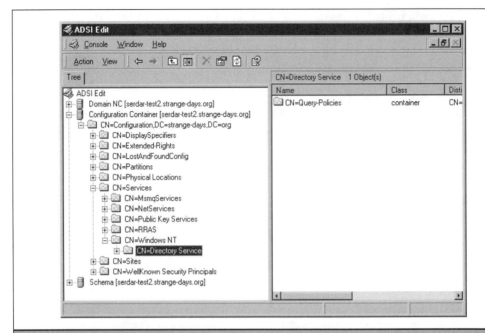

**Figure 7-3.** The sub-branch of the Configuration Container that holds the Directory Service object

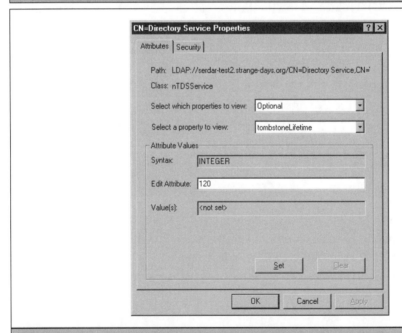

**Figure 7-4.** Changing the tombstoneLifetime property in the Directory Service object

2000/2003

# Modifying the Maximum Number of Active Directory Search Objects

| High |
|---|
| **Moderate** |
| Low |

By default, Active Directory caps the maximum number of objects to process during a search, but this number can be raised to increase search performance on a fast server.

## Overview

When searches are conducted in Active Directory, the AD engine processes up to 10,000 objects at a time during the search. This affects everything associated with Active Directory—the browse displays, the MMC Users and Computers snap-in, and so on. If you have a particularly large organization (and a robust server), you may want to ramp up the number of objects to search at once to make searches conclude a little faster.

## The Party Line                                    Company X

```
Microsoft prefers that you keep the default number of searches
to 10,000 as a way of not flooding the system with search
request processing. For slower machines, this is probably
true, but if you are dealing with a two- or four-way system
(or a single, extremely fast system), the number of searches
can be ramped up a bit.
```

## *The Undocumented Solution*

*The way to modify this behavior is twofold. First, you can modify the Group Policy for a particular object to change its search parameters; second, you can edit the Registry.*

CHAPTER
7

IIS and Active Directory

## What You'll Need

The MMC Active Directory Users and Computers snap-in

Here are the steps to change the number of searches via Group Policy:

1. From the Start menu, select Programs | Administrative Tools | Active Directory Users and Computers to open the Users and Computers console for Active Directory.

2. Right-click the container whose search parameters you want to modify and select Properties. Select the Group Policy tab, as shown in Figure 7-5.

3. Select the Group Policy Object, and select Edit. In the MMC console that appears, select User Configuration from the left-hand panel and drill down to Administrative Templates | Desktop | Active Directory, as shown in Figure 7-6.

4. Double-click Maximum Size Of Active Directory Searches, select Enabled, and set the number to the maximum size of the search to run on that object. Figure 7-7 has an example of this. Click OK when done, and close all instances of MMC.

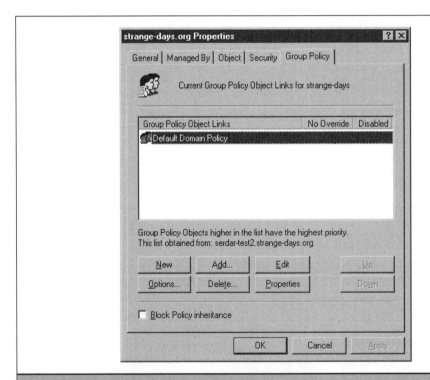

**Figure 7-5.**   The Group Policy tab for the modified object

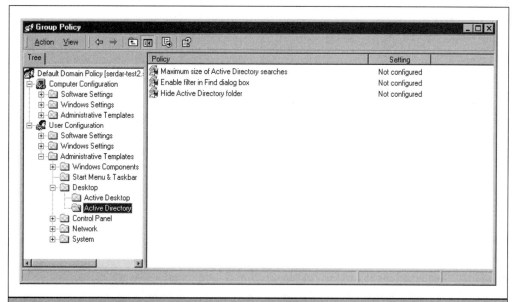

**Figure 7-6.** Group Policy for the modified object

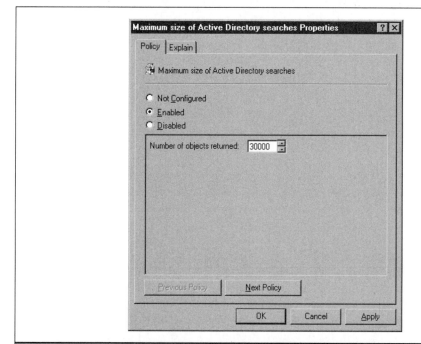

**Figure 7-7.** Changing the maximum size of Active Directory searches to 30,000

## What You'll Need

- A Registry editor
- Administrative access to the machine from which the search is conducted

Follow these steps to change the number of searches per user via the Registry:

1. Open the Registry and navigate to HKEY_CURRENT_USER\Software\ Policies\Microsoft.
2. Add a new key named **Windows**, and under that, another new key named **Directory UI**.
3. Within Directory UI, add a new DWORD value named **QueryLimit**. Set the value of QueryLimit to the number of searches.

For both methods, the change will take effect when the user logs on the next time.

---

**NOTE** If you want to perform a find operation in Active Directory from your desktop, you can do this by creating a new shortcut that contains this command: **%SystemRoot%\SYSTEM32\rundll32.exe dsquery,OpenQueryWindow**.

---

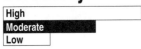 2000/2003

# Restoring SYSVOL and Netlogon Shares for an Active Directory Domain Controller

| High |
|---|
| Moderate |
| Low |

Domain controllers brought out of restore mode can misbehave thanks to a quirk in File Replication Services that causes certain system shares to also become unavailable.

## Overview

When a domain controller is restored, its File Replication Service (FRS) database (stored in *%SystemRoot%*\Ntfrs\Jet) is not restored. This is because another replica in the network is assumed to have a more current database. In other words, this is done to prevent an older copy of the FRS database from corrupting other machines.

After the restore operation, FRS will try to locate a replica to synchronize with. Until this happens, the SYSVOL and Netlogon shares will not be accessible. If you restore *all* the domain controllers in an organization, this can be a big problem—none of them will be able to find a replica, since *all of them will be searching*. (Note that this generally happens only if you restore the only domain controller in a domain, but it can also happen if you restore all domain controllers at once, too.)

**NOTE** Under these circumstances, running dcdiag.exe produces the following error:
Warning: DcGetDcName(GC_SERVER_REQUIRED) call failed, error 1355.
If you're wondering if this is what's wrong, try running dcdiag.exe to see if it produces this problem.

# The Party Line                                              Company X

Microsoft's approach to this problem is more preventative
than anything else: don't set the only domain controller
in your organization to restore without promoting another
machine first.

## *The Undocumented Solution*

*There is another answer, one which involves designating one domain controller among all others to be authoritative for the SYSVOL replica. This requires editing the Registry.*

## What You'll Need
A Registry editor

Follow these steps to fix the FRS replica problem:

1. Go to the server that functions as the primary domain controller emulator or FSMO role holder.
2. Stop the File Replication Service on that server.
3. Open the Registry and navigate to HKEY_LOCAL_MACHINE\SYSTEM\ CurrentControlSet\Services\NtFrs\Parameters\Backup / Restore\Process at Startup. (Note that "Backup / Restore" is the name of the key.)
4. Edit the DWORD BurFlags and set it to **D4 (hex)**. *Don't set this on more than one server.*
5. Exit the Registry and restart the File Replication Service.

CHAPTER
7

IIS and Active Directory

## 2000/2003 Detecting and Removing Duplicate Security Identifiers in an Active Directory Domain

| High |
| Moderate |
| Low |

Duplicate Security Identifiers (SIDs) within an Active Directory domain can cause serious problems for Exchange Server and many other programs, but removing them is not always a straightforward process.

## Overview

Windows uses two types of identifiers for objects: SIDs and RIDs (Relative Identifiers). RIDs refer to the portion of an SID that identifies a user or group in relation to the authority that issued the SID. One of the most common examples of this is the SID CREATOR OWNER (S-1-3-0). This is made up of the authority SECURITY_CREATOR_SID_AUTHORITY (3) and the relative identifier SECURITY_CREATOR_OWNER_RID (0).

Whenever you create a domain controller, Windows assigns a pool of RIDs to that controller (taken from the RID FSMO role holder), so that each SID issued by that domain controller is unique. If for whatever reason you seize the RID role from that machine, the same RID pool could be allocated to different domain controllers. This is not something that might be noticeable immediately, but it *can* show up in the long run and create real trouble.

To detect if the problem exists, run **NTDSUTIL** from the command prompt and type the following commands (pressing ENTER after each line),

```
Security Account Management
Connect To Server <nameofserver>
```

where *<nameofserver>* is the name of your server.

At the Security Account Maintenance prompt, type

```
check duplicate sid
```

You should receive

```
Duplicate SID check completed successfully.
Check dupsid.log for any duplicates.
```

dupsid.log should be placed in whatever folder NTDSUTIL was run from.

# The Party Line

Microsoft discusses this problem and its solution in a KnowledgeBase article (419021), although it does not cover all of the possible reasons why this solution may not work. (As of this writing, the document itself is no longer available except in the Japanese edition of the KnowledgeBase, but it does not seem to have been moved or merged with any other documents.)

## *The Undocumented Solution*

*The solution listed here is culled from Microsoft's documents with some additional comments.*

## What You'll Need

The NTDSUTIL utility, which should be present on any domain controller

To clean up a duplicate SID:

1. Start NTDSUTIL and connect to the server as described in the previous steps (by typing **connect to server <servername>**).
2. Once you are connected, type **cleanup duplicate sid** and press ENTER. You will receive confirmation of the removal.
3. Type **q** and then press ENTER twice to quit the program.

If you are using Exchange 2000, use the Active Directory Cleanup Wizard instead, which searches the Active Directory for duplicate accounts and then allows you to merge those accounts together into a single account.

The bad news is that the wizard does not always find duplicate SIDs, because of some limitations on its behavior: It can't merge objects between forests or merge enabled objects in different domains within the same forest (you must move them into the same domain first). For these reasons you may need to run the auditing previously described and then selectively delete duplicate accounts, rather than merge or perform automatic cleanup on them.

Another problem that is somewhat related to this one is when there are two different SIDs sharing the same alias or object name. When this happens, a domain will display an alias with :*<sid#>* appended to it. This may happen if an object with the same exact name is created on two domain controllers in between two replications intervals, or when one of the controllers is down. In such a case, the offending object may need to be renamed for clarity's sake.

#  Removing Orphaned Domains from Active Directory Without Demoting Domain Controllers

A domain and its servers are referred to as "orphaned" from Active Directory when there is no active domain controller for the domain.

## Overview

An "orphaned" domain can happen if the only domain controller for a domain has failed and cannot be recovered at all, or if some domain controllers were physically removed (shut off, unplugged from the network) without being demoted first. This rarely happens, but when it does, it can be messy.

---

## The Party Line                                      Company X

Microsoft strongly recommends having contingency plans against a failure of this magnitude, but they do have a rather sneaky technique for removing orphaned domains in the event of a catastrophe. It is, however, not a very clean solution: once you do this, the machines from the domain in question will not be able to access Active Directory without being reinstalled.

---

## *The Undocumented Solution*

*Deleting an orphaned domain is a two-step process. First, the computer entries have to be removed for the domain in question, and second, the domain itself has to be manually removed.*

## What You'll Need

- Administrator access on the Flexible Single Master Operation (FSMO) holder for the domain forest
- The NTDSUTIL utility, which should be installed by default on the FSMO holder

Follow these steps to delete an orphaned domain:

1. Go to the FSMO holder and launch the Sites and Servers MMC snap-in.

---

**NOTE**    In Windows 2000, the forest root is in Active Directory Sites and Services. In Windows Server 2003, the forest root is in Active Directory Domains and Trusts.

---

2. Remove the computer entry for each computer in the affected domain. Again, once you do this, they will not be able to access Active Directory without being reinstalled.
3. Close the Sites and Servers console.
4. From the command line, launch NTDSUTIL by typing **ntdsutil.**
5. Type **metadata cleanup** and press ENTER.
6. Type **connections** and press ENTER. Make sure you are logged in as a member of the Enterprise Administrators group for the FSMO holder.
7. Type **connect to server** *<servername>,* where *<servername>* is the server name for the FSMO holder. Press ENTER. If you get an error when connecting, make sure you are logged in with the correct credentials.
8. Type **quit** and press ENTER to bring up the Metadata Cleanup menu.
9. Type **select operation target** and press ENTER.
10. Type **list domain** and press ENTER to bring up a list of all domains and their associated numbers. The number is how the domain in question is to be removed.
11. Type **select domain** *<number>* to choose the appropriate domain, and press ENTER.
12. Type **quit** and press ENTER to bring up the Metadata Cleanup menu again.
13. Type **remove selected domain** and press ENTER to remove the domain in question.
14. Type **quit** and press ENTER to leave NTDSUTIL.

---

**NOTE**    All the domain controller entries for the domain have to be removed first, or an error— DsRemoveDomainW-Error 0x216—will occur if you try to remove the domain.

---

**CHAPTER 7**

IIS and Active Directory

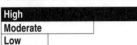 # Removing Data from Active Directory After an Unsuccessful Domain Controller Demotion

| High |
|------|
| **Moderate** |
| Low |

An unsuccessful domain controller demotion can leave garbage data in Active Directory that can cause problems and possibly contribute to AD corruption in the future.

## Overview

When a server is demoted from being a domain controller, an Active Directory object named "NTDS Settings" corresponding to that server is removed. NTDS Settings objects exist as children to the server object in the Active Directory Sites and Services Manager. Among the attributes in this object are data that describe its Global Catalog status, how the domain controller is identified to its replication partners (even if it has none at the time), naming contexts for the machine, and other important AD metadata.

If a server is demoted incorrectly or the demotion process does not work, the NTDS Settings object may not be removed correctly. In such a case, the object will need to be manually yanked.

---

## The Party Line                                         Company X

Microsoft strongly recommends against removing AD objects "by hand" unless you have a very good reason to do so. They're right, but removing an improperly deleted AD server reference object is as good a reason as any.

---

## *The Undocumented Solution*

*As with removing an orphaned domain, the way to delete an NTDS Settings object is by using the NTDSUTIL utility.*

## What You'll Need

- The NTDSUTIL utility, included when you have Active Directory running
- Administrative access to the server that is the Flexible Single Master Operation (FSMO) holder

Here are the steps:

1. From the command line, launch NTDSUTIL by typing **ntdsutil**.

2. Type **metadata cleanup** and press ENTER.

3. Type **connections** and press ENTER. Make sure you are logged in as a member of the Enterprise Administrators group for the FSMO holder.

4. Type **connect to server** *<servername>*, where *<servername>* is the server name for the FSMO holder. Press ENTER. If you get an error when connecting, make sure you are logged in with the correct credentials.

5. Type **quit** and press ENTER to bring up the Metadata Cleanup menu.

6. Type **select operation target** and press ENTER.

7. Type **list domain** and press ENTER to bring up a list of all domains and their associated numbers.

8. Type **select domain** *<number>* to choose the appropriate domain, and press ENTER.

9. Type **list sites** and press ENTER. Select the appropriate site by typing **select site** *<number>* and pressing ENTER.

10. Type **list servers in site** and press ENTER. Select the server in question by typing **select server** *<number>* and pressing ENTER.

11. Type **quit** and press ENTER to bring up the Metadata Cleanup menu.

12. Type **remove selected server** and press ENTER. If you get an error (such as "Error 8419 (0x20E3): The DSA object could not be found"), the object may have already been deleted.

13. Type **quit** and press ENTER to leave NTDSUTIL.

14. Using your DNS administration tools, remove the cname record in the _msdcs.<rootdomainforforest> DNS zone. You need to clean out the DNS record to make sure the old DNS record is not used with any newly promoted servers.

15. Delete the computer account for the server from Active Directory using ADSIEdit, in OU=Domain Controllers, DC=domain.

16. Delete the FRS member object in CN=Domain System Volume (SYSVOL share), CN=file replication service, CN=system.

17. If this was the last member of a deleted domain, also delete the trustDomain object for the child in CN=System, DC=domain, DC=domain, Domain NC.

CHAPTER
7

IIS and Active Directory

#  Handling Windows 2003 DNS Requests over 512 Bytes

| High |
|---|
| **Moderate** |
| Low |

Windows 2003's DNS server can send UDP packets larger than 512 bytes to a remote DNS server, but some routers and firewalls are not configured to handle UDP packets of this size.

## Overview

Windows 2003 behaves slightly differently than Windows 2000 when it comes to sending UDP packets greater than 512 bytes. If a router or firewall rejects these packets because of their size (as is often the case), Windows 2003 will *not* retransmit them, as Windows 2000 did.

---

## The Party Line                                    `Company X`

```
Microsoft has two recommendations: modify the router
or firewall in question (not always a realistic option,
since the firewall or router may not be configurable by the
administrator), or use the DNSCMD tool to change this behavior.
```

---

## *The Undocumented Solution*

*One of the support tools on the Windows 2003 CD-ROM is named DNSCMD. It modifies various behaviors of the Microsoft DNS server. One of the functions that can be changed is to force DNS to send UDP packets that are less than 512 bytes in size at all times.*

To do this, install the DNSCMD tool and type

```
dnscmd /Config /EnableDnsProbes 0
```

This turns off the DNS server's advertising for EDNS (which allows UDP packets larger than 512 bytes), and will also cause it to stop honoring such packets when they are received.

# Moving or Backing Up DNS Information on Windows Servers

`2000/2003`

| High |
|---|
| Moderate |
| Low |

> **NOTE** Thanks to jsiinc.com for details on this technique.

Rather than reconstruct DNS information, some of which is vital to Active Directory, it may be easier and better to simply relocate it when moving from one server to another.

## Overview

Microsoft's DNS server maintains information not only for conventional DNS lookups but for zone information used by Active Directory. For that reason, keeping backup copies of the DNS zone data can be useful. It's also possible to relocate the DNS zone information from one Windows server to another.

> ## The Party Line                       Company X
>
> ```
> Microsoft has no built-in provision for backing up, restoring,
> or migrating DNS information other than performing a whole
> system backup.
> ```

### The Undocumented Solution

*As it turns out, it is not only possible to move or back up DNS zone information, but it's relatively easy as well.*

## What You'll Need

A Registry editor

> **NOTE** This technique only works with Microsoft's own DNS server. It will not work with ports of BIND or other third-party DNS servers.

CHAPTER
7

IIS and Active Directory

Here are the steps needed to perform DNS backup or migration:

1. If you're migrating to a new machine, install DNS on the target server but leave it unconfigured.

2. Go to the current DNS server and change any Active Directory integrated zones to standard primary. This will create the zone files needed for the copy.

3. Stop the DNS server service(s).

4. Copy out the *%systemroot%*\system32\DNS folder from the source server. If you are copying to a new system, you can copy it directly into the same folder on the target system. If not, this is the first part of your backup.

5. Open the Registry and export the branch HKEY_LOCAL_MACHINE\System\ CurrentControlSet\Services\DNS\Zones to a .REG file. This is the second part of your backup.

6. If you are moving servers, launch the .REG file on the target server to import it.

7. Shut off the old server and change the new server's IP address (if needed) to match the old one.

8. Restart the DNS Server service on the target machine.

9. Type **iconfig /registerdns** to reload the server's A and PTR records.

10. Type **netdiag /fix** to register the SRV records.

11. If the new server is a domain controller, convert the Active Directory standard primary zones back to integrated zones.

---

**NOTE**   This technique does not copy over any interface, forwarder, root hint, or logging or security information. It only copies zone data.

---

# `2000/2003` Using Third-Party DNS Servers

Even though Microsoft provides its own DNS server with Windows 2000 and 2003, many administrators may opt to use a simple port of BIND or a third-party DNS server product.

## Overview

One common use for Windows 2000 and 2003 Server is as an Internet gateway—a proxy server or connection-sharing system. Normally, when Windows is configured for this, it uses the DNS servers of the provider or ISP rather than a local DNS server (unless it's specifically configured to use a local DNS server instead). Many people who rely on remote-hosted DNS servers for lookups find that they're simply not that reliable. During heavy traffic, lookups can timeout constantly. Windows (both server and workstation) is supposed to cache DNS lookups, although even caching doesn't always provide reliable results.

Windows 2000 and 2003 both come with an internal DNS server as a standard feature, which is also used by Active Directory to manage its own zone information. (If you install AD, you must either install the Microsoft DNS server or assure the machine that you have one running.) On a smaller server, one devoted to sharing and/or routing, running Microsoft's DNS server on top of everything else might be burdensome. The best answer for this (and other) scenario(s) may be to simply run a third-party DNS solution.

## The Party Line                              `Company X`

```
Microsoft doesn't disallow the use of third-party DNS, but
it doesn't go out of its way to recommend such a thing,
either. Much as they bundle IE as their web browser, the
Microsoft DNS server is bundled with Windows 2000 and 2003
as being their DNS solution of choice.
```

## *The Undocumented Solution*

*The original DNS server is BIND, now currently in its ninth iteration. Since BIND is a universal standard, platform binaries exist for almost every conceivable operating system—including 32-bit Windows. Both binaries and source code for BIND can be downloaded directly from the ISC at http://www.isc.org/products/BIND/bind9.html. Many administrators who are already used to using BIND in a UNIX environment find it a lot more dependable than Microsoft's DNS.*

There are also third-party versions of BIND. One of the best and least expensive is BIND-PE (http://ntcanuck.com). BIND-PE is small enough and designed intelligently enough to run not only on Windows server products, but workstations as well—this is useful if you're using a Windows XP Professional machine as a gateway, for instance. The program installs and configures itself automatically, and all the administrator needs to do is redirect all DNS lookups to 127.0.0.1 or localhost. The one drawback to the program: it's provided free but has no technical support at all. Nevertheless, it is elegant and well-written enough that none is really needed.

# Editing Registry Settings for Crash Logging

| High |
|---|
| **Moderate** |
| Low |

The behavior of the Dr. Watson debug/crash dump tool can be modified to suit the needs of a particular administrator.

## Overview

Many Windows administrators are by now familiar with the infamous Dr. Watson (drwtsn32.exe), the crash dump and error debugging tool that pops up whenever a Win32 program goes awry. As Windows has matured, though, Dr. Watson tends to pop up less—my current Windows 2000 server hasn't Dr. Watsoned once on any program since it went live!—but that doesn't mean an administrator shouldn't be aware of some of its less-documented behaviors.

---

## The Party Line                    Company X

```
Most of the documentation on how Dr. Watson behaves is written
for programmers rather than administrators. There's far less
overlap between programmers and system administrators than you
might think, so administrators usually wind up hearing very
little about Dr. Watson's configurability.
```

---

## *The Undocumented Solution*

*What follows is a list of some of the modifiable, and not always well-documented, behaviors of Dr. Watson.*

## What You'll Need

A Registry editor

Here is a rundown of some modifications to make to Dr. Watson:

1. Dr. Watson writes log files into a specific folder, but this folder can be redirected. To change it, open the Registry and navigate to HKEY_LOCAL_MACHINE\ SOFTWARE\Microsoft\DrWatson. Edit the REG_SZ entry named LogFilePath to point to a new repository for the crash logs.

2. Many third-party programs, such as Lotus Notes (and Microsoft's Visual Studio) replace Dr. Watson with another debugger entirely. Some administrators resent this (understandably!) and want to switch back to the original Dr. Watson. To do this, open the Registry and navigate to HKEY_LOCAL_MACHINE\SOFTWARE\ Microsoft\Windows NT\CurrentVersion\AeDebug. Edit the Debugger value (a REG_SZ value) to read:

```
drwtsn32 -p %ld -e %ld -g
```

3. If Dr. Watson stops writing crash events to the Application log, that may be because its own internal crash tracking has exceeded a pre-set limit. Open the Registry and navigate to HKEY_LOCAL_MACHINE\SOFTWARE\Microsoft\ DrWatson. Look for the values NumberOfCrashes and MaximumCrashes. MaximumCrashes is the maximum number of times per session that a crash can take place before Dr. Watson stops writing events to the system log (although it will continue to write crash events to its *own* log). You can increase the MaximumCrashes value to get around this.

4. Finally, if you want to *disable* Dr. Watson completely, open the Registry and navigate to HKEY_LOCAL_MACHINE\SOFTWARE\Microsoft\Windows NT\CurrentVersion\AeDebug. Set the DWORD named Auto to **0**. (Setting it to **1**, or typing **drwtsn32 -i** at the command line, restores Dr. Watson.)

---

**NOTE**    If Dr. Watson is causing a fault in user32.dll, odds are the program causing this exception is running as a service in an account that does not have local logon rights.

---

**CHAPTER**
**7**

IIS and Active Directory

# CHAPTER 8
## *Upgrades and Updates*

**In This Chapter:**

- ☐ Upgrading VBScript and JScript Components
- ☐ Upgrading Windows Database Components
- ☐ Managing Multiple Updates Across Many Machines
- ☐ Manually Setting the Service Pack Level
- ☐ Disabling Windows File Protection
- ☐ Working with Changes to Task Scheduler from SP3 to SP4
- ☐ Deploying Microsoft Office Updates

The saying goes, "Update early, update often." That's the phrase I hear bandied about a lot in the IT community, and it has never been truer. On the one hand, the sheer breadth and connectedness of the user and administrator populace means that if a product has a bug or an exploit, word of it gets out very fast. On the other hand, when it comes to such problems, Microsoft generally attends to the more urgent ones quickly.

Even though Microsoft has automated the process of updating Windows and many of its component products, an administrator still needs to know the ins and outs of how to use these tools correctly. Even the most self-evident ones, such as Windows Update, have quirks and eccentricities that need to be called out, and there are many update tools that most administrators don't even know exist. On top of that, there are third-party products that can also take a good deal of the pain out of updating.

The number of guises a Microsoft update can come in is, in itself, striking. Microsoft Update packages are the most obvious, which include service packs for all their operating systems. Then there are post-service pack hotfixes, not all of which are made available through Microsoft Update. In addition, there are upgrades to system components like DirectX, VBScript, the database connectivity layer, and, of course, upgrades for their own separately packaged products: Microsoft Office, SQL Server (both 7.0 and 2000), Exchange Server, and on and on.

This chapter deals with managing and handling upgrades, and as a result it varies slightly from the usual format of the other chapters. In some cases, there is no dichotomy between Party Line and Undocumented Solution—rather, they will be consolidated, with a detailed explanation of what the Party Line consists of, and how to use it effectively.

# 2000/2003 Upgrading VBScript and JScript Components

The Windows Scripting Host subsystem in Windows has become one of its cornerstone technologies, supporting everything from shell scripts to several Active Server Pages (ASP) technologies. Keeping it up-to-date is also essential. When it comes to security holes, it's unfortunately one of the biggest thorns in Microsoft's side, no thanks to the sheer magnitude of exploits that use VBScript as their mode of operation.

## Overview

Both the VBScript and JScript engines are part of Microsoft Windows Script, a set of interlocked technologies that provide scripting capability for system components and the OS itself. ASP programmers should be intimately familiar with either JScript or VBScript as one of their main languages—both are driven by the Windows Script subsystem.

As of this writing, the most recent version of the Windows Script engine is 5.6, released April 23, 2003. Ever since its inception, it has undergone a good deal of rewriting and revising, and seems to have achieved a relatively stable plateau of development for the time being. The reason for its lack of continued development since then may be because Microsoft is positioning C# (via Windows 2003) as the ultimate replacement for VBScript. In the meantime, however, the support for VBScript in Windows is quite solid, so don't expect VBScript or JScript to disappear anytime soon.

An out-of-the-box installation of Windows 2000, even one patched with the most recent service pack, may not sport the latest Windows Script engine. To make sure that it's being run, visit http://msdn.microsoft.com/library/default.asp?url=/downloads/list/webdev.asp to download a copy of the script engine for the appropriate platform.

> **NOTE**   If you *want* to install a prior version of Windows Script as a way of testing backwards compatibility or to see how support for a particular feature (or elimination of a given bug) has fared, you can do this. When you click the link to download the latest Windows Script engine, select Windows Script for the appropriate OS, and then select Download Other Script Versions in the box on the right-hand side of the subsequent page. You will be able to download Windows Script engines from 5.1 on. Earlier versions of Windows Script are no longer supported or provided.

Most of the changes from version to version of Windows Script involve either bug fixes or addressing memory leaks. The latter is actually the most significant; the early versions of Windows Script were plagued with bugs that caused, among other things, improperly disposed programmatic objects to leak memory. When running desktop scripts, this is not that big an issue, since the script engine is loaded and unloaded on each script run, but for an environment like ASP—where the script engine is cached in memory and runs more or less continuously—this can be deadly. Windows Server 2003 and IIS 6.0 sport features to better deal with components that leak memory, such as "rolling over" script engine requests into a newly- loaded iteration of the script .DLL. But the best solution is, of course, to fix the underlying leak. One way to avoid this in VBScript and JScript is simply to adhere to good programming practice: any object created with the **set** command needs to be set to **nothing.** For instance, in VBScript,

```
Set Foo=Server.CreateObject("ADODB.RecordSet")
```

needs to be cleaned up with

```
Close Foo
Set Foo=Nothing
```

More recent versions of the Windows Script engine recover far more gracefully from undisposed objects, although it's never a bad idea to implement solid code hygiene. In the event such a bug returns in the future, good code is an excellent first line of defense.

## 2000/2003 **Upgrading Windows Database Components**

| High |
| Moderate |
| Low |

Microsoft's database middleware, like its scripting components, is relied on heavily in many instances, and should be kept up-to-date to prevent performance issues.

## Overview

Built into Windows is a set of data access technologies that Microsoft collectively refers to as MDAC (Microsoft Data Access Technologies). Also included in this software layer are the Microsoft Data Engine (MSDE) and, more recently, ADO.NET. All of these components work together to help programs get data from databases, or from other programs that work with data such as SQL Server.

MDAC exists to allow any two programs that talk to each other in a common way to share formatted data. The most common use for MDAC is to have a front-end program (such as an ASP or ASP.NET application) access a back-end data repository (SQL Server, Oracle, or even a plain, old comma-delimited file). Rather than have to deal with each program, data source, or data type separately every time you sit down to write a new program, MDAC simplifies the connection between the two so you only have to use one common interface. Many system administrators who are not themselves programmers are not entirely clear about what MDAC is for, or why it's needed, or why it needs to be kept up-to-date. Given how many web sites are data-driven, MDAC and its associated pieces are more important than ever.

As of this writing, the most recent version of MDAC is 2.8. However, there are a number of different downloads available in Microsoft's Data Access Downloads section (in http://msdn.microsoft.com/library/default.asp?url=/downloads/list/dataaccess.asp). Not all of them may be relevant to your needs, so download and install only the ones you believe most useful.

### Microsoft Data Access Components (MDAC)

The core MDAC components are the most commonly used drivers for accessing data sources from programs, such as SQL Server, FoxPro, and MS Access. Non-Microsoft products such as Oracle or Sybase need their own MDAC drivers, and need to be downloaded separately. (When installed, they will integrate with the existing MDAC driver set.)

---

**NOTE**    If you are running SQL Server 7.0 or 6.5 clustered installations, do *not* install MDAC 2.6 RTM or later. Doing so will break the cluster.

---

## MDAC Utility: Component Checker Version 2.7

Component Checker Version 2.7 is an immensely useful little utility that audits your system and determines which MDAC components you have present. If you are testing a system or a whole slew of systems, you can use this to determine what, if anything, needs to be installed. When unpacked and executed, the program gives you several choices for how the analysis is to be run: an automatic check, a check against a specific version of MDAC, or a scan without an analysis, as shown in Figure 8-1.

Once the Component Checker is run (which may take several minutes), the results are provided in a tree format, along with an at-a-glance summary report. In the example shown in Figure 8-2, the only component found on this machine that was out-of-date was the Microsoft Jet database engine (MSJTES40.DLL), used for accessing Microsoft Access databases and also for handling many of the internal databases that Windows works with. Each type of component, both ODBC and OLEDB, is also broken out, so you can determine what components are installed and functional. If you are experiencing problems with a particular ODBC or OLEDB component, running this scan might help determine if it's not installed correctly.

## Microsoft Data Access Components 2.6 SDK

For programmers only, the Microsoft Data Access Components 2.6 SDK is used to build applications that use data access components "under the hood." ASP programmers using VBScript or JScript do *not* need to use this—this is only for C++, C# or Visual Basic programmers who want direct access to the components. (VBScript and JScript already have built-in programmatic interfaces for MDAC.)

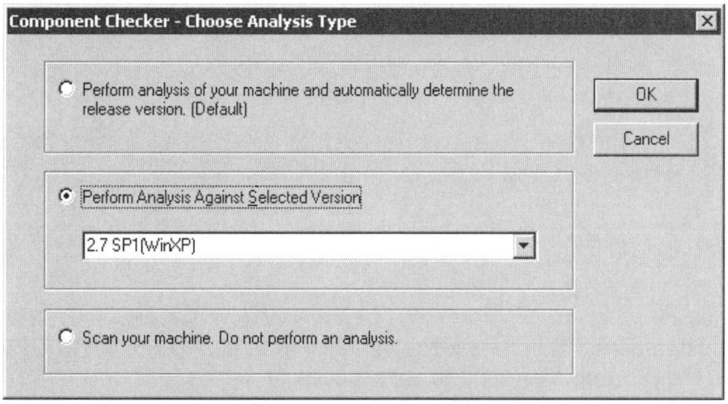

CHAPTER
8

Upgrades and Updates

**Figure 8-1.** The scanning/analysis options offered by the MDAC Utility

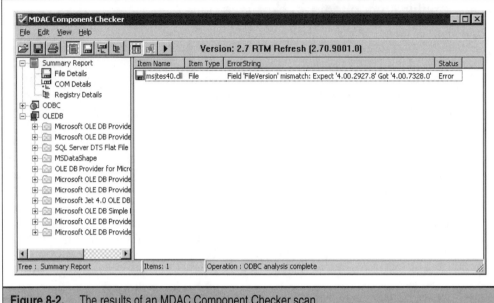

**Figure 8-2.**    The results of an MDAC Component Checker scan

## Microsoft SQL Server 2000 Desktop Engine

The Microsoft SQL Server 2000 Desktop Engine (MSDE), built using SQL Server 2000's core technology, is used for creating applications that require a robust and redistributable data engine for certain functions. This is again for programmers and developers; if you have a copy of SQL Server running locally on your server, you don't need to use this, since updates to SQL Server will also update its data engine.

## Jet 4.0 Service Pack 7

Jet 4.0 Service Pack 7, the most recent service pack for the Jet database engine, is used in Access, and also used in Windows itself for many common functions. Having an updated copy of the Jet engine is actually a good idea even if you don't use Access, because many other applications, both desktop- and server-based, rely on it, as well as DHCP and WINS.

---

**NOTE**    If you are using an Alpha processor, note that the last version of MDAC available for Alpha is 2.61.7326.6 (the pre-2.6 SP1 edition). Development for Alpha has been discontinued in favor of IA-64 at this point, and Windows 2000–2003 have never supported Alpha.

---

## Visual FoxPro ODBC Driver Setups

MDAC 2.6 and later no longer come with Visual FoxPro drivers, since Visual FoxPro has been discontinued. Nevertheless, the program remains in wide legacy use. If you are using FoxPro for any of your development, or if you have legacy products that require it, you need to download the MDAC drivers for Visual FoxPro separately and install them *after* upgrading the rest of MDAC.

## 2000/2003 Managing Multiple Updates Across Many Machines

| High |
| Moderate |
| **Low** |

Keeping Windows up-to-date across many machines can be tiring and difficult without proper support, but various tools exist to spare an administrator from having to do the job by hand.

## Overview

When an administrator only has one server to deal with, managing upgrades is difficult enough. As detailed here, the process of keeping a Windows server up-to-date doesn't just consist of visiting Windows Update every so often; many of the more important updates that relate to servers are not published there. Manually plowing through all of the disparate sites that Microsoft keeps—Windows Update, the MDAC site, the security bulletin site, and on and on—can become exhausting.

> ## The Party Line                    Company X
>
> Microsoft has future plans for eventually consolidating all of these variegated update locations into one super-update system, but that hasn't happened yet. In the meantime, administrators still have to scurry from one site to another.

*CHAPTER 8*

*Upgrades and Updates*

## The Undocumented Solution

*There's a better way than picking up all the pieces by hand. As a matter of fact, there are several, including both Microsoft and third-party products that perform auditing of needed downloads in Windows for you.*

## Microsoft HFNetChk 3.82

HFNetChk, or Hotfix Network Check, from Microsoft, allows an administrator to audit one or more machines to determine whether or not they have particular security or post–service pack hotfixes installed. The program downloads a copy of an XML database, maintained by Microsoft, and compares that information against a manifest of currently installed system components. If anything is missing or not up-to-date, the program produces a report about what is missing and where to obtain it, as seen in Figure 8-3. The program even alerts you about updated versions of itself.

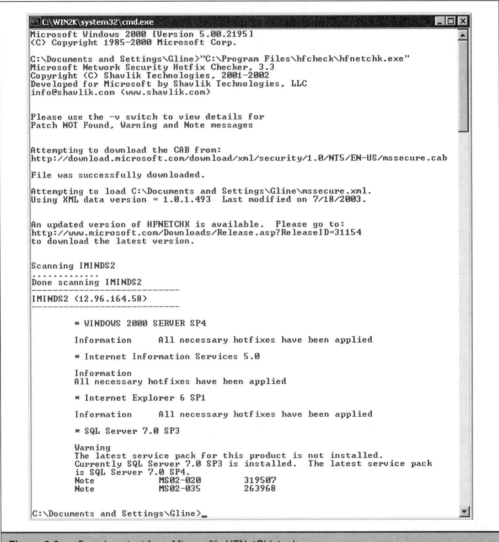

**Figure 8-3.**    Sample output from Microsoft's HFNetChk tool

---

**NOTE**    If you are using the Microsoft Baseline Security Analyzer (MBSA) version 1.1.1 or later, you already have HFNetChk installed—it should be available in the same directory as that program. MBSA is considered to be somewhat problematic, however, but at least you can resort to the command-line HFNetChk with it.

---

## Gravity Storm Software Service Pack Manager 2000

A particularly well-regarded and extremely powerful third-party product for patch and upgrade management is Service Pack Manager 2000 from Gravity Storm Software (http://www.securitybastion.com/). Its detection and reporting capabilities for upgrades and needed security fixes are not limited to Windows 2000 or 2003 alone; it can also report on known security vulnerabilities and stability problems in Windows NT/2000/XP/2003 and additional Microsoft products, such as IIS, Exchange, SQL, ISA, IE, Outlook, and Windows Media Player. The newest version of the product as of this writing, 6.9.5.0, has many features HFNetChk doesn't have, including: template-based custom reporting (so you can show hotfixes or machines that match or that are excluded from specific criteria); custom user and machine groups that can be defined by the administrator; intelligent severity ratings for the hotfixes (so that, for example, one hotfix that is eclipsed by another, later hotfix is given a low priority); on-the-fly filtering of results; remote maintenance features (which allow you to install a hotfix or service pack over the network to one or more machines); and many more. Administrators in an environment with as few as ten or more machines will find it a boon. I was able to use it effectively in a setup where I had only six.

A sample Service Pack Manager screen can be seen in Figure 8-4. The program can query via network group, IP address range, or predefined machine listings, and produces easily tabulated and analyzed results either in the program itself or in a formattable report.

## BigFix Patch Manager 3.0

Another highly-regarded patch manager product is BigFix Patch Manager (http://www.bigfix.com), now in its 3.0 revision. Patch Manager is written from a security-enhancement point of view rather than from a latest-update perspective. The program monitors Microsoft Security Bulletins, not only through conventional Windows Update, but through TechNet and the Windows Corporate Update sites.

What's unique about Patch Manager is that it's proactive: it monitors all the machines on the network continuously and redeploys approved patches if a machine gets modified in such a way that it falls out of compliance. The program also includes comprehensive reporting that can be accessed via either the BigFix Enterprise console or a web browser. It's also programmable—with the BigFix Development Environment an administrator can create and deploy custom changes and product updates. Administrators looking to use their patch-management system for something slightly more ambitious than just pushing out updates should look into this.

**CHAPTER 8**

**Upgrades and Updates**

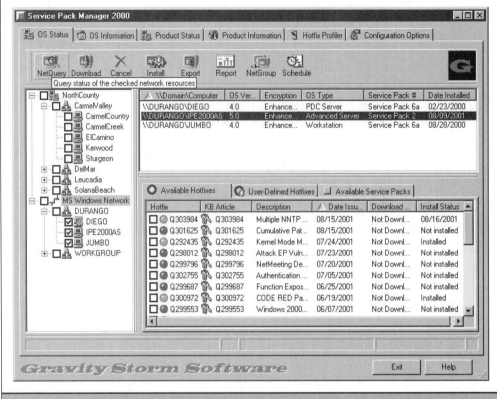

**Figure 8-4.**   Service Pack Manager 2000 6.9.5.0 in action, probing a network for needed service packs and hotfixes on a group of machines

2000/2003 # Manually Setting the Service Pack Level

The Service Pack level in Windows can be manually changed for the sake of testing, to correct problems with a misapplied service pack, or to force backwards compatibility.

## Overview

The Service Pack level of Windows 2000 and 2003 is a key system setting. Normally, this is only changed whenever a new service pack is applied or when the current one is rolled back (if, for instance, a new service pack breaks compatibility with applications or doesn't install correctly). The administrator is not allowed to directly edit the value of the current service pack, which is stored in the Registry and not exposed through an administrative interface.

## The Party Line

**Company X**

Microsoft has good reason to keep service pack revision information out of harm's way, as it were: changing it willy-nilly can create real problems, ranging from program incompatibility to an unbootable system.

## *The Undocumented Solution*

*With a little care, you can change the Service Pack level if it's needed. The Service Pack level is recorded in the Registry as a simple editable value, and can be changed by an administrator. Just remember to observe the highest level of caution and not attempt this on a production machine without sufficient safeguards, as the results can be unpredictable.*

**CHAPTER 8**

**Upgrades and Updates**

### What You'll Need

A Registry editor

Here are the steps for modifying the Service Pack level:

1. Open the Registry and navigate to HKEY_LOCAL_MACHINE\SOFTWARE\ Microsoft\Windows NT\CurrentVersion.

2. Edit the REG_SZ value named CSDVersion. To set this to a specific Service Pack level, change it to **Service Pack <level>**, where <level> is a number. For instance, to force Service Pack 1, set the value to **Service Pack 1**.

3. Reboot.

**NOTE** If on rebooting you experience a crash, reboot using the Last Known Good configuration to reset the Service Pack level.

# Disabling Windows File Protection

| High |
| Moderate |
| Low |

Windows File Protection technology could once be disabled easily but now requires more active intervention to circumvent.

## Overview

Microsoft introduced Windows File Protection into Windows 2000 and later editions of Windows as a way of preventing key system files from being overwritten, either by mistake or by a hostile program or user.

A backup copy of all the system files kept safe by WFP is held in a protected directory on the system (by default, *%systemroot%*\system32\dllcache), and if the system detects that a key file has been overwritten or changed, it is replaced with a backup copy. It is also possible to scan a system on demand and detect if components have been changed or overwritten. The system is set up to automatically protect all files with the extensions ax, cpl, cpx, dll, exe, fon, inf, ocx, rsp, sys, tff, and tlb.

Windows allows the WFP cache to be updated whenever a service pack, a post-SP hotfix, or a Windows Update package is installed. Another (sneakier) way to change the system file is to manually copy an updated file into the dllcache folder, and then attempt to replace the system file itself. This provokes a file replacement from the dllcache folder—and since WFP doesn't know that the cached copy has been modified, it simply copies it out faithfully. (This is only possible for an administrative user; a program cannot do this.) Unfortunately, this method is not very dependable.

In certain circumstances, the administrator may need to bypass WFP *completely*—for instance, to forcibly insert a modified version of a system .DLL for regression testing or experimentation. The original shipped version of Windows 2000 allowed you to disable WFP by simply editing a Registry setting, but all versions of Windows 2000 containing Service Pack 2 and later (this includes Windows 2003 and Windows XP, all editions) do not allow you to do this.

## The Party Line                                    Company X

Microsoft instituted tight controls over WFP behavior as a way of guarding against possible security problems. The whole point of WFP in the first place was to prevent unscrupulous users and malicious programs from trashing system files. As a result, Windows 2000 from Service Pack 2 onwards, Windows XP, and Windows 2003 all have WFP switched on permanently. Group Policy and editing the Registry alone have no effect on WFP background scanning.

## *The Undocumented Solution*

*There is a way to disable WFP, but it is risky, for several reasons. It requires that the administrator manually patch a system .DLL file, an "after-market modification," which will in effect void your OS's warranty! However, if you are doing this under controlled circumstances, then you can afford to experiment freely.*

**NOTE**   Make a full system backup, or at least keep backups of the patched .DLL files, before attempting any of this.

# What You'll Need

- A Registry editor
- A hex editor, for editing files on the binary level

Here are the steps for disabling Windows File Protection in Windows 2000:

1. Make a backup copy of the file SFC.DLL in the *%systemroot%*\system32 directory.

2. Make a backup copy of the file SFC_OS.DLL, also in the *%systemroot%*\ system32 directory.

3. Make *another* copy of SFC.DLL (called **SFC_1.DLL**) and open that copy in a hex editor.

4. Go to offset 6211 hex in the file and look for the hex values 8B and C6. If you cannot find these values there, *do not continue.*

5. If you do find them, change 8B C6 to 90 90 and save the changes.

6. Type the following commands to copy the system files back in:

```
copy %systemroot%\system32\sfc1.dll %systemroot%\system32\sfc.dll /y
copy %systemroot%\system32\sfc1.dll
%systemroot%\system32\dllcache\sfc.dll /y
```

   Be sure to replace *%systemroot%* with the path to your \WINDOWS or \ WINNT directory.

7. If you are prompted to insert your Windows CD-ROM, click Cancel.

8. Restart Windows.

Here are the steps for disabling Windows File Protection in Windows 2003:

1. Make a backup copy of the file SFC.DLL in the *%systemroot%*\system32 directory.

2. Make a backup copy of the file SFC_OS.DLL, also in the *%systemroot%*\ system32 directory.

3. Make *another* copy of SFC_OS.DLL (called **SFC_OS_1.DLL**) and open that copy in a hex editor.

4. Go to offset E2B8H hex in the file and look for the hex values 8B and C6. If you cannot find these values there, check the offset E3BB. If you cannot find 8B C6 there either, *do not continue*. Odds are, changes have been made that make this tip invalid, and there is no sense in randomly hacking the file.

5. If you do find them, change 8B C6 to 90 90 and save the changes.

6. Type the following commands to copy the system files back in:

```
copy %systemroot%\system32\sfc_os1.dll %systemroot%\system32\sfc_os.dll /y
copy %systemroot%\system32\sfc_os1.dll %systemroot%\system32\dllcache\sfc_os.dll /y
```

   Be sure to replace *%systemroot%* with the path to your \WINDOWS or \ WINNT directory.

7. If you are prompted to insert your Windows CD, click Cancel.

8. Restart Windows.

Once you have done one of the preceding, do the following:

1. Open the Registry and navigate to HKEY_LOCAL_MACHINE\SOFTWARE\ Microsoft\Windows NT\CurrentVersion\Winlogon.

2. Edit the DWORD value SFCDisable and set it to FFFFFF9D hex.

3. Restart Windows once more.

# [2000] Working with Changes to Task Scheduler from SP3 to SP4

**NOTE**   Thanks to jsiinc.com for this tip.

Among the many changes to Windows 2000 in Service Pack 4 is a change in the way scheduled tasks run, which can cause existing scheduled tasks to break.

## Overview

Administrators who upgrade Windows 2000 to Service Pack 4 and have scheduled tasks running on the system in question may find that the scheduled tasks don't work correctly after the upgrade. Usually the way this manifests itself is that the status for the task is listed as "Could not start."

---

### The Party Line                                    Company X

```
Deinstalling Service Pack 4 does not solve the problem.
Installing SP4 converts the credentials database on the
system to a new format; removing the service pack does not
cause the credentials database to revert.
```

---

### *The Undocumented Solution*

The best workaround for this problem is to disable the Task Scheduler service before installing SP4, then re-enable it after SP4 has been installed. You will also need to re-enter each task's security credentials.

2000/2003 # Deploying Microsoft Office Updates

| High |
| Moderate |
| Low |

Microsoft Office is the one other product, aside from Windows, that is most widely used *and* frequently updated. Knowing how to do this can save you a lot of effort.

## Overview

Because of Microsoft Office's size and complexity, Microsoft issues updates and fixes for their *other* flagship product on a fairly regular basis. Most of these changes get rolled into regular service packs for Office, but keeping on top of the changes, to say nothing of rolling them out, can be daunting.

   Microsoft provides a way to install a group of updates across a whole slew of machines through a program called OHotFix, available at http://www.microsoft.com/office/ork/

xp/journ/Ohotfix.htm. OHotFix requires some configuration to get working—it doesn't "seek and deploy," to coin a phrase, automatically—but it is much easier to work with than performing dozens or hundreds of manual updates on different machines.

---

**NOTE**   OHotFix requires that Windows Installer version 1.1 or later be present on the target machines.

---

## What You'll Need

- The OHotFix tool
- The patches and updates for Office to be rolled out
- A network share that is accessible to all the machines that need to be patched
- The ability to set logon scripts for the machines in question, usually via policies

Here are the steps for using OHotFix:

1. Create a shared folder on a server that will be accessed by all the machines to be updated.

2. Unpack the OHotFix files into this directory: OHOTFIX.EXE, OHOTFIX.INI, and OHOTFIXR.DLL. The .INI file contains a great many options for OHotFix's behavior that you may want to read through and modify depending on your needs. (The file has its own internal documentation and is very detailed.)

3. Unpack the Windows Installer update files into another folder using the following syntax:

   ```
   <updatename>.exe /c /t:C:/<targetfolder>
   ```

   where *<updatename>* is the name of the update file, and *<targetfolder>* is another directory to unpack the update into.

---

**NOTE**   Don't unpack the update directly into the OHotFix folder; unpack it into another folder first to avoid overwriting anything.

---

4. Copy the MSP files from the unpacked update into the shared folder. If other copies of OHotFix or its attendant files are unpacked, do *not* copy them over.

5. Using policies, set up a logon batch script to map a drive letter to the share, run OHotFix.exe, and then disconnect the share when the updater finishes running.

OHotFix will run all available fixes in alphabetical order, and will also detect whether or not a given fix is present so it will not apply them unless it is needed. This way, new fixes can simply be unpacked and "dumped" into the shared folder as needed, and Office will be updated automatically on the next user logon.

# APPENDIX A

## Links

Internet links are by their very nature volatile. That said, it never hurts to have a few more of them to refer to if needed. Here I've compiled a short list of reference sites which are meant to be in keeping with the theme of the book, and which I recommend.

Many of these sites are either based in the United States or are biased towards American readers. For that I apologize in advance, although a number of them are working to broaden their coverage to relate to international English-speaking readers.

# Tips and Tricks

Microsoft is far from being the only source of information about their products. A whole host of independent and loosely affiliated sites have sprung up about Windows and its products, as well as the hardware it's run on. I've collected many of the best here, with some discussion about why they're significant or which readership they're aimed at. I've tried to focus on the IT/professional/administrator sites, but there are many other sites that are as good, if not better, which are devoted to a more general readership. Read for flavor.

## 15seconds.com

Also known as "4 Guys From Rolla" (4guysfromRolla.com), the 15 Seconds site is devoted to the intelligent and ingenious implementation of ASP and ASP.NET on Windows 2000 and 2003. I cut my teeth on ASP thanks to these fellows—their advice and lessons are delivered in plain English, and they delve into every conceivable topic on the board. They also take the time to explore (and explode) some of the myths and rumors about ASP behavior, such as what recordset types are more efficient than others, and what the fastest database retrieval methods really are (ODBC vs. non-ODBC, for instance). Anyone seriously interested in learning ASP in a hands-on, nuts-and-bolts way needs to read this site. There's also plenty of good information about server-level optimizations, but their emphasis on getting good performance is via good programming practice.

## ActiveWin.com

A subdivision of the ActiveNetwork, ActiveWin covers all Windows titles, including Windows 2000 and Windows Server 2003. The Windows 2003 section is a mite thin at the moment, with little more than a collection of KnowledgeBase articles and a bunch of links back to Microsoft's own site, but the Windows 2000 section is a veritable goldmine of goodies, all broken out by topic. Among the subjects covered: clustering, Windows 2000 on laptops, step-by-step guides, licensing, required utilities, and tons more. They also go into detail about what's fixed (or not fixed) in each Service Pack, so I expect to see similar coverage for Windows 2003 once they really get that section rolling.

# Annoyances.org

Aside from the wonderful name (and it really is fitting here), Annoyances.org is one of *the* most thorough, in-depth, nitty-gritty problem-solver sites of any kind, anywhere. Register with the site, and you can post your own annoyance and describe it in detail—and have a quorum of experts post solutions for your problem. It's sort of like a massive interactive FAQ/message board, so if you find what looks like a solution to your problem, you can post it if it works—or post it if it doesn't—and potentially help other people who may be in the same bind as you! The vast majority of existing solutions, however, will probably be more than enough.

# Bootdisk.com

The venerable boot floppy lives on, despite every attempt to move past it or kill it off. And is that a bad thing? Maybe not, because you never know when you'll need a boot floppy to save the day. BootDisk.com is a repository for every conceivable variety of boot disk—DOS, non-DOS, you name it. A great resource for disks when you need to flash a BIOS, quick, and the disk builder supplied by the manufacturer isn't bootable (among many other horrible scenarios!).

# Experts-Exchange.com

Experts Exchange has some of the same flavor as Annoyances.org, but it's more professional and IT staffer–oriented than that site. The basic approach is the same, though: post a problem and have both the problem and the suggested answers peer-reviewed. When an answer comes along that is satisfying enough for you, you mark it so that other people searching for the same problem can see what answer you settled on and why. All problems are organized by topic and can be keyword searched. As with Annoyances.org, this is a fantastic reference for knotty problems of the "why does this have to happen to me?" ilk that don't seem to have any real solution.

# Is-it-true.org

Subtitled "Wayne's Windows Administrator Support Site," this is another excellent, hierarchically organized reference site with an emphasis on esoteric information about Windows NT and 2000, network hardware, and network security. Not much Windows 2003 information here (it's stored in the form of Windows XP tips, actually), but what there is here is quite splendid and easily searchable—although, like many sites of this ilk, sometimes it's just more fun to go stumbling across the treasures contained within.

# Jsiinc.com

A gold mine, plain and simple. The web site of JSI, Inc., an Atlanta-based computer consulting firm run by Jerold Schulman, is one of the best places anywhere to get amazingly meaty, useful information about all breeds of Windows. The site contains a "Tips and Tricks" section with over seven *thousand* tips (searchable, of course). In fact, many of the tidbits I found for this book were corroborated through his database. I used a few of the best with his permission, and I suppose the best way I can thank him is by recommending his site (and his business) without hesitation.

## learnasp.com

This was the other site I learned ASP (now ASP.NET) from. Charles Carroll's incredibly detailed, encyclopedic discussion of ASP and its derivatives breaks down into a series of "lessons," each demonstrating how to do a specific thing in ASP. Much of the best ASP advice you'll ever learn comes from this site, and Carroll has kept his material fresh and relevant with the appearance of ASP.NET as well. They also run a number of high-traffic mailing lists for discussion problems which are not specifically discussed in the site itself—post wisely and read thoroughly before posting, however, since the signal-to-noise ratio is kept very low.

## Onecomputerguy.com

"The main goal of this site is to provide clear, accurate and easy to understand information regarding Windows95/98/ME/2000/XP," reads the notice on the first page of Bob Cerelli's excellent, ad-free site, Onecomputerguy.com. Compiled within are gobs of tips on every subject imaginable, spelled out in plain English and of interest to everyone from the novice to the expert. Many of the XP tricks apply to Windows 2003, too, although there is, as yet, no 2003 section.

## PCQandA.com

If it's immediate, one-on-one (or one-on-fifty!) help you're looking for, the massive and massively friendly community of PCQandA.com is one of the best places to turn. Thousands of active users looking for answers (or giving them) log in daily, and the answers provided are courteous, technically spot-on, and in plain English (always a big help!). The "folks like you" feeling of the place is one of its biggest attractors; it's nice to get hard answers to hard tech questions without feeling like a mere number.

## searchwin2000.com

*Disclaimer: I write for this site.* SearchWin2000.com bills itself as "the web's best Windows 2000–specific information resource for enterprise IT professionals." That does indeed about sum it up; this site is a massive and very elegantly assembled collection of news, expert advice, tips, resources, external links, moderated discussions and live conferences. Membership is free but not mandatory.

## Windows.about.com

The venerable About.com pantheon of sites sports its own Windows subdivision, as you might imagine. But this is no bland me-too site: it's run by Douglas Ludens,

MCSE and CNE, and Director of Information Technology for MPI Research. Tips and resources in every conceivable category are here: clustering, Active Directory, ISA Server, Terminal Services, reviews of topically relevant books, and even tips specifically for the Alpha implementation of Windows NT. It's hard to go wrong.

## WinGuides.com

Subtitled "Empowering the Windows operating system," WinGuides is an elegantly designed and extremely in-depth set of resources on tweaking and tinkering with Windows. The emphasis is actually slightly more on desktop than server tweaking, but there's enough backend coverage to make it worth the trip with such subjects as security and Windows Script Host (my favorite for Most Underrated Windows Feature).

## Woram.com

My former *Windows* Magazine co-worker (or would that be co-conspirator?), John Woram, runs his own site, packed with interesting Registry-related tips and data. His emphasis is actually on Windows 9*x*, but he has kept on top of other Windows editions as well.

# News and Coverage

There's no shortage of news sites for technology out there, but all of them have their own specific biases, preferences, angles of coverage, and quirks. These are some of the best, most notable, and also the most talked-about (or even infamous) news sites which include Windows coverage as at least part of their territory.

## 2cpu.com

Are two CPUs better than one? These folks seem to think so, and have created a closely-knit community of enthusiasts and experts devoted to dual-CPU systems, both desktops and servers. Extremely in-depth discussion about which multi-CPU motherboards and processors are the best at what tasks, the right memory to use for specific types of multiprocessor systems, and quite a bit more. OS-specific discussion forums include Windows 2000 and 2003, with plenty of traffic in each.

## Anandtech.com

A close cousin to TomsHardware.com in both look and approach, Anandtech (run by computer engineering major Anand Lal Shimpi) does meaty, in-depth reviews of everything they can get their hands on: new CPU iterations, motherboards, chipsets, video cards, whole systems, storage, audio subsystems, memory, you name it. Claims are put to the test in explicit detail, and every component is put through exhaustive, rigorous benchmarking. The articles are dense, data-packed, loaded with photos, and never lacking in meaty details. "Nuts-and-bolts" folk will want to start here.

## ArsTechnica.com

Dubbed "the PC enthusiast's resource," ArsTechnica.com is more of a general issues-and-news discussion site than it is an in-depth technical resource. What's good is that it does have a very nice set of technical resources, the "Ars Technopaedia," which contains detailed explanations of thorny technical concepts like pipelining, superscalar execution, Moore's law, wireless network security, video capture, and many other subjects that are normally "just out of reach" but which here are made accessible and (gasp!) even easy. The prose is level-headed and genial, too.

## Bink.nu

Originally WindowsXP.nu, Bink.nu is a news-and-tips site run by Steven Bink, a Windows 2000+XP MCSE and MVP from Amsterdam. I owe him many thanks for some of his tips which have been featured here, but he's also a regular correspondent on all things Microsoft. (As I write this, he has a piece on his site about Visual Studio .NET 2005.) He also eats his own dog food, as the saying goes: the whole site runs on Windows Server 2003 and it says so quite proudly on the homepage.

## Cnet.com

The 900-pound gorilla of tech news, there's very little C | Net *doesn't* cover. Although it's written primarily for a consumer rather than an IT audience, that aspect actually helps it make some topics that a given IT person may not be familiar with more accessible—for instance, if you're an Exchange administrator suddenly pressed into service to set up wireless networking. Tons of the usual product reviews, news, and columnists round out the site's populist appeal, although real nuts-and-bolts coverage isn't typically their game.

## hardOCP.com

Dedicated to the hard-core high-performance crowd, Hard | OCP focuses on motherboards, chipsets, video cards and gameplay. They do tend to cover details of interoperability between components that might be overlooked elsewhere, so if you're assembling a high-end system by hand and want to learn more about the pieces of the puzzle, you can draw on them for additional details. They also run good instructional articles on modding and overlocking.

## kuro5hin.org

The folks at kuro5hin.org (pronounced "ku-ro-shin") are very much in the same arena as those at Slashdot.org, but are generally smarter and less condemnatory of particular OSes or platforms. A great deal of discussion of non-IT issues, such as science, tech culture, media, and even fiction can be found here. It's a nice way to get some wider perspective on things during your lunch break, and even a few good laughs.

# LabMice.net

The site would be worth checking out for the name alone, but there's more than just a cutesy moniker at work here. LabMice.net covers Windows 2000, XP, and 2003 from the IT manager's point of view—what's worth fixing, what's worth looking into, and what's worth playing around with. Among their resources is an excellent device-driver research repository (for finding just the right driver for that network card), and many well-organized links back into Microsoft resources. There's also a fun section named Cybercheese, with links to such goodies as Wil Wheaton's personal page (Wesley Crusher, nerd-at-large!) and the amazing HowStuffWorks.com site.

# Lockergnome.com

Tips, tips, and more tips! LockerGnome publishes a slew of free technology newsletters targeted at specific subjects (Windows, Mac, Linux, Internet developers, bargain hunters, and so on), but what's nice is that there's a lot of crossover interest from one newsletter to another. They also have a slew of other quirky offerings, such as GnomeJobs and GnomePersonals (meet that special IT expert you've been looking for, or hire them full-time, or both). They also hold a regular event, known as GnomeDex, and have tons of tutorials available as PDF downloads for easy offline perusal.

# NTBugTraq.com

One of the longest-lived and most respected sites for Windows NT/2K/XP/2K3 security exploits and bugs is NTBugTraq.com. Editor Russ Cooper is frequently quoted by major news outlets for his opinions and analysis of Microsoft product security, and the list has over 30,000 members and continues to grow. The list archives stretch back to March 1997 and are accessible for free and without a user account. Anyone serious about Windows security should get on the list and read it religiously. Journalists curious about the history of a given problem can dig through the archives for some real insight.

# SecurityFocus.com

A very comprehensive and opinionated security news and research site that covers not only Microsoft but Unix, as well as and many other platforms and subjects. Regular tracking of vulnerabilities, discussions of new books, guest articles, opinion columns, hands-on testing (a major resource), and more conventional news ("Probing the Half-Life of Bugs") from other sources make for interesting and broad-ranging reading.

# ServerFiles.com

ServerFiles.com is a directory of software *specifically* for network administrators and IT professionals. This site maintains a very thorough and categorically rich set of links to a staggering variety of material. They keep detailed notes on each program and allow for user feedback and comments as well. The one guiding rule is that this has to be stuff for servers and backend systems, not stand-alone desktops. If you're wondering if a particular application exists for your needs, start here—you may find more candidates that fit the bill than you imagined.

## Slashdot.org

No discussion of IT-related news sites would be complete without some mention of Slashdot.org, one of the most essential and infamous news portals in existence. Essential, because having something covered on Slashdot means potentially having it brought to the attention of millions of readers a day; infamous, because Slashdot's reputation for being anti-Microsoft often precedes it. That said, they often cover subjects that are simply not mentioned in many other places. The site runs on open-source portal code designed to help its readers filter out the signal from the noise, although it requires the diligence of its own readers to be effective.

## TechTutorials.com

TechTutorials.com is a regularly updated and peer-reviewed collection of links to resources on learning how to do almost everything in the tech world. Many tutorials listed are offsite links, but TechTutorials also maintains its own stash of tutorials, all of which are clearly worded and sport plenty of good illustrations.

## TheRegister.com

With a subhead like "Biting the hand that feeds IT," how can you go wrong? This is tech news from the UK with venom in its stinger. The upside is that they see right through the hype and self-serving hot air of most tech pronouncements and PR puff pieces; the downside is that they sometimes leap to conclusions about things. But in a field dominated by dry, humorless, and often witless writing, they're a welcome relief. (The O'Reilly book parodies are worth the visit alone.)

## TheTechZone.com

The Tech Zone is a friendly, close-knit, and splashily designed site for enthusiasts as well as IT folks, which has an active forum and plenty of in-depth product information. It also has a PriceWatch-like price-tracking system for bleeding-edge hardware. The articles cover the gamut from building your own Peltier-cooled beer mug (!) to creating an all-SCSI system from scratch.

## Tomshardware.com

Almost no other independent IT/hardware review site has garnered the respectability and breadth of readership that Tom's Hardware Guide has. There's a reason for that: Dr. Thomas Pabst, the chief editor of the site, knows his stuff inside and out. He is also unafraid to speak his mind: in the summer of 2000, he challenged Intel to stop shipping the 1.13 GHz PIII, citing reproducible problems in stability with the chipset. Incredibly, Intel obliged, realizing that alienating someone of his readership and clout would be lethal. There are many print magazines that are simply not this good. Anyone who is even casually interested in new hardware releases (or wants to get the most out of their current hardware) should stop by.

## Windows2000Faq.com

Windows 2000 Faq, also known as John Savill's FAQ for Windows, is a question-and-answer format site with no end of good stuff to dig through. John takes questions (and answers) from readers with an eye for the most useful and popular stuff, and organizes them by topic. Some recent questions: "How can I prevent users from disabling the Remote Desktop Sharing settings in Microsoft NetMeeting?" and "What alternatives do I have to Windows 2000 Server Terminal Services?"

# Shopping

Sooner or later, everyone's got to go shopping. I've encountered a great many IT folks, both formal and informal (for instance, those pressed into service as the resident IT person when there was no one else handy who fit the bill), who are constantly asking where to get the best prices on hardware and software. I've found a few, and rather than keep a good thing a secret, I've passed them along.

## Access Micro

In business since 1996, Access Micro (www.accessmicro.com) covers a lot of territory: simple parts, full systems, corporate and government volume sales. They also have their own brand of Intel- and Athlon-based desktops and notebook computers (from around US$1000 on up). Systems can be customized and shipped to order to a very high degree, on a par with what you'd expect from Dell or many of the other build-to-order outfits.

## Directron.com

This California-based factory-direct supplier of everything PC-related under the sun not only has excellent prices and customer satisfaction, but one of the better-organized sites I've ever seen. Whenever you choose to buy an item, you can also choose to add a great many related items: if you buy a motherboard, for instance, you can outfit it with CPUs, cables, power supply, chassis, and so on—without having to click away to another page. It makes shopping for a complete package of things painless and swift. I've ordered from them many times in the past and have never been disappointed. Do-it-yourselfers love the place, but others who are simply looking to pick up a few things cheap (a new monitor, say, or a batch of network cards) should take heed.

The site's one downside is that it doesn't stock particular brands consistently because of fluctuations in availability, but what it does have is usually good.

## Micro Warehouse

Micro Warehouse is a very browser- and shopper-friendly site that's run as part of the Ziff-Davis empire. It also features editorials in the form of the "MW Advisor." Prices are comparable to other sellers of this ilk, but Micro Warehouse stocks a broad range of common brands more consistently than some other sites (useful if you're doing comparison shopping), and also carries big-ticket items, like plasma displays, not sold elsewhere.

## Newegg.com

Another factory-direct site, with well organized shopping, good prices, and an incredible breadth of material to choose from is Newegg.com. It also has more consistent brand availability than Directron, although it doesn't quite have the quirky pleasures of stumbling over that site's offerings. System builders and people looking for an IT bargain should certainly check it out.

## PacificCable.com

The right cable for the right job can leave you grinding your teeth. Ever tried to find a replacement three-lobe Compaq-only notebook power supply cable? I did and it nearly drove me to drink at one point. PacificCable.com is a reseller that's devoted to nothing but cabling for computers—and they carry every conceivable variety and type of cable: fiber, SCSI, gender changers, KVM switch cables, token-ring, S-Video, coaxial, you name it. If they don't have it, chances are good they can find it, or even make it for you.

## Pricewatch.com

PriceWatch is not actually a store, but a "meta-shopping" site. They aggregate price listings from thousands of hardware and software vendors around the United States, and index them by product, category, vendor, and other topics. If you're searching for the best possible price on a particular piece of hardware (new or slightly used), this is one of the best places to start.

# APPENDIX B

## *Freeware, Shareware, and Trialware*

There is no end of freeware and shareware out there for Windows. Not all of it is good, though, and most of it is pitched at end users rather than administrators. That said, for this appendix I've done some research and come up with a slew of useful and diverse tools of interest to Windows 2000 and 2003 administrators. Almost all of these are free or are of low enough cost that they can be purchased with little more than pocket change (and if you like what you see, do the authors a favor and support them!).

## What's Available

At this point, there are legitimate demo versions of almost every program imaginable. Even Windows itself can be tried out in a 120-day evaluation version, and so can the vast majority of programs out there. Everything listed here is free unless otherwise described, although many of the non-free tools have separate site and user licensing agreements.

There is also probably no end of sites that catalog and list freeware and shareware. I've mentioned a few of them in the previous appendix, so if you don't see something you're looking for here, try browsing a bit.

## ArGoSoft Mail Server

One common complaint about Windows 2000's IIS 5.0 is that while it has an SMTP server, it does not have a POP server (Windows 2003 does). Enter ArGoSoft Mail Server (at http://www.argosoft.com), a free SMTP/POP server. It's a basic program, without many frills, but it gets the job done, and is intelligently written and secure enough to prevent hijackers from using your system as an open relay. Included with the program is a .DLL that allows scripting through your choice of language (Visual Basic and VBScript are the most common), so the mail system can be managed entirely from code. New to the most recent revision of the server is an optional web-based management interface. More advanced versions of the program (which run from $49 to $88) include features like mailing lists, ORDB and MAPS support, trusted/untrusted IP listing, multiple IP homing, and much more.

## BootIt Next Generation

When PartitionMagic and other non-destructive partition-editing programs first appeared, it really *did* seem like magic. System administrators and server hacks loved it: they could re-do the partitions of their systems without having to tediously tear everything apart and reinstall it. But it came with a price tag—a literal one, one which many of them couldn't always shell out for.

BootIt Next Generation does almost everything PartitionMagic can—maybe even more in some ways—and is free for downloading at http://www.terabyteunlimited.com/. Actually, the download is a 30-day evaluation version, but I strongly encourage users to drop the money on a copy. Among the features in the program: support for hard drives and partitions up to 2 terabytes in size, non-destructive resizing for all Windows partition types, partition management, support for many Linux partition types, imaging directly to removable media, boot management, user/password partition locking, and much more.

## HHD HexEditor 2.0

Hex editors used to be far more prevalent in the DOS days than they are now. The kind of low-level hacking done through hex editing is still done by experts, but the number of levels of abstraction between us and our software makes hex editing less urgent. That said, you never know when you will need this particular tool, or when it'll save you from unexpected disaster.

There are a billion and one hex editors out there, but HHD HexEditor 2.0 (available at http://www.hhdsoftware.com/hexeditor.html) is easily the best of the bunch for several reasons. It deals transparently with large files (up to 2GB as of this revision), works with multiple files at once, can undo revisions easily, allows drag-and-drop/cut-and-paste without complications, and many other things.

## WinHex

Another extremely powerful hex editor, WinHex (http://www.winhex.com), comes loaded with tons of bonus features, including: a directory browser for all supported Windows file systems; file splitting/merging; file comparing on the binary level; encrypt/decrypt; drive imaging; template-based data structure editing (for common, repeated tasks); unlimited file sizes, and tons more. It's well worth the registration cost.

## ISAPI_Rewrite

One of IIS's drawbacks is that it doesn't have anything like Apache's mod_Rewrite built in. Found at http://www.isapirewrite.com/download/, ISAPI_Rewrite fixes that by providing a free URL manipulation engine, written as an ISAPI .DLL, which uses regular expressions to allow administrators to create many sophisticated redirection systems. Among the applications: block remote linking of files and images (a *very* common complaint these days), optimize dynamic content to be indexed by search engines, manage access to static files using custom scripts and a database, proxy content from one site to another, make dynamic host-header–based sites using a single physical site (which is possible in IIS, but ISAPI_Rewrite adds another level of flexibility), return browser-dependent content even for static files, and on and on. The free version of the DLL is limited, but there's a 30-day trial for the full version, and the price is $69.

## JV16 PowerTools

The Swiss Army Knife—make that *Dutch* Army Knife—of all-in-one utilities, JV16 (available at http://www.jv16.org) packs an amazing amount of power and usefulness into their little program. I have found myself depending on it almost daily for everything from simple maintenance to sophisticated Registry spelunking. The Registry tool lets you remove dead Software key entries, invalid program installation entries, invalid registered

APPENDIX
B

Freeware, Shareware, and Trialware

file types, file shell extensions, IE context menu additions, and Open With menu additions. The File tool can automatically search the user and system Temp directories (I use this one constantly!), and the Backup tool allows you to back up *all* of the changes and deletions you make non-destructively. This program is solid gold, and it's available as a 30-day trialware edition.

## Lavasoft AdAware

One of the first and most powerful of the ad-ware/spy-ware buster programs, Lavasoft's AdAware (at http://www.lavasoft.de) has progressed to revision 6 in a relatively short amount of time. Spy-ware has become a menace as big as worms or viruses, and to have spy-ware plant itself on a *server* is even worse. AdAware runs through every relevant file in your system and compares it against a table of possible spyware signatures, which is thorough but also time-consuming. For a different (and in my opinion functionally better) approach, see the "Spybot—Search and Destroy" section later in this appendix.

## MailWasher

Whether you call it UCE (unsolicited commercial e-mail), spam, or just plain junk, that nonsense cluttering up all our inboxes has got to go. MailWasher (available at http://www.mailwasher.net) works side-by-side with *any* existing POP3 mailbox or mail client and lets you pre-screen it according to any criterion you can think of. It will also compare incoming mail against known good or bad lists (including net-based blacklists). The same company also makes more advanced versions for corporate users, but as an individual solution many people (myself included) get a lot out of it.

## PDF995

Adobe Acrobat is an open standard, so third-party developers have come up with their own PDF export and editing tools. Among the best is the PDF995 Suite (available at http://www.pdf995.com)—the core product is ad-supported freeware and the price for the full suite is far cheaper than what you would expect to pay for the Adobe product! Both standard and expanded PDF encryption is supported, along with workflow and document management systems, easy PostScript-to-PDF processing, integration with MS Word, document properties, *n*-up printing, and tons more. The output is totally indistinguishable from Adobe's own PDF creation system and works transparently through a printer driver—just print the needed document out to PDF. Anyone who deals with PDF on a regular basis should at least know about it.

## Resplendent Registrar

The Registry editor in Windows is a perfect example of a bundled Windows application that could have been done so much better. In fact, many third-party programmers have done exactly that—written replacement Registry editors that beat the MS version's pants off. Among the best is Resplendent Registrar, which includes heaps of features not found in REGEDIT or REGEDT32: multilevel undo, highly sophisticated security and permissions editing, bookmarking of common Registry entries, activity monitoring, defragmentation, comparing, global search and replace, and much more. The "Lite" version comes without some of the more advanced features but also without the $44.95 price tag of the full version. Both can be found at http://www.resplendence.com/docs/.

## ServerState

Administrators responsible for more than one server's health usually need some way of making sure all their servers are up and responding (or at least accessible). One good, inexpensive program to do this is ServerState, which can monitor servers that run on just about any port (HTTP, POP3/SMTP and Telnet being some of the built-in options) and notify the administrator via e-mail when a server is no longer responding. The program also runs in the tray and can notify the administrator silently from there. It can be downloaded from the following address: http://www.freewebs.com/phearnet/.

## SiSoftware Sandra

SiSoftware Sandra is a *very* detailed benchmarking and system information application, a "for experts, by experts" program that reveals a staggering amount of data about your system. Every conceivable component, hardware or software, system statistic and setting can be analyzed and reported through Sandra, and the program also contains a series of built-in benchmarks for testing many common aspects of a system's performance (disk throughput, CPU power, network speed, memory bandwidth, and so on). Among the test suites are a "burn-in" suite that is designed to run everything non-stop for any given length of time. The free evaluation version has some of its components turned off but is still capable of delivering. Each can be found at http://www.sisoftware.co.uk/.

## Spybot—Search and Destroy

A slightly more sophisticated cousin to AdAware, Spybot—Search and Destroy not only compares files against a criterion filter but takes proactive steps (which the program calls "inoculation") to stop spy-ware from ever getting into the system. Spybot also traps more programs and takes less time to search for them. It's also completely free to *all* users and comes in multiple-language editions available at http://security.kolla.de/. (Apparently a fair number of people have sunk low enough to copy the program except for the name and resell it as their own work.)

## Sysinternals

The SysInternals site at http://www.sysinternals.com/ntw2k/utilities.shtml is, frankly, a gold mine. I can't think of another place where you can get this many *useful* and powerful Windows 2000 utilities, most of them for free (with their source code), all in one place.

No system administrator should be without the stuff found here. Here are just *some* of the utilities available:

- **NewSID**   Changes the SID on a given system, either to something new or to one derived from another machine.

- **Fundelete**   Enhances the Recycle Bin to catch files deleted from the command line.

- **PageDefrag**   Defragments the Registry and the paging files.

- **Contig**   Defragments single files as needed.

- **CacheSet**   Changes the Cache Manager's working set size on-the-fly.

- **TDIMon**   Allows monitoring of TCP and UDP activity in real time.

- **PSTools**   A suite of utilities for listing the processes running on local or remote computers, running processes remotely, rebooting computers, dumping event logs, and more.

- **Process Explorer**   Lists all applications, currently loaded .DLLs, and their application associations.

- **NTFSDOS**   Allows access of NTFS partitions from DOS (read-only).

- **Handle**   Allows you to see which files are open by what processes (useful for figuring out why you can't delete a file!).

## VisualRoute 7.2A

VisualRoute is, as they say, a visual PING tool and so much more. Aside from being able to graphically plot the route of a network packet, you can use it to pinpoint Internet threats, perform bottleneck analysis, and obtain domain and network contact information for quick problem reporting. The free version, available from http://www.visualware.com/business/products/visualroute/index.html, can only trace from a set of pre-defined servers, but this still yields a great deal of useful information. A 15-day trial version is also available.

## WinImage

WinImage is a very powerful disk utility that lets you create disk images from, or to, any disk media—floppies, CDs, hard drive partitions, and more. WinImage also supports many different standard and non-standard image formats, including the Microsoft DMF format. Supported features include the ability to "inject" files and directories into an image after the imaging process is finished, perform batch operations and disk image format conversions, enable Unicode support, and much more. It's available at http://www.winimage.com.

# WinRAR

WinRAR packs a whole mess of compression tools into one handy utility. Almost every common compression and archive format—tar, gzip, ZIP, LZH, CAB—is supported natively by the program, which can be downloaded from http://www.win-rar.com/index.php?lang=eng. Their own RAR archiving system is one of the best out there, albeit heavily CPU-intensive, but it's great for compressing data like server logs and uncompressed image binaries. The program even allows you to explore ISO images and extract files from them without having to burn them first.

# WS_FTP LE 5.08

Everyone needs a decent FTP client, and the command-line Windows client isn't going to cut it. WS_FTP LE (for "lite edition") covers everything you need in a simple package. If you need a corporate license, the full version is modestly priced. Many advanced features, such as file resume, firewall and host types, date/time preservation, and many more additions are in the newest version, which can be found at http://www.ipswitch.com.

# Xteq X-Setup

Xteq X-Setup is quite possibly *the* ultimate system-tweaking tool—not just because of the range of tweaks and modifications it covers, but because of its open, scriptable architecture. Third-party developers can create their own plug-in tweak modules (and you can, too), and the results can be scripted so that your favorite tweaks can all be applied at once to a given system. The tweaks apply not only to desktop systems but servers as well. Check their site (http://www.xteq.com) for constant updates.

# INDEX

❖   **E**

❖   **F**

❖   **G**

## ❖ N

❖   **O**

### ❖ T

## ❖  X

## INTERNATIONAL CONTACT INFORMATION

**AUSTRALIA**
McGraw-Hill Book Company
Australia Pty. Ltd.
TEL +61-2-9900-1800
FAX +61-2-9878-8881
http://www.mcgraw-hill.com.au
books-it_sydney@mcgraw-hill.com

**CANADA**
McGraw-Hill Ryerson Ltd.
TEL +905-430-5000
FAX +905-430-5020
http://www.mcgraw-hill.ca

**GREECE, MIDDLE EAST, & AFRICA**
**(Excluding South Africa)**
McGraw-Hill Hellas
TEL +30-210-6560-990
TEL +30-210-6560-993
TEL +30-210-6560-994
FAX +30-210-6545-525

**MEXICO (Also serving Latin America)**
McGraw-Hill Interamericana Editores
S.A. de C.V.
TEL +525-1500-5108
FAX +525-117-1589
http://www.mcgraw-hill.com.mx
carlos_ruiz@mcgraw-hill.com

**SINGAPORE (Serving Asia)**
McGraw-Hill Book Company
TEL +65-6863-1580
FAX +65-6862-3354
http://www.mcgraw-hill.com.sg
mghasia@mcgraw-hill.com

**SOUTH AFRICA**
McGraw-Hill South Africa
TEL +27-11-622-7512
FAX +27-11-622-9045
robyn_swanepoel@mcgraw-hill.com

**SPAIN**
McGraw-Hill/
Interamericana de España, S.A.U.
TEL +34-91-180-3000
FAX +34-91-372-8513
http://www.mcgraw-hill.es
professional@mcgraw-hill.es

**UNITED KINGDOM, NORTHERN,**
**EASTERN, & CENTRAL EUROPE**
McGraw-Hill Education Europe
TEL +44-1-628-502500
FAX +44-1-628-770224
http://www.mcgraw-hill.co.uk
emea_queries@mcgraw-hill.com

**ALL OTHER INQUIRIES Contact:**
McGraw-Hill/Osborne
TEL +1-510-420-7700
FAX +1-510-420-7703
http://www.osborne.com
omg_international@mcgraw-hill.com

# Sound Off!

Visit us at **www.osborne.com/bookregistration** and let us know what you thought of this book. While you're online you'll have the opportunity to register for newsletters and special offers from McGraw-Hill/Osborne.

*We want to hear from you!*

# Sneak Peek

Visit us today at **www.betabooks.com** and see what's coming from McGraw-Hill/Osborne tomorrow!

Based on the successful software paradigm, Bet@Books™ allows computing professionals to view partial and sometimes complete text versions of selected titles online. Bet@Books™ viewing is free, invites comments and feedback, and allows you to "test drive" books in progress on the subjects that interest you the most.

OSBORNE DELIVERS RESULTS! OSBORNE
www.osborne.com